Good News for Writers

Good News for Writers

A College Reader

Clela Allphin-Hoggatt
Los Angeles Mission College

Shirley LaRue Mann
Los Angeles Mission College

1817

HARPER & ROW, PUBLISHERS, New York
Grand Rapids, Philadelphia, St. Louis, San Francisco,
London, Singapore, Sydney, Tokyo

Sponsoring Editor: Jane Kinney
Project Editor: Donna DeBenedictis
Art Direction: Heather A. Ziegler
Cover Coordinator: Mary Archondes
Cover Design: Heather A. Ziegler
Production: Paula Roppolo

GOOD NEWS FOR WRITERS: A College Reader

Library of Congress Cataloging-in-Publication Data

Allphin-Hoggatt, Clela, 1932–
Good news for writers : a college reader / Clela Allphin-Hoggatt, Shirley LaRue Mann.
p. cm.
ISBN 0-06-040239-3
1. College readers. 2. English language—Rhetoric. I. Mann, Shirley LaRue. II. Title.
PE1417.A39 1990
808'. 0427—dc20 89-38703
CIP

89 90 91 92 9 8 7 6 5 4 3 2 1

Contents

Thematic Contents

Memories and Reflections

Natural Environment

Work and Play

Science and Technology

Social and Political Issues

Philosophical Values

Crime and Society

Education

Language and the Arts

Preface

This anthology of news stories from a dozen or more of the nation's top newspapers centers around themes, rhetorical modes, and on-going issues that add novelty, talent, and familiarity to a textbook targeted for intermediate writers in prefreshmen skills courses.

A real advantage of this type of selection is that the original length of the articles is within the range of intermediate writers (rather than excerpts or abridged versions), the directness and clarity of journalism aids students to focus on the structure of organization, the economy of language clears up the tendency of beginning writers to overwrite, and, finally, it encourages students to read newspapers instead of relying on TV spot news.

In addition to contemporary journalists and wordsmiths, we have included several pieces by Jack London, Ernest Hemingway, and H. G. Wells, all of whom learned their craft through the newsroom.

Description, narration, characterization, and example form the backbone of all good writing. Therefore, Chapters 1, 2, 3, and 4 provide the basic tools for students. The next chapters—5 through 10—help students to organize their essays according to a purpose for writing. In Chapter 11, "Writing About Books," more advanced students have an opportunity to extend their writing skills to specific assignments that often occur across the curriculum.

We begin each chapter with an overview on a particular strategy of writing and a checklist for students to follow when using that strategy for their own writing assignments. Each reading is followed by two sets of exercises: questions on content and technique, and writing assignments.

A *Manual for Instructors* is available through the publisher. It provides teaching suggestions, summaries of each article to aid the instructor in quickly selecting the one or two most appropriate for a class discussion, suggested answers for the questions on content and technique, samples of student essays, and a bibliography of helpful sources.

We would like to acknowledge the sources of the articles: *Atlanta Journal-Constitution*, Associated Press, *Baltimore Sun, Boston Globe, Chicago Tribune, Christian Science Monitor, Dallas Morning News, Denver Post, Fort Worth Star-Telegram*, Hearst Syndicate, *Kansas City Star, Kansas City Times*, King Syndicate, Knight-Ridder, *London Evening Chronicle, Los Angeles Daily News, Los Angeles Herald-Examiner, Los Angeles Times*, Los Angeles Times Syndicate, McClatchy News Service, *New York Herald Tribune, New York Post, New York Sun, New York Times*, North American Syndicate, *Orlando Sentinel, Rocky Mountain News, Sacramento Bee, San Diego Union, San Francisco Chronicle, Seattle Times, Times Picayune*, Tribune Media Services, Universal Press Syndicate, *Wall Street Journal, Washington Post*, and Washington Post Writers Group.

We would also like to acknowledge the following reviewers of the text: June Bobb, Queens College of New York; Phyllis G. Kremen, VPL Rutgers University; Donald Mager, Johnson C. Smith University; Russell Murphy, University of Arkansas, Little Rock; Lisa M. Stepanski, Emmanuel College; Harriet Williams, University of South Carolina.

Clela Allphin-Hoggatt
Shirley LaRue Mann

Chapter 1

Description

LUANN by Greg Evans
Reprinted with special permission of NAS, Inc.

Description lays the foundation for almost every type of writing, whether it is fictional or factual. Think how dull fiction would be if nothing were described. The writing would be as flat as the synopsis of a soap opera or the directions for assembling a bookcase.

The best approach to describe a person or thing is by appealing to the reader's senses, particularly to the sense of sight. Imagine a novel where the protagonist is only a name. Yet when the professional writer describes the principal character as short, curly-haired with a mustache, and yellowed teeth, we see an individual whose physical appearance comes alive on the page.

The same techniques also are used in nonfiction works with sight as probably the most important sense utilized. In Judith Morgan's piece on Europe, you can see how vivid the images are: "Masses of daffodils trumpet spring . . ."; ". . . golden light of the cyprus-lined gardens." In addition, the writer learns to use the senses of smell, touch, and taste to communicate. Consider the appeal to the reader's sense of smell in this sentence from Russell Baker's article about growing up: "The heat of summer was mellow and produced sweet scents which lay in the air so damp and rich you could almost taste them."

In every reading in this chapter, the senses are appealed to by creating sharp pictures that linger long after the stories are read. For example, note this description from H. G. Wells's article on the tank: "They resemble large slugs with an underside a little like flattened rockers of a rocking horse, slugs between twenty and forty feet long." When Jim Murray writes about Dave Butz's football helmet, he says it looks like "a condemned building or a short stretch of bad road." In writing about the great San Francisco earthquake, Jack London gives us this picture of the homeless: "Some were wrapped in blankets. Others carried bundles of bedding and dear household treasures. . . . Baby buggies, toy wagons and gocarts were used as trucks while every other person was dragging a trunk."

On the other hand, description need not be realistic to be vivid, as in Stephen Crane's picture of a man having a seizure: "It was as if an invisible hand had reached up from the earth and had seized him by the hair."

In these selections and in other pieces you have read, the writers use description because it truly forms the bedrock of good writing.

WHEN YOU WRITE DESCRIPTION

- Select a subject that lends itself to detail through the use of more than one of our senses: sight, sound, touch, taste, and/or smell.
- Focus on a single scene, activity, or image.
- Create a dominant feeling, such as beauty, excitement, horror, or wonder.
- Arrange the details in a logical order: from top to bottom, right to left, near to far, or vice versa.
- Write your description so that any reader can picture it.

When a Man Falls

Stephen Crane

Stephen Crane describes a man on the street who suddenly falls to the pavement. This street scene in New York appeared in the *New York Press* on December 2, 1894.

WORDS TO KNOW

admonitions warnings

convulsion involuntary muscle contraction

prostrate stretched out with face toward the ground

scurried ran nimbly

The boy who had been walking with the man who fell was standing helplessly, a terrified look in his eyes. He held the man's hand. . . .

Those that were nearest to the man upon the sidewalk at first saw his body go through a singular contortion. It was as if an invisible hand had reached up from the earth and had seized him by the hair. He seemed dragged slowly, relentlessly backward, while his body stiffened convulsively; his hand clenched, and his arms swung rigidly upward. A slight froth was upon his chin. Through his pallid, half-closed lids could be seen the steel colored gleam of his eyes that were turned toward all the bending swaying faces and this inanimate thing upon the pavement burned threateningly, dangerously, shining with a mystic light, as a corpse might glare at those live ones who seemed about to trample it under foot.

As for the men near, they hung back, appearing as if they expected it to spring erect and clutch at them. Their eyes, however, were held in a spell of fascination. They seemed scarcely to breathe. They were contemplating a depth into which a human being had sunk, and the marvel of this mystery of life or death held them chained. . . .

A doctor had come. He and the policeman bended down at the man's side. Occasionally the officer upreared to create room. The crowd fell way before his threats, his admonitions, his sarcastic questions and before the sweep of those two huge buckskin gloves.

At last the peering ones saw the man on the sidewalk begin to breathe heavily, with the strain of overtaxed machinery, as if he had just come to the surface from some deep water. He uttered a low cry in his foreign tongue. It was a babyish squeal, or like the sad wail of a little storm-tossed kitten. As this cry went forth to all those eager ears, the jostling and crowding recommenced until the doctor was obliged to yell warningly a dozen times. The policeman had gone to send an ambulance call. . . .

When they picked up the limp body, from which came little moans and howls, the crowd almost turned into a mob, a silent mob, each member of which struggled for one thing. Afterward some resumed their ways with an air of relief, as if they themselves had been in pain and were at last recovered. Others still continued to stare at the ambulance on its banging, clanging return journey until it vanished into the golden haze.

QUESTIONS ON CONTENT AND TECHNIQUE

1. From Crane's description, what do you think is probably happening to the man?
2. Where are some sentences that describe through action?
3. What is Crane's attitude toward the crowd?
4. This article was written in 1894. Would it be realistic today? Explain.
5. Crane likens the crowd to "a silent mob, each member of which struggled for one thing." What is that one thing?

WRITING ASSIGNMENTS

Description

1. Describe a crowd (for example, at a ball game, at an accident, or at a natural disaster).

2. Do you remember being unconscious and then coming to with a person or crowd standing over you? If you have had that experience or one similar, describe the person or persons and surroundings as they appeared to you.

Memories and Reflections

1. Often crowds turn hostile. If you have ever witnessed such an occurrence, write an essay exploring the reasons.
2. Relate an emergency as if you were an ambulance driver, doctor, or police officer, and mention some problems that you might face.

Summer Beyond Wish

Russell Baker

Russell Baker is a nationally known humorist whose syndicated columns have entertained many readers.

WORDS TO KNOW

constituted established

meandered wandered aimlessly

wisteria a woody vine

A long time ago I lived in a crossroads village of northern Virginia and during its summer enjoyed innocence and never knew boredom, although nothing of consequence happened there.

Seven houses of varying lack of distinction constituted the community. A dirt road meandered off toward the mountain where a bootleg still supplied whiskey to the men of the countryside, and another dirt road ran down to the creek. My cousin Kenneth and I would sit on the bank and fish with earthworms. One day we killed a copperhead which was basking on a rock nearby. That was unusual.

The heat of summer was mellow and produced sweet scents which lay in the air so damp and rich you could almost taste them. Mornings smelled of purple wisteria, afternoons of the wild roses which tumbled over stone fences and evenings of honeysuckle.

Even by standards of that time it was a primitive place. There was no electricity. Roads were unpaved. In our house there was no plumbing. The routine of summer days was shaped by these deficiencies. Lacking electric lights, one went early to bed and rose while the dew was still in the grass. Kerosene lamps were cleaned and polished in an early-morning hubbub of women, and children were sent to the spring for fresh water.

This afforded a chance to see whether the crayfish population had multiplied. Later, a trip to the outhouse would afford a chance to daydream in the Sears, Roebuck catalog, mostly about shotguns and bicycles.

With no electricity, radio was not available for pacifying the young. One or two people did have radios that operated on mail-order batteries about the size of a present-day car battery, but these were not for children, though occasionally you might be invited in to hear "Amos 'n' Andy."

All I remember about "Amos 'n' Andy" at that time is that it was strange hearing voices come out of furniture. Much later I was advised that listening to "Amos 'n' Andy" was racist and was grateful that I hadn't heard much.

In the summer no pleasures were to be had indoors. Everything of delight occurred in the world outside. In the flowers there were hummingbirds to be seen, tiny wings fluttering so fast that the birds seemed to have no wings at all.

In the heat of midafternoon the women would draw the blinds, spread blankets on the floor for coolness and nap, while in the fields the cattle herded together in the shade of spreading trees to escape the sun. Afternoons were absolutely still, yet filled with sounds.

Bees buzzed in the clover. Far away over the fields the chug of an ancient steam-powered threshing machine could be faintly heard. Birds rustled under the tin of the porch roof.

Rising dust along the road from the mountains signaled an approaching event. A car is coming. "Car's coming," someone would say. People emerged from houses. The approaching dust was studied. Guesses were hazarded about whom it might contain.

Then—a big moment in the day—the car would cruise past.

"Who was it?"

"I didn't get a good look."

"It looked like Packy Painter to me."

"Couldn't have been Packy. Wasn't his car."

The stillness resettled itself as gently as the dust, and you could wander past the henhouse and watch a hen settle herself to perform the mystery of laying an egg. For livelier adventure there was the field that contained the bull. There, one could test his courage by seeing how far he dared venture before running back through the fence.

The men drifted back with the falling sun, steaming with heat and fatigue, and washed in tin basins with water hauled in buckets from the spring. I knew a few of their secrets, such as who kept his whiskey hidden in a Mason jar behind the lime barrel, and what they were really doing when they excused themselves from the kitchen and stepped out into the orchard and stayed out there laughing too hard.

I also knew what the women felt about it, though not what they thought. Even then I could see that matters between women and men could become very difficult and, sometimes, so difficult that they spoiled the air of summer.

At sunset people sat on the porches. As dusk deepened, the lightning bugs came out to be caught and bottled. As twilight edged into night, a bat swooped across the road. I was not afraid of bats then, although I feared ghosts, which made the approach of bedtime in a room where even the kerosene lamp would quickly be doused seem terrifying.

I was even more afraid of toads and specifically of the toad which lived under the porch steps and which everyone assured me would, if touched, give me warts. One night I was allowed to stay up until the stars were in full command of the sky. A woman of great age was dying in the village and it was considered fit to let the children stay abroad into the night. As four of us sat there we saw a shooting star and someone said, "Make a wish."

I did not know what that meant. I didn't know anything to wish for.

QUESTIONS ON CONTENT AND TECHNIQUE

1. What time period would you guess that the author is describing?
2. How does the use of multiple senses affect the reader? Which is the most common? The least common?
3. Baker closes his article with "I didn't know anything to wish for." How do you interpret those last words? Relate them to the title.
4. What does the use of dialogue add to the piece?
5. "I also knew what the women felt about it [the hidden whiskey], though not what they thought." What do you think Baker means?

WRITING ASSIGNMENTS

Description

1. Write a descriptive essay on a season during your childhood with emphasis on sounds.
2. Try to remember a special place of your childhood. Describe this scene with as much sensory detail as possible.

Memories and Reflections

1. Baker writes, "Even then I could see that matters between women and men could become very difficult and, sometimes, so difficult that they spoiled the air of summer." Recount a quarrel within your family.
2. Baker, as a child, feared the toad under the porch. Relate your childhood fear and how you overcame it.

The Helmet

Jim Murray

Jim Murray is a sportswriter who has won the Pulitzer Prize.

WORDS TO KNOW

pillbox a low concrete fortification for machine guns and tank weapons

subdural situated under a hard membrane like that of a scorpion or spider

San Diego—A radio announcer said his helmet looked like a used car. Someone else thought it looked more like a condemned building or a short stretch of bad road.

Dave Butz himself looks like an abandoned pillbox that was well used in the war. But if you saw only his helmet, you would know that what Dave Butz does for a living is (a) dark, (b) dirty, and (c) dangerous. And that not everyone in the world would want to do it.

It doesn't look like it, but Dave Butz gets issued a new helmet every year. He has to. Because by the end of the season, his old one no longer meets the safety standards of the National Football League which are just slightly above those of a Japanese kamikaze pilot.

His helmet is in the position where one more blow to it could probably produce a subdural hemorrhage, split personality and, doubtless, permanent impairment in his hearing—or all three of the above.

Butz's helmet is so bad, it has to be touched up periodically during the season with fresh paint, like a tank that needs re-camouflaging after a direct hit.

Butz retires his helmets at the end of every season. He arranges them in neat rows, like mothballed ships, in his trophy room. During the season, he has to hide them from the Board of Health, the National Safety Council and Ralph Nader.

The Redskins have a portrait of a plains Indian on the sides of their helmets. By the fourth quarter, Butz's Indian looks not unlike Custer. Or the loser in a fight. When the Denver Broncos say that to beat the Washington Redskins in the Super Bowl, they have to kick their Butz, they mean the man not the anatomy.

Butz's helmet takes a pounding because the man in it usually does. He draws a crowd of hostiles, like an ant at a family picnic.

The Washington Redskins are one of the few teams in pro football to still employ the four-man defensive front. They are able to do this because they do not have the manic fear of the forward pass that infests most coaching staffs. Their reasoning is that no one can throw the football successfully with his arm in Dave Butz's mouth. . . .

Butz is logging his 15th year in the NFL and has the helmets to prove it. That's an awful lot of dents in the plastic, but the face is unmarked. The nose isn't broken, the knees look zippered. Even the hands don't have the swollen, broken look of most guys who make a living separating quarterbacks from the ball or from their senses, whichever comes first. . . .

You'll have no trouble recognizing Dave Butz on the field on Super Sunday. He'll be the one whose helmet looks as if it has just been dropped from a 10th-story window or brought up from the wreck of the Titanic.

QUESTIONS ON CONTENT AND TECHNIQUE

1. How does the description of the helmet give the reader an image of its wearer?
2. Find the fragments in the article and join them effectively to the sentence preceding or following.
3. What does Murray mean by "safety standards . . . slightly above those of a Japanese kamikaze pilot"?
4. "He draws a crowd of hostiles, like an ant at a family picnic." Find other similes and explain their structure. (See glossary if necessary.)

WRITING ASSIGNMENTS

Description

1. Describe a piece of wearing apparel or possession that indicates something about your occupation or your personality.
2. Describe only the setting, not the action, of a sports event that you have witnessed.

Work and Play

1. Americans idolize athletes. Discuss the reasons for the popularity of a current sports idol.
2. Murray writes, ". . . what Dave Butz does for a living is (a) dark, (b) dirty, and (c) dangerous." Find another occupation that holds these three d's and explain.

San Francisco Is Gone!

Jack London

Jack London, who lived near San Francisco, was sent to the scene of the earthquake and wrote an eyewitness account May 5, 1906, for *Collier's Weekly.*

WORDS TO KNOW

conflagration a great fire

enumeration a listing

imperial relating to empire

lurid gruesome

nabobs men of great wealth

vestiges remains

The earthquake shook down in San Francisco hundreds of thousands of dollars' worth of walls and chimneys. But the conflagration that followed burned up hundreds of millions of dollars' worth of property. There is no estimating within hundreds of millions the actual damage wrought. Not in history has a modern imperial city been so completely destroyed. San Francisco is gone! Nothing remains of it but memories and a fringe of dwelling houses on its outskirts. Its industrial section is wiped out. Its social and residential section is wiped out. The factories and warehouses, the great stores and newspaper buildings, the hotels and the palaces of the nabobs, are all gone. There remains only the fringe of dwelling houses on the outskirts of what was once San Francisco.

Within an hour after the earthquake shock the smoke of San Francisco's burning was a lurid tower visible a hundred miles away. And for three days and nights this lurid tower swayed in the sky, reddening the sun, darkening the day, and filling the land with smoke.

On Wednesday morning at a quarter past five came the earthquake. A minute later the flames were leaping upward. In a dozen different quarters south of Market Street, in the working-class ghetto, and in the factories, fires started. There was no opposing the flames. There was no organization, no communication. All the cunning adjustments of a twentieth-century city had been smashed by the earthquake. The streets were humped into ridges and depressions and piled with debris of fallen walls. The steel rails were twisted into perpendicular and horizontal angles. The telephone and telegraph systems were disrupted. And the great water mains had burst. All the shrewd contrivances and safeguards of man had been thrown out of gear by thirty seconds' twitching of the earth's crust.

By Wednesday afternoon, inside of twelve hours, half the heart of the city was gone. At that time I watched the vast conflagration from out on the bay. It was dead calm. Not a flicker of wind stirred. Yet from every side wind was pouring in upon the city. East, west, north, and south, strong winds were blowing upon the doomed city. The heated air rising made an enormous suck. Thus did the fire of itself build its own colossal chimney through the atmosphere. Day and night this dead calm continued, and yet, near to the flames, the wind was often half a gale, so mighty was the suck. . . .

Before the flames, throughout the night fled tens of thousands of homeless ones. Some were wrapped in blankets. Others carried bundles of bedding and dear household treasures. Sometimes a whole family was harnessed to a carriage or delivery wagon that was weighted down with their possessions. Baby buggies, toy wagons, and gocarts were used as trucks, while every other person was dragging a trunk. Yet everybody was gracious. The most perfect courtesy obtained. Never in all San Francisco's history were her people so kind and courteous as on this night of terror.

All the night these tens of thousands fled before the flames. Many of them, the poor people from the labor ghetto, had fled all day as well. They had left their homes burdened with possessions. Now and again they lightened up, flinging out upon the street clothing and treasures they had dragged for miles.

They held on longest to their trunks, and over these trunks many a strong man broke his heart that night. The hills of San Francisco are steep, and up these hills, mile after mile, were the trunks dragged. Everywhere were trunks, with across them lying their exhausted owners, men and women. Before the march of the flames were flung picket lines of soldiers. And a block at a time, as the flames advanced, these pickets retreated. One of their tasks was to keep the trunk pullers moving. The exhausted creatures, stirred on by the menace of bayonets, would arise and struggle up the steep pavements, pausing from weakness every five or ten feet.

QUESTIONS ON CONTENT AND TECHNIQUE

1. If you were to hear today the words "San Francisco is gone!" what would you immediately think?
2. The last paragraph is especially well written. Why does it work so well?
3. London basically describes what two circumstances?
4. Find repetitive phrases in the description and defend or attack their use.
5. London notes that despite the tragedy everyone was courteous. Do you believe people would react that way today? Explain.

WRITING ASSIGNMENTS

Description

1. London particularly mentions the reluctance of the poor to leave their possessions. Can you describe a scene of someone concerned about his or her belongings?
2. Describe a traumatic event that you have witnessed.

Philosophical Values

1. Imagine a natural disaster (for example, an earthquake, a tornado, or a flood) in your city, and describe the behavior of the people.
2. You have only a few minutes to evacuate your home. What possessions would you take, and why?

I Like This Place

Herb Caen

Herb Caen, a longtime lover of "Frisco," writes of its contrasts in his column for the *San Francisco Chronicle.*

WORDS TO KNOW

boozers heavy drinkers

precipices steep cliffs

urchins mischievous children

I like and am sickened by the look of it. Streets crashing head-on into hills, houses clinging by their fingertips to precipices, dead piers alive with the ghosts of clipper ships that came around the Horn with all canvas aloft. I like a cable car lurching at top speed (nine miles an hour) from Powell into Jackson, bringing back memories of the conductor who hollered, "Look out fer da koive!"—and then HE fell off. A kid buying a gardenia for his girl at a Powell St. flower stand, around the corner from rag-snapping bootblacks and newsboys too old and tired to holler the headlines that reflect their own misery. Heartbreak city. A thin woman emerging from a rat's nest on Turk, scuttling to the corner liquor store for a pint in a paper bag, and shuffling back to her barred door in her bedroom slippers; then you notice what else she's wearing: nightgown and bathrobe. Sixth St., the most dangerous, with its constant threat of sudden death, flash of a knife, blood on the dirty sidewalk. A city is at once beautiful and cruel, cold and generous, a place of grace and disgrace. At Polk and Pine, some mother's son is waiting at the corner for whomever and whatever, at so much a pound. A teenager with a baby face, blond ringlets, a beanie with a propeller. A BEANIE.

* * *

I like this place. It's hard, with a heart. Unspoken tragedies, secret gallantries, untold generosities. The city is old, rundown, falling apart. It has led a tough life, from gold miners through gold diggers to yuppies in designer clothes who never heard of Hangtown, oyster pirates or dancing the Grizzly Bear. It's the old-timers who keep the mysteries alive and remember the people who made the town great. Sure, they're boring and they live in the past, but their eyes have seen the glory of the coming of Sunny Jim and Dodie Valencia, good-time girl, and the politicians and fixers cutting deals right out in the open at Shorty Roberts' joint at the beach. Real cash, which was worth money in those days, changed hands between the cracked crab and the porterhouse steak, rare. From Chinatown, the bag man headed straight for City Hall with a black satchel crammed with green-backs. The bag was placed on the mayor's desk. Not a word was exchanged. The alleys of Chinatown were safe for pai-gow for another month.

I like the look of this town. Not the tall buildings—the little ones, preferably wooden and rickety and a little off-plumb. South o' Market has a lot of these one- and two-story jobs, sagging on the dead ends named Clara and Harriet and Kate. We never did find out who these ladies were, but they were not hookers. Probably buxom, red-cheeked Irish lasses whose men worked on the waterfront and came home tired, with a whiskey breath, ready for their corned beef and cabbage. The streets were cobbled, the carriages rattled, the streetlamps gradually cast a golden glow over the city as the urchins sang, "When the lamps begin to light, then the fleas begin to bite." San Francisco was infamous for fleas, especially in the Sunset, where they popped out of the sand and infested everything.

* * *

Sounds of the city. Tires screeching as they try to get a toehold on the Taylor St. hill at the crest of Nob Hill. A freighter hooting its way through a flock of sailboats that scatter like swans. Horns in the

Stockton Tunnel, bells in distant church towers, whistles from hard-hats at pretty girls. Cab drivers honking at tourists driving slowly, lost reading maps that won't help them at all. Cabbies are always in a hurry except when they're cruising in search of a fare, in which case they don't give a damn who's behind them. "I've been reading you for years," writes a cabbie, "and you've never had a good word to say for cab-drivers." I sympathize with their job. It's dangerous. And dangerously boring. And the rattiest of rat races, fighting for the buck, generally undertipped. But their driving is the worst. Cutting in, cutting out, speeding, idling, getting on everybody's nerves—but I wouldn't take the job for anything. Good luck, buddy, and keep the change.

* * *

A good town where too much has happened in a short time. A trenchcoat city where any guy wearing a hat could be Sam Spade, looking for the falcon, and the plainclothes cops cruise in unmarked cars that holler "Police!" A city that cares about the good life, which is right around the corner from the bad one: swinging restaurants, real bars with real boozers, a pretty good cultural scene (not as good as it might be) and a lot of beautiful neighborhoods in a small space, some of them among the world's most elegant. There's a lot of elegance, spiced with the originality of a free-spirited city. Crazy clothes on weird people. The bike messengers look elegant in their own way, and the deadpan disco dancers in the SoMa joints, and the hotel doormen, extremely elegant. It's a town that is forever grabbing you by the throat and saying, "Look around, see what's going on, feel it, experience it. You don't have to enjoy it. Just don't turn your back on it, OK?" OK, OK, I'm lookin'. I'm likin'. Now leave me alone.

QUESTIONS ON CONTENT AND TECHNIQUE

1. How do the contrasts in the article affect you?
2. Caen uses the technique of personification. (See glossary if necessary.) In what ways does it enrich the piece?
3. Why does Caen use many sentence fragments?
4. How does the writer suggest the problems of the city? What are they?

WRITING ASSIGNMENTS

Description

1. Take any one of the people that Caen describes briefly and develop a complete character study (for example, ". . . some mother's son waiting at the corner . . .").
2. "I like this place." Describe a place that you like, using sights, sounds, smells, and activities.

Work and Play

1. "A city is at once beautiful and cruel, cold and generous. . . . " Using your own city as an example, show how a community can possess a dual personality.
2. "Look around, see what's going on, feel it, experience it." Choose and write about an activity that you observed, felt drawn to, and experienced or tried.

Springtime in Europe

Judith Morgan

Judith Morgan, of La Jolla, California, is a magazine and newspaper writer. She contributed this piece to the *Los Angeles Times*.

WORDS TO KNOW

balmy mild

gnarled twisted

schmaltz sentimentalism

sublime splendid

Spring is a season of bountiful starts, a season of pomp and show. Each year at this time my mind takes off for Europe, even when my body stays at home.

I envision myself driving along the winding roads of Brittany, that salt-breezy province of France.

I am meeting a friend for a seafood lunch—oysters, perhaps, or *lotte*—in the port town of Concarneau. We'll dine inside the old walls at Le Galion, where the tables are set with white candles on crisp, blue linen and the stone hearth is blazing with poppies and buttercups.

Soft, taped music eases from Beethoven to the Missa Criolla. We will not be rushed.

I dream of a spring day in the white beech woods near Arhus on the east coast of Denmark's Jutland. I am meeting a friend at a thatched-roof country inn called Moesgaard Skovmolle Kro.

A millstream trickles over a wooden waterwheel near the door, which is framed with hollyhock. We share a platter of smoked salmon to start, then laugh on through cloudberries and Brie. We will not be rushed.

I yearn to be in Italy on a green hill above Florence, where the magnificent hotel Villa San Michele has just reopened for its March-to-November season.

A year ago I was there, savoring the quiet corridors of this former monastery with its facade by Michelangelo. An altar, sweet with roses, fills an end of the reception room. The restaurant serves the most sublime menu I found in Florence, from the Tuscan bread and the bean and garlic soup called *ribollita* to tender beefsteak *alla fiorentina.*

I sat in the golden light of the cypress-lined gardens and admired the city below, the city crowned by the massive dome of Santa Maria del Fiore, a cathedral simply called the Duomo.

The 28-room inn is on the winding road to the village of Fiesole, a pocket of sunshine and serenity topped by the chapel of St. Francis, which was guarded when I was there by pairs of strutting white doves.

From this terrace the view of Florence and the glint of the River Arno is as enchanting, though not so intimate, as from the tall, shuttered windows of the Villa San Michele.

The small piazza of Fiesole is marked by huge plane trees, their gnarled trunks sprouting hair-like branches of new leaves.

In their shade are sidewalk cafes: cane chairs and slat tables at the Bar Etrusca, orange tablecloths and wicker chairs at the Falli Bar next door.

The pleasant Italian custom is to pause here for vibrant conversation, or to read a newspaper while savoring an espresso *doppio.* On a balmy spring evening this is the place to sit and admire the *passegiata,* the traditional promenade of those who live in Fiesole.

My heart also journeys to Salzburg and is ensconced once more in the splendid old Hotel Goldener Hirsch just steps from Mozart's birthplace.

Masses of daffodils trumpet spring, but they are not alone. This is the *spargel* season in Austria, when mounds of fresh asparagus—white and green—are featured on menus. At market stalls by the Collegiate Church, shoppers eagerly crowd to buy fresh *spargel* by the kilo, and then splurge on baskets of wild strawberries.

Last April my room was a country haven of hand-painted

wooden armoires, shaggy lamp shades and thick down comforters buttoned into white slipcases; my window opened onto the pedestrian street called Getreidegasse, a narrow lane where shop signs of wrought iron coil artfully overhead.

I leaned out to see a baker hurry around the corner carrying a tray of rolls and cakes. Girls paraded in beribboned straw hats, and student musicians played violins as coins were tossed into upturned caps at their feet.

The Goldener Hirsch is a warren of creaky floors and twists of hall. The name means *golden stag*; there are antlers on the walls of the bar in this Old World hostelry, which stands as proof that you can successfully mix schmaltz and elegance, a mix that is not unlike spring.

QUESTIONS ON CONTENT AND TECHNIQUE

1. What effect do all the foreign phrases have on you, the reader?
2. Select a phrase showing each of the following: sight, sound, touch, taste, smell.
3. Why does Morgan repeat "We will not be rushed"?
4. Of the descriptive passages, which appealed most to you? Why?
5. For what group of people is the author writing?

WRITING ASSIGNMENTS

Description

1. Select your favorite season and describe it by using sensory details and examples.
2. Take one year in your childhood and through multiple images share that year with your reader.

Work and Play

1. Go to a restaurant, park, workplace, or shopping mall and create a collage of images.
2. Do you suppose life is carefree for the people that Judith Morgan sees—the waiters, laborers, musicians? Write about springtime in Europe during the tourist season from one of their points of view.

The Tank

H. G. Wells

In 1903, H. G. Wells prophetically warned readers of *The Strand Magazine* about the monsters of wars to come. Later, after the invention of the tank, Mr. Wells wrote this description in the *London Daily Chronicle,* December 18, 1916.

WORDS TO KNOW

apoplectic related to a stroke

contrivances inventions

embargo ban on trade

integument covering membrane structure

perambulator baby carriage

piquant provocative or charming

The young of even the most horrible beasts have something piquant and engaging about them, and so I suppose it is in the way of things that the land ironclad which opens a new and more dreadful and destructive phase in the human folly of warfare should appear first as if it were a joke. Never has any such thing so completely masked its wickedness under an appearance of genial silliness. The Tank is a creature to which one naturally flings a pet name; the five or six I was shown wandering, rooting, and climbing over obstacles, round a large field near X, were as amusing and disarming as a litter of lively young pigs.

At first the War Office prevented the publication of any pictures or descriptions of these contrivances except abroad; then abruptly the embargo was relaxed, and the press was flooded with photographs. The reader will be familiar now with their appearance. They resemble large slugs with an underside a little like the flattened rockers of a rocking horse, slugs between twenty and forty feet long. They are like flat-sided slugs, slugs of spirit, who raise an inquiring snout, like the snout of a dogfish, into the air. They crawl upon their bellies in a way that would be tedious to describe to the general reader and unnecessary to describe to the inquiring specialist. They go over the ground with the sliding speed of active snails. Behind them trail two wheels, supporting a flimsy tail, wheels that strike one as incongruous as if a monster began kangaroo and ended doll's perambulator. (These wheels annoy me.) They are not steely monsters; they are painted the drab and unassuming colors that are fashionable in modern warfare, so that the armor seems rather like the integument of a rhinoceros. At the sides of the head project armored cheeks, and from above these stick out guns that look like stalked eyes. That is the general appearance of the contemporary Tank.

It slides on the ground; the silly little wheels that so detract from the genial bestiality of its appearance dangle and bump behind it. It swings round about its axis. It comes to an obstacle, a low wall let us say, or a heap of bricks, and sets to work to climb with its snout. It rears over the obstacle, it raises its straining belly, it overhangs more and more, and at last topples forward; it sways upon the heap and then goes plunging downward, sticking out the weak counterpoise of its wheeled tail. If it comes to a house or a tree or a wall or suchlike obstruction it rams against it so as to bring all its weight to bear upon it—it weighs some tons—and then climbs over the debris. I saw it, and incredulous soldiers of experience watched it at the same time, cross trenches and wallow amazingly through muddy exaggerations of shell holes. Then I repeated the tour inside.

Again the Tank is like the slug. The slug, as every biological student knows, is unexpectedly complicated inside. The Tank is as crowded with inward parts as a battleship. It is filled with engines, guns, and ammunition, and in the interstices, men.

"You will smash your hat," said Colonel Stern. "No; keep it on, or else you will smash your head."

Only Mr. C. R. W. Nevinson could do justice to the interior of a

Tank. You see a hand gripping something; you see the eyes and forehead of an engineer's face; you perceive that an overall bluishness beyond the engine is the back of another man. "Don't hold that," says someone; "it is too hot. Hold on to that." The engines roar, so loudly that I doubt whether one could hear guns without; the floor begins to slope and slopes until one seems to be at forty-five degrees or thereabouts; then the whole concern swings up and sways and slants the other way. You have crossed a bank. You heel sideways. Through the door which has been left open you see the little group of engineers, staff officers, and naval men receding and falling away behind you. You straighten up and go uphill. You halt and begin to rotate. Through the open door, the green field, with its red walls, rows of work sheds, and forests of chimneys in the background, begins a steady processional movement. The group of engineers and officers and naval men appears at the other side of the door and farther off. Then comes a spring downhill. You descend and stretch your legs.

About the field other Tanks are doing their stunts. One is struggling in an apoplectic way in the mud pit with a cheek half buried. It noses its way out and on with an air of animal relief.

They are like jokes by Heath Robinson. One forgets that these things have already saved the lives of many hundreds of our soldiers and smashed and defeated thousands of Germans.

Said one soldier to me: "In the old attacks you used to see the British dead lying outside the machine-gun emplacements like birds outside a butt with a good shot inside. Now, these things walk through."

QUESTIONS ON CONTENT AND TECHNIQUE

1. What are the various comparisons that Wells uses to describe the tank? Why so many comparisons instead of just one?
2. For what purpose does Wells describe the tank driver?
3. Wells does not write simply "the tank moves." How does he vary this idea without repeating words?
4. What do you think is his attitude toward tanks? Explain.

WRITING ASSIGNMENTS

Description

1. Write an essay describing your vehicle (truck, car, or bicycle) and give it human characteristics.

2. Use an animal image to describe any object that you own.

Science and Technology

1. Assume you are watching the six o'clock news and a bulletin flashes across the scene—War Has Been Declared Against______! Fill in the blank and describe your feelings and actions.
2. "One forgets that these things [tanks] have already saved lives." Explain whether you agree or disagree with this statement.

Chapter 2

Narration

Tell me a story.

People have been saying that ever since primitive people learned to communicate with more than screeches and shouts.

Narration is simply a story about someone doing something to achieve a goal. It probably began when a hunter lorded over his fellow cave dwellers with a tall tale about how he slew a mighty mammoth. Others followed and soon semiprofessional storytellers developed an oral system whereby tales were passed down through generations, in the manner of Homer, whose *Iliad* and *Odyssey* later became part of classical literature.

In many ways narration is the most direct writing method. The writer basically tells us what happened to someone. The event may be no more than a trip to the local video store, but in skillful hands, the technique of narration can become both absorbing and complex, and far more convincing than the strongest argument.

For example, consider the impact of accounts of the Holocaust, contrasted to *The Diary of Anne Frank*, or the power of antislavery tracts versus *Uncle Tom's Cabin*. In both instances, these narratives stirred many more people than the most logical treatises on the subjects because recounting the actions of a character inevitably gets the reader wound up in the character's emotions; nothing is more compelling than the force of emotions.

Almost all of the selections in this chapter show how narration can stir emotions, from Jimmy Breslin's story on meeting a plane carrying the wounded from Vietnam, to Bill Stokes's simpler but moving piece about the duck caught in a frozen creek.

Since virtually any subject can be covered by using narration, its impact as a writing tool is powerful.

WHEN YOU WRITE NARRATION

- Tell the story usually in a time sequence.
- Decide if you (as narrator) are telling the story in first person (I) or if you (as observer) are telling the story in third person (he, she, or they), and then maintain that point of view throughout your narrative.
- Be certain that your narrative has a beginning, a middle, and an end.
- Write carefully so that your reader understands the situation, becomes excited about the outcome, and accepts the solution as credible.

Duck-Killing Cold: An Image That Has Never Flown South

Bill Stokes

Bill Stokes is a staff writer for the *Chicago Tribune*.

WORDS TO KNOW

eons periods of indefinite time

exuberant joyously unrestrained

parasites organisms living on another

prepubescent before sexual maturity

tentacles stalk of plant that holds it to object

The story of how the tiny duck died was written in the ice around it. It told of an ever decreasing area of open water until finally the brutal cold closed in and sealed the bird into the steel-hard ice of the creek.

Sometime during the night, the cold had invaded the duck's body like an infestation of minute, murderous parasites. It had crawled through the feathers, the down and the skin, and into the flesh where the exquisite arrangement of organs and fluids made the bird a miraculous product of the eons.

At some point, the duck had bowed to it, dipping its head low where it froze in a submissive tilt as its blood congealed and its heart stopped beating.

We found it that way the next day as we skated up the twisting channel. There were three or four of us, prepubescent boys with red cheeks and damp noses, and the discovery of the duck stopped our exuberant exploration.

We stood on wavering ankles and stared down at the bird, our breaths forming a cluster of miniature clouds and our eyeballs threatening to roll from our heads. Nobody spoke for a second or two and then somebody muttered a boyish version of a curse in a whispery voice. We knelt around it, our bony knees and elbows down on the ice, and tried to look the dead duck in the eye.

"Maybe it's not dead yet," somebody said.

We wanted that to be true. We were too full of life, too much on the brink of living, too engrossed in the grand potential of a lifetime to give any consideration to death. We could not, in fact, even manage a remote grasp of it.

But here it was, in front of us as certainly as the dried bird nest in the willow thicket and the mink tracks through the cattails. The resistance went on, however; somebody suggested we get a hatchet and chop the duck out of the ice and take it to somebody's home where it might thaw out and come back to life.

One of us touched the duck's head with a mittened hand and it was as solid as a baseball. We all touched it then, like timid worshipers at a strange shrine.

"Why didn't it go south?" somebody asked.

"Maybe it was wounded by a hunter and couldn't fly," someone else said.

The cold from the ice crept up into our elbows and our knees as we knelt there and then the connection was somehow made: The cold had killed the duck. The frigid temperature that had come slinking in from the north suddenly took on villainous dimensions and a kind of horror frost was formed in our boyish brains. The brutal, duck-killing cold would kill us too if we were ever trapped in it and could not get back into our warm homes.

We skated away then, slowly and subdued. And we went to our respective homes early, even before the short winter day creaked to a dark, bone-chilling end.

Then the other day, when the awful cold descended and caressed us all with its life-sucking tentacles, the frozen duck was there again, and I realized that I had been seeing it off and on over the years. The image does not fade; instead, it seems to be more vivid each time it appears.

QUESTIONS ON CONTENT AND TECHNIQUE

1. How is the title related to the theme of the article? See the glossary if necessary.
2. Explain the significance of the last paragraph.
3. Identify the simile in the second paragraph. Use the glossary if necessary. What purpose does it serve? Write a simile of your own.
4. What ten words if removed would make the piece dull and lifeless?
5. The author writes of the cold as if it were a living thing. How does he develop this personification? Refer to the glossary if necessary.

WRITING ASSIGNMENTS

Narration

1. Using sensory detail, describe a memorable childhood experience.
2. Write a narrative in which you recall the death of a family member, friend, or pet.

Memories and Reflections

1. Discuss the moment of your own awareness of death.
2. Select and explain an event that bound you to your friends.

Violence in Films? Check Out Theaters

Mike Royko

Mike Royko, a syndicated columnist of the *Chicago Tribune,* goes to the movies with his wife and then narrates the following incident.

WORDS TO KNOW

magpie long-tailed black and white bird

The last time I went to the movies, a young man sitting next to me laughed uproariously at almost every line of dialogue. That would have been okay if the movie was a comedy, but it was serious and sad.

After a half-hour of this distraction, I finally turned to him and asked if he would please show a bit of restraint.

He responded by swearing and shrieking about how I didn't have the right to tell him what to do, that he had paid for his ticket, who did I think I was, and so on.

My wife, who has a keen eye for such things, whispered: "He's on something and he's high. I think you'd better ignore him."

Out of the corner of my eye, I looked the lad over. He was short, scrawny and had delicate arms and wrists. I had him by 60 pounds, 6 inches, more upper-body strength, a vicious nature and the element of surprise. He was a perfect adversary.

So I whispered to my wife: "All it will take is one or two good pops to the side of his head, and I'm sure his manners will improve."

That seemed a reasonable solution. It was obviously too late for me to tell him to say no to drugs. I might even have been doing him a service by helping clear his head.

But she said: "No, you don't know what he has in his pockets."

She was right. I had forgotten that in this, the age of the new barbarian, it was risky business for me to have even asked him to keep quiet. And if I slugged him, who knows, he might have whipped out a semiautomatic weapon and done in the entire audience.

So we left. As I went through the lobby, I saw a man who appeared to work there, and I said: "In about the 10th row, there is a loony bird making all kinds of noise."

He nodded, smiled weakly, but didn't move. Ah, for the days of old. When I was a theater usher on Cermak Road and in the Loop, we would have been charging down the aisle. We carried industrial-sized flashlights. First, a beam of light in the noisemaker's eyes. If that didn't silence him, a command that he leave. If he resisted, fine, that was why we carried the heavy flashlights. They left a neat crease in the brow.

Times change. There is no longer any devotion to duty. The twerp just slouched there, nodding and smiling. He was probably on something, too.

That was the last time I went to the movies. I had sworn off several times earlier because of the chatterers, jabberers, hooters, howlers and other noisy goofs. Each time I weakened and went back.

But when it reached the point that I had to defer to a scrawny hophead geek, I knew it was time to become a couch potato.

Oh, you can still go to a Woody Allen movie and tell some magpie to shut up. Most of the young men in the audience are frail creatures with trimmed beards who feel they must explain the plot to their yuppie mates.

At everything else, though, the yahoos have the upper hand because, as my wife said, you don't know what's in their pockets.

Just the other day, her wisdom was confirmed by an incident in a crowded Baltimore theater.

A man sitting in the back row found his view of the screen blocked by a guy who was standing in the aisle.

He tapped him on the shoulder and asked him to move.

The man in the aisle indignantly said, "Don't touch," whipped out a pistol and opened fire, wounding a woman in both legs.

All that for a tap on the shoulder. What would he have done if someone had jostled his popcorn?

It's been more than a year since I swore off going to the movies, and I've found pluses and minuses.

The pluses are that eventually everything comes out on cassette or one of the cable movie channels. I can also ignore the film critics because by the time I get around to seeing a movie, I've forgotten what they said.

The minuses are that the most creative special effects—spaceships swooping between planets, fiends slashing off heads at the senior prom and sharp-toothed little gremlins chomping on housewives—aren't as effective on a TV screen.

So I occasionally consider giving it one more try, maybe at the last show on a Tuesday night at a theater in a deserted-looking mall.

And I've thought about carrying something in my own pocket, possibly a length of lead pipe.

But that isn't really a good idea. Actually, it is, but I could wind up in front of a knee-jerk judge who would take the narrow view and say: "I can understand your irritation at being subjected to the torment of constant giggling from the group behind. But giggling does not justify the crushing of three skulls."

As someone said, the law is an ass.

QUESTIONS ON CONTENT AND TECHNIQUE

1. What factors in the article indicate Royko's age?
2. Do you think he is justified in his verbal attack on certain people? Which ones?
3. Does Royko achieve his effect through understatement or overstatement of the situation? What is his purpose?
4. Royko uses such words as "yahoo," "new barbarian," "twerp," and "hophead geek." How do you react to these terms?
5. Do you think Royko really believes what he states in the last sentence? Explain.

WRITING ASSIGNMENTS

Narration

1. Narrate an incident where you became very annoyed with a person in a public place, for example, a salesperson, a customer, an employee.
2. Royko and his wife differ on how to handle the disturbing young man in

the theater. Relate an incident where you and a companion had different opinions on how to handle a problem.

Crime and Society

1. Using sensory detail that places your reader on the scene, describe an argument, a fight, or an accident that you have witnessed.
2. Discuss violence you have seen personally or on film and its effect on you.

Super Fantasy

Bob St. John

Bob St. John wrote this column for the *Dallas Morning News*.

WORDS TO KNOW

lore traditional knowledge

lurking lying in wait

That year we lived in an apartment at the end of a long hall in an old two-story, red brick building. It was somewhat dark in the hall, even during the daylight hours. But when the weather was bad the hall became our playground. When you're a kid even dimly lit halls can become whatever you want them to be—so it was a river, a raceway, a jungle with dark creatures lurking in doorways, or a dangerous trail.

The worst experience in the hall was when I was playing Superman. I would ride my tricycle down the hall, picking up speed and then sticking out my arms and legs and pretending to fly. "Up, up and away!"

I can clearly remember that time and that tricycle. I must have been, oh, 18 or 19. Just kidding. I think I was 3, but the particular episode has become my only contribution to family legend and lore. The elderly in our family used to sit around telling stories about how great this or that person was and what a hero somebody else was . . . and then they'd tell about me being Superman on my tricycle.

It was the closest I ever came to flying. I was racing down the hall as Superman when my cousin, Rita Jane, visiting us that day, yelled something as I passed going faster than a speeding bullet. I turned my head to look back at her . . . and suddenly was airborne, going off the hall and over the steep stairs, I can do it! I can do it! I can flyyyyy!

The flight ended all too quickly in a heap at the bottom of the stairs. Fortunately, I landed on my head. My mother said she heard this awful noise and ran to and down the stairs and the first thing I said was, "I always wanted to fly like Superman." The tricycle was a mess, being bent to the right. But we had to make do in those days so I learned to ride it by leaning at a 45-degree angle to the left. Later I rode a bicycle which was not bent by leaning 45 degrees to the left and sometimes I catch myself doing the same thing when driving a car. Anyway.

Superman did it to so many of us. This came to mind because it's the 50th anniversary of the character we first saw in comics by Jerry Siegel and Joe Shuster. We saw the comics, following the action in the pictures before we could read, and listened to *The Adventures of Superman* on the radio. "Faster than a speeding bullet, more powerful than a locomotive . . . Look! Up in the sky! It's a bird! It's a plane! It's . . . Superman!"

We knew about Krypton, the *Daily Planet*, Superman's disguise as Clark Kent, and Lois Lane, Perry White and Jimmy Olsen. I sometimes still catch myself looking at atlases and maps, trying to locate Metropolis. We wore our fathers' long socks as Superman boots and towels or our mothers' aprons around our necks as capes.

When we grew older and started to school we watched the younger kids playing Superman. There was a little kid named Billy Mac Something-or-Other who wore his mother's apron around his neck when he first started to school. He always claimed he could fly, too. And he couldn't even swim! Neither could I, so when people teased him about not being able to swim, I'd take up for him.

One day during a school outing at the lake a few of us slipped away from the group and got into the water. They swam and I waded out until the water was up to my shoulders. And then Billy Mac Something-or-Other appeared in a tree over the water.

"I IS SUPERMAN!" he screamed and prepared to fly.

"You ain't even Waterman!" said Choo-Choo Charlie Moore, the oldest, meanest, fastest, biggest kid in our elementary school. "You can't swim a lick!"

"Up, up and awayyyy!" screamed Billy Mac and dove out of the tree, flapping his arms. He hit the water like an anchor and disappeared.

I yelled at Choo-Choo Charlie to save poor little Billy Mac. Choo-Choo Charlie was the best swimmer. The word was that he'd learned to swim at a very early age when he tossed his father into the water and had to figure out some way to go in and save him. Anyway, Choo-Choo Charlie agreed to save the kid and be a hero.

There was another kid in our group who jumped out a second story window with his mother's apron tied around his neck. But he broke his foot so I guess it was a shame he didn't land on his head. The kid just wanted to fly. And the favorite dreams I have are the ones about being able to fly so I guess even now, I always wanted to fly like Superman.

QUESTIONS ON CONTENT AND TECHNIQUE

1. Where and how does St. John give you a sense of "place"?
2. What do you think is the role of fantasy in children's lives? In adult lives?
3. How does the author evoke emotion in the reader?
4. What techniques does St. John use to reveal that he is telling the story from a child's point of view?

WRITING ASSIGNMENTS

Narration

1. Modeling your story after the author's, relate one of your family legends.
2. Narrate a childhood incident where you pretended to be a hero.

Memories and Reflections

1. Recount your fantasy of a secret ambition or achievement.
2. What fictional character from a comic strip, novel, or film played a significant role in your childhood? How did this character influence you?

38 Who Saw Murder Didn't Call the Police

Martin Gansberg

Martin Gansberg was a reporter and editor of *The New York Times.*

WORDS TO KNOW

apprehensive fearful

deliberation careful thinking

reticence inclination to silence

For more than half an hour 38 respectable, law-abiding citizens in Queens watched a killer stalk and stab a woman in three separate attacks in Kew Gardens.

Twice the sound of their voices and the sudden glow of their bedroom lights interrupted him and frightened him off. Each time he returned, sought her out and stabbed her again. Not one person telephoned the police during the assault; one witness called after the woman was dead.

That was two weeks ago today. But Assistant Chief Inspector Frederick M. Lussen, in charge of the borough's detectives and a veteran of 25 years of homicide investigations, is still shocked.

He can give a matter-of-fact recitation of many murders. But the Kew Gardens slaying baffles him—not because it is a murder, but because the "good people" failed to call the police.

"As we have reconstructed the crime," he said, "the assailant had three chances to kill this woman during a 35-minute period. He returned twice to complete the job. If we had been called when he first attacked, the woman might not be dead now."

This is what the police say happened beginning at 3:20 A.M. in the staid, middle-class, tree-lined Austin Street area:

Twenty-eight-year-old Catherine Genovese, who was called Kitty by almost everyone in the neighborhood, was returning home from her job as manager of a bar in Hollis. She parked her red Fiat in a lot adjacent to the Kew Gardens Long Island Rail Road Station, facing Mowbray Place. Like many residents of the neighborhood, she had parked there day after day since her arrival from Connecticut a year ago, although the railroad frowns on the practice.

She turned off the lights of her car, locked the door and started to walk the 100 feet to the entrance of her apartment at 82-70 Austin Street, which is in a Tudor building, with stores on the first floor and apartments on the second.

The entrance to the apartment is in the rear of the building because the front is rented to retail stores. At night the quiet neighborhood is shrouded in the slumbering darkness that marks most residential areas.

Miss Genovese noticed a man at the far end of the lot, near a seven-story apartment house at 82-40 Austin Street. She halted. Then, nervously, she headed up Austin Street toward Lefferts Boulevard, where there is a call box to the 102nd Police Precinct in nearby Richmond Hill.

She got as far as a street light in front of a bookstore before the man grabbed her. She screamed. Lights went on in the 10-story apartment house at 82-67 Austin Street, which faces the bookstore. Windows slid open and voices punctured the early-morning stillness.

Miss Genovese screamed: "Oh, my God, he stabbed me! Please help me! Please help me!"

From one of the upper windows in the apartment house, a man called down: "Let that girl alone!"

The assailant looked up at him, shrugged and walked down Austin Street toward a white sedan parked a short distance away. Miss Genovese struggled to her feet.

Lights went out. The killer returned to Miss Genovese, now trying to make her way around the side of the building by the parking lot to get to her apartment. The assailant stabbed her again.

"I'm dying!" she shrieked. "I'm dying!"

Windows were opened again, and lights went on in many apartments. The assailant got into his car and drove away. Miss Genovese staggered to her feet. A city bus, Q-10, the Lefferts Boulevard line to Kennedy International Airport, passed. It was 3:35 A.M.

The assailant returned. By then, Miss Genovese had crawled to the back of the building, where the freshly painted brown doors to the apartment house held out hope of safety. The killer tried the first door; she wasn't there. At the second door, 82-62 Austin Street, he saw her slumped on the floor at the foot of the stairs. He stabbed her a third time—fatally.

It was 3:50 by the time the police received their first call, from a man who was a neighbor of Miss Genovese. In two minutes they were at the scene. The neighbor, a 70-year-old woman and another woman were the only persons on the street. Nobody else came forward.

The man explained that he had called the police after much deliberation. He had phoned a friend in Nassau County for advice and then he had crossed the roof of the building to the apartment of the elderly woman to get her to make the call.

"I didn't want to get involved," he sheepishly told the police.

Six days later, the police arrested Winston Moseley, a 29-year-old business-machine operator, and charged him with the homicide. Moseley had no previous record. He is married, has two children and owns a home at 133-19 Sutter Avenue, South Ozone Park, Queens. On Wednesday, a court committed him to Kings County Hospital for psychiatric observation.

When questioned by the police, Moseley also said that he had slain Mrs. Annie May Johnson, 24, of 146-12 133d Avenue, Jamaica, on Feb. 29 and Barbara Kralik, 15, of 174-17 140th Avenue, Springfield Gardens, last July. In the Kralik case, the police are holding Alvin L. Mitchell, who is said to have confessed to that slaying.

The police stressed how simple it would have been to have gotten in touch with them. "A phone call," said one of the detectives, "would have done it." The police may be reached by dialing "0" for operator or SPring 7-3100.

The question of whether the witnesses can be held legally responsible in any way for failure to report the crime was put to the Police Department's legal bureau. There, a spokesman said:

"There is no legal responsibility, with few exceptions, for any citizen to report a crime."

Under the statutes of the city, he said, a witness to a suspicious or violent death must report it to the medical examiner. Under state law, a witness cannot withhold information in a kidnapping.

Today witnesses from the neighborhood, which is made up of one-family homes in the $35,000 to $60,000 range with the exception of the two apartment houses near the railroad station, find it difficult to explain why they didn't call the police.

Lieut. Bernard Jacobs, who handled the investigation by the detectives, said:

"It is one of the better neighborhoods. There are few reports of crimes. You only get the usual complaints about boys playing or garbage cans being turned over."

The police said most persons had told them they had been afraid to call, but had given meaningless answers when asked what they had feared.

"We can understand the reticence of people to become involved in an area of violence," Lieutenant Jacobs said, "but when they are in their homes, near phones, why should they be afraid to call the police?"

He said his men were able to piece together what happened—and capture the suspect—because the residents furnished all the information when detectives rang doorbells during the days following the slaying.

"But why didn't someone call us that night?" he asked unbelievingly.

Witnesses—some of them unable to believe what they had allowed to happen—told a reporter why.

A housewife, knowingly if quite casual, said, "We thought it was a lover's quarrel." A husband and wife both said, "Frankly, we were afraid." They seemed aware of the fact that events might have been different. A distraught woman, wiping her hands in her apron, said, "I didn't want my husband to get involved."

One couple, now willing to talk about that night, said they heard the first screams. The husband looked thoughtfully at the bookstore where the killer first grabbed Miss Genovese.

"We went to the window to see what was happening," he said, "but the light from our bedroom made it difficult to see the street." The wife, still apprehensive, added: "I put out the light and we were able to see better."

Asked why they hadn't called the police, she shrugged and replied: "I don't know."

A man peeked out from a slight opening in the doorway to his apartment and rattled off an account of the killer's second attack. Why hadn't he called the police at the time? "I was tired," he said without emotion. "I went to bed."

It was 4:25 A.M. when the ambulance arrived for the body of Miss

Genovese. It drove off. "Then," a solemn police detective said, "the people came out."

QUESTIONS ON CONTENT AND TECHNIQUE

1. What reasons did people give for not getting involved?
2. Were there perhaps underlying reasons for their reluctance to help? Explain.
3. Do you feel that witnesses who fail to report a crime should be held legally responsible? Why?
4. Gansberg gives little "gory" detail that might have been included. Where instead does he put the emphasis on detail?
5. What point of view does the author use? Why?

WRITING ASSIGNMENTS

Narration

1. Narrate a terrifying experience of your own.
2. Write an essay about an event where someone did become involved and helped you.
3. Relate a misdemeanor or crime that you observed.

Social and Political Issues

1. Take the role of any one of the 38 who were inside the apartment dwelling and did not call the police. Explain the reasons why you didn't want to get involved.
2. If this stabbing had occurred in your community, tell how the residents might have reacted.

Wheels of Misfortune

Bob Sylva

Bob Sylva does a magnificent job of detailing this old Cad.

WORDS TO KNOW

brazen bold

languishing listlessly waiting

neophyte beginner

opulence wealth

portly somewhat stout

For the past couple of days, this sinfully red Cadillac has been languishing in a gritty parking lot off a bad stretch of Broadway.

Like a tenderloin jazz haunt or an aging starlet with platinum hair, there's nothing quite so gloriously tawdry as a used Caddy. And this one's wheels are canted against the pavement in brazen fashion.

Unavoidably, the lipstick red plushmobile with the albino vinyl top catches your eye. It possesses a certain disreputable allure, a kind of once overstated opulence, now merely a vulgar parody. On closer inspection, it also boasts great blisters of rust. A peek inside the studio apartment of tufted red leather reveals around 149,000 miles on the clock. This baby has been around the block. And then some.

Parked beneath a shady elm tree, the Cadillac Sedan de Ville looks sad and abandoned, splotched by pigeon droppings and covered by road dust. A hand-lettered cardboard sign is lashed to the front grille like a makeshift bug screen. It raises a whimper of enthusiasm, urging: "Buy Today. Only $300. Best Deal Now!" The car's windshield is soaped with an earlier offering, now faded, which entreats—"$400. '73. New Tuneup. New Tires. Needs $100 work."

This is more than a good deal. This is more than a story about a beached land yacht. This has the makings of a minor mystery (emphasis on minor), a cautionary tale about status seeking and ominous-sounding engine noises.

Sam Stein (not his real name) is standing next to the red Caddy. He casts it a cursory glance, at once dark, aggrieved, and nearly hemorrhaging with disapproval. Stein is but 24 years old. He is an aspiring chef in the city's suddenly frothing culinary scene. He is tall, blond, soft-spoken and slightly portly. Given his stature and sense of style, Stein, whose earlier form of transportation was a ten-speed, perhaps felt it appropriate to acquire a conveyance more in keeping with his current ambitions. Yes, a Cadillac.

As fate would have it, last month a friend had just swapped his '63 Volvo for a '73 Cadillac Sedan de Ville. (The guy was unloading the Caddy because he was going through a divorce and the car reminded him of his wife. Thus, the car was cursed from the start.) This same friend offered the car to Stein for $550. Stein, something of a neophyte when it comes to auto ownership—his last car was a lowly Chevy—coveted the Cadillac. He was particularly enamored of its power windows. "I liked the way they went up and down," declares Stein. "It was a beautiful car."

So he coughed up $200 as a down payment and was on the hook for the difference. That first day of Cadillac ownership was a dream. Stein recalls it vividly: "I took it to the car wash, filled it up with $20 worth of gas, and dropped by the restaurant to show it to some friends. Then I cruised through the park." It's easy to imagine Stein, one hand on the wheel, a smug look on his face, gliding about town in red leather comfort, lowering and raising his windows at the flick of a switch. Then disaster struck.

Taking a friend to work the next day, Stein heard a loud knocking sound in the engine compartment. His first intuition was maybe the radiator was low on water (Stein is clearly no auto mechanic). Ignoring the noise, he completed his errand, and then proceeded to return home via the freeway. Stein: "I'm not accustomed to driving big cars on the freeway. I was in the fast lane, and suddenly the engine seemed to be losing power. I looked in the mirror, and I couldn't see any of the cars behind me, it was so smoky. I saw an exit sign ahead, so I punched the gas once and the car seemed to say, 'No, I don't like that at all.' It just started going slower and slower."

Until it stopped. On the freeway median. Stein got out of the car. It was 107 degrees out. Traffic whipped by. There was a weird, toxic smell in the air. "I literally felt like I was going to throw up or pass out," exclaims Stein, who tried futilely to fuss with the radiator cap. "Plus, I had spent all that money on the car." After no one stopped to help him, Stein went back inside the car and sat and sulked. Finally, a CHP officer showed up and arrangements were made to tow the car.

And so it sits. In this parking lot. With a cardboard death sentence on its bumper. "I wouldn't know how to describe how it runs," says Stein, stymied. "It runs very angry and upset."

Understandably, there have been no takers. "One guy," says Stein, "called me once at 7 in the morning. I said I was sleeping. He said he'd make it worth my while. So I went (to the lot) and he offered me $200. He said he was a mechanic, and would come back later that day with the money. He never showed up."

Asked if he regrets buying the car, a chastened Stein says, "Yes. I'm in between jobs now. I don't have the money to fix it up. I have no choice but to see it." He regards the car ruefully. "I like big cars," he says. "I like the leather interior. I thought I would live in that car. I just wish it ran."

QUESTIONS ON CONTENT AND TECHNIQUE

1. How does the image in the second paragraph affect you?
2. What encouraged Stein to buy the car?
3. Sylva paints a romantic picture of the Cad. Briefly describe it as a used car dealer would see it.
4. In one sentence, summarize the entire episode.

WRITING ASSIGNMENTS

Narration

1. Nearly everyone has at one time or another bought an item on whim or impulse that later was regretted. Narrate your own experience.
2. "It's easy to imagine Stein, one hand on the wheel, a smug look on his

face . . ." Narrate a time when you wanted to impress your friends and it became a moment of embarrassment.

Philosophical Values

1. Give examples of current status symbols in society today. Explain what needs they serve and their effects on others.
2. Stein was impressed with the appearance of the Cadillac rather than its mechanical reliability. What factors in society encourage this trait? Give examples and carefully examine the causes and effects.

SAT Shows Reporter Improves with Age

Gary Putka

Gary Putka is a staff reporter of *The Wall Street Journal.*

WORDS TO KNOW

elliptical orbit circle longer than it is wide

obsession persistent and disturbing idea or emotion.

Brookline, Mass.—Legs twitch. Chewing gum cracks. A few wide-eyed souls scan crib sheets for a last-minute edge. One of them is me.

It is minutes before the start of the Scholastic Aptitude Test in test center 22–240, Brookline High School in suburban Boston. A reporter and about half a million high-school seniors around the country are about to take the biggest test of the college admissions season.

Are we ill at ease? "I'm out here like an island," exclaims a girl in an isolated desk, to nobody in particular. In the next row a student averts his eyes from the proctor and stares at his hands.

For my fellow test takers, this Saturday morning will decide something important. For me, it will decide nothing except whether I beat my original scores of 17 years ago.

Together we will take a test, given seven times a school year to a total of 1.5 million students, that has become a national educational obsession. Educators will read our scores for signs that U.S. schools are improving or slipping. More colleges than ever will use the results to reject applicants or recruit them. The U.S. secretary of education will plot new SAT numbers on his wall charts.

For higher anxiety on the road to higher education, nothing matches the SAT. Students are flocking in record numbers to cram classes and shelling out more for computer software, practice manuals and advice books promising "sure-fire," "proven" and "revolutionary" ways to beat the test. Some even pop pills to calm their nerves.

The boom in preparation for the SAT is raising new concerns about its fairness. The poor can't afford the better cram courses. Some students say this is no way to run an equitable admissions system.

Fortified with tips from some of the cram artists, I am ready to go. I have consulted with Stanley H. Kaplan, the dean of the SAT coaches. I have reviewed "Cracking the System," the bible of the Princeton Review group, one of the SAT's biggest critics, whose $595 cram course is a hot item.

I have also plumbed "How to Beat Test Anxiety," by Barron's Educational Series. For only $4.95, it advises me to wrinkle up my nose, pucker my lips, grit my teeth (but not too tightly), smile for a while, open my mouth wide, drop my jaw and roll my eyes around to relax. My anxiety grows when I find that I can accomplish only four of these at any one time.

It is 8:40 now and the test hasn't started. My stomach growls. "Are you a proctor or something, or are you just old?" asks a blue-jeaned girl in braces.

"I'm writing a story."

"Sure," says someone behind me.

"Begin work," barks the test proctor.

Ripping open my test booklet, I go straight to the first question, following Mr. Kaplan's favorite rule: Ignore the instructions. He and other coaches teach students to review them beforehand to save time on the test. The first question is always easy, designed to curb test anxiety:

If $25 \times 360 = 100 \times n$, then $n =$

(A) 6
(B) 9
(C) 50

(D) 60
(E) 90

Dividing 9,000, the product of 25 and 360, by 100, I come up with E, the correct answer. But even Joe Bloggs, the Princeton Review's mythical test-taking everyman, gets the first question right.

The format of the SAT has changed since my first time around. Instead of five 30-minute sections, there are now six. Four sections count on each test, two verbal and two mathematical, with a total of 145 multiple-choice questions. The two other sections test writing skills and experiment with new questions for future tests. Scores, one each for verbal and mathematics, go from 200 to 800.

Soon, my mouth feels awfully dry. I have a few moments left for the last five questions in the section. I get them all wrong, starting with this one:

Each plant of a certain variety yields 50 seeds in the early fall and then dies. Only 40% of the seeds produce plants the following summer and the remainder never produce plants. At this rate, a single plant yielding seeds in 1986 will produce how many plants as descendants in 1989?

(A) 60
(B) 400
(C) 8,000
(D) 16,000
(E) 32,000

This is the kind of stumper, needing lots of figuring, that coaches urge you to skip until the end, since easier questions count as much. I can't find any easier ones and go for E. The answer is C: The 50 seeds of 1986 yield 20 plants in 1987. They produce 1,000 seeds, which yield 400 plants in 1988. They produce 20,000 seeds, which yield 8,000 plants in 1989. I had an ingenious way of coming up with 32,000 [which his editors deleted because they didn't understand it].

Halfway through the first verbal section, I hear a voice. "Put the watch under the desk," the proctor demands. A boy in a Brown University sweatshirt looks stunned. Under the rules, watches are permitted on wrists but not on desks or as alarms. "It's broken. It won't fit on my wrist," he says. But he removes it, looking shaken. "It's not a beeping watch," he shouts. "It's not a beeping watch." Other students pretend he isn't there.

A reading passage about the elliptical orbits of comets sends me spinning. At another point I pick "leisurely" as the opposite of "harrowing" instead of the wanted answer, "delightful."

I am getting angry. Some questions seem to have more than one good answer. Others seem intended to deceive. And in questions with only four choices, A–B–C–D, in the test booklet, there are five choices, A–B–C–D–E, on the answer sheet. Twice I pick the last choice in the booklet correctly but am marked wrong when I fill in the last oval on the answer sheet. Educational Testing Service, the test's writers, says it would be too expensive to print new forms.

Sometimes in its striving for difficult questions, particularly in math, ETS goofs. In a couple of celebrated cases in recent years, it has rescored tests based on challenges from students who saw more than the test writers did.

On my test, the last question in one mathematics section wasn't exactly a picture of clarity, not to me anyway:

If one of the solutions of the equation $x^2 + x + c = 0$ is 2, what is the other solution?

(A) -3
(B) -2
(C) 0
(D) 3
(E) It cannot be determined from the information given.

I choose E, since the question hasn't told me whether I'm solving for *x* or *c*. But the wanted answer is A, -3. That's because the solution for *x* is -3, since -3 squared, or 9, plus (-3) plus $(-6) = 0$.

But the question didn't say whether it was *x* or *c* that equaled 2. Later, when I get my test results and questions, I query ETS about this. Jame Braswell, an ETS senior examiner for math questions, says it is a commonly accepted convention in algebra to state equations with *x* as a variable and *c* as a constant. "I know no one that would say *c* is what you're solving for," says Mr. Braswell. But he acknowledges that "it would have been better" if the question had more clearly stated that one of the solutions is $x = 2$.

I leave the test center exhausted. Outside a few boys with blue hair and army boots unwind by wrestling on the frozen ground. I corner Jonathan Pessin, the Brookline senior who lost the watch battle. "I'm glad it's over," he says. . . .

We won't know until September what Joe Bloggs, the average SAT taker, scored this year. Last year he came up with 430 in verbal, 476 in mathematics, for a 906 total out of 1600. My 1400 score (750 verbal, 650 math) was 140 points more than my first try 17 years ago—quadruple the average gain that ETS predicts for repeaters. All the gain was on the verbal side. I dropped 20 points in math.

Mr. Braswell says my test scores mean I would probably make a better college student today than I did 17 years ago. That wouldn't be hard. I took six years to graduate. John Katzman, the president of the Princeton Review, disagrees with Mr. Braswell's assessment. "The only thing the SAT measures," he says, "is your ability to take the SAT."

QUESTIONS ON CONTENT AND TECHNIQUE

1. What is the effect of the first paragraph on you?
2. Locate some of the transitional words or phrases that Putka uses to keep the story line flowing.
3. By including two of the SAT questions, the author accomplishes a purpose. What is it?
4. The author uses certain words and phrases that indicate the toll that anxiety is taking on others' bodies. What are they?
5. What do you think is Putka's attitude toward the validity of the SAT? Attack or defend.

WRITING ASSIGNMENTS

Narration

1. Narrate an incident where you were nervous: job interview, final exam, newcomer at a party.
2. Write a narrative about your first day in this class or another. Make it interesting for your reader by including your emotions.

Education

1. Recall the young man who had the watch on the desk and attempted to explain the infraction of the rules. Write of an incident where you misunderstood or didn't follow instructions and where the outcome was similar to this incident.
2. Putka improved his test score 140 points more than his "first try 17 years ago." Can you relate a second time you attempted a test, contest, or problem and showed significant improvement?
3. Explain how you react under pressure in one of the following situations: job, test, quarrel, crisis.

How He Saw the War in Viet Nam

Jimmy Breslin

Through his syndicated column, Jimmy Breslin, a former sportswriter, has won many readers with his distinctive style. He has collected some of these essays in the book *The World of Jimmy Breslin.*

WORDS TO KNOW

colostomy surgically making an opening for the colon through the abdominal wall

Travis Air Force Base, California

The ground-crew man kept waving his black-gloved hands for them to keep coming, and they moved slowly over the white concrete runway toward him. The blue truck came first. The big jet transport, which had no windows on its sides, was behind it. Then there were two red firetrucks which always come out when they land a plane that carries people who are wounded.

Otherwise, there was no change in the routine of the air base. Transport planes taxied onto runways and took off. Straight across the field, in front of low sand-colored hills, B-52 bombers waited in the dusk with their nuclear bombs inside them. The ground-crew man's black gloves still waved and the truck led the plane right up to a knot of people who stood with their hands over their ears. The jet's engines roared and the kerosene fumes were thick in the air. Then its engines ran out in a whine.

A wide cargo door in the side of the plane came open. A nurse stood in the doorway with a clipboard in her hands. She was dark-haired and tanned, and wearing blue slacks and shirt and a heavy flying jacket with captain's bars on it.

"How many do you have?" one of the officers on the runway said.

She looked down at the mimeographed sheets. "Twenty-six from Viet Nam." She shook her head. "No, I missed one. Twenty-seven from Viet Nam"

"All litters?" the officer said.

"No, we have twelve ambulatory," she said. "And one psychiatric."

The ground crew pushed a covered chute up to the plane. The officers who had been standing on the runway started walking up the chute. A hospital bus backed up to the chute; white-uniformed medics ran out of the bus and up the ramp and into the plane.

The litters were stacked in tiers. The inside of the plane was warm. Only sheets covered their broken bodies. The medics carried them up to the hatch and into the cold Northern California breeze. Each time, the nurse told the medics to put the litter down.

"You have to cover up," she said, and she bent down and pulled olive-drab blankets over them and tucked the blankets in. Then she looked at them. "Now lie on your back, please," she said. The young, smooth faces went back and the white pillows came up around their cheeks. They were silent. Their eyes, opened very wide, looked straight up.

They came, one after another, in casts and with bloodstains on their sheets, and the nurse's tanned hands pulled olive-drab blankets over their broken bodies and she talked quietly and looked into the face of each of them. Then he would be gone and the medics would put another piece of the war in Viet Nam at her feet. And she would bend over and reach for blankets.

She did not bend over when they brought Sergeant Philip Vogel out. He was the last. Both of his legs were in casts that were dark from the blood seeping through them. The bandages on his body began at his chest. A sheet covered part of him. Plastic bags and tubes from a colostomy showed from under the sheet.

"Don't put anything on my legs, please," Philip Vogel said.

She shook her head. "No, I won't put anything over you," she said. She stood and looked at him. "Get him out of the cold right away," she said. The medics took Philip Vogel down the ramp and into the bus. The doors shut and the bus rolled away and went off the runway and up a hill to the light green hospital building.

They bring them in like this almost every night at Travis Air Force Base. Broken bodies from a small war in a place in Asia. They come in on jet planes that land unnoticed while the nation watches programs on television. They used to come home as heroes. Now they are a way of life.

They put Philip Vogel in a room on the first floor of the hospital. They gave him a cigarette and lit it up for him and then the medic went to get a doctor for him. Vogel's brown eyes looked up at the ceiling. There was no animation in his long, straight face. He took the cigarette out of his mouth and, without being asked a question, he started talking.

"On the second night," he said. "They attacked us on the second night. According to the S-2 there were four hundred guerrillas. It was only my second day there and I got hit. A hand grenade. The VC hit me with a hand grenade. No, what's the use of saying that? I was in a foxhole one night at 10:30 on guard duty and the guy with me was asleep in the higher portion of it. I heard a noise. I didn't want to fire and give away my position. I tried to get out a hand grenade and it didn't clear the bunker and it came back and got me. It bounced right back. Right back at my feet and got me everywhere. I have a colostomy. I'm twenty-five and I have a colostomy. I was going to marry a girl. She's in Pennsylvania. If I ever heal up I can marry her. We got the most modern weapons in the world. I never saw one of them. Never saw one. They move in the grass like snakes. Hey, aren't you gonna do anything about my feet, man?"

The medic heard him and came into the room. He started to take the pillow out from under Vogel's feet. Somebody across the hall began to scream that he couldn't breathe. Then there was a gagging sound. The medic let go of the pillow and ran out of the room.

Vogel looked around the room. "May I have an ashtray, please?" he said.

"Where are you from?" he was asked.

"Baltimore."

"What are you going to do with yourself when you're finished with this?"

"Do? I don't know what I'm going to do. I like the Army. The Army's good. I didn't want to go to Viet Nam. The second lieutenant, he was running to different men's positions. He got shot right in the head. I saw it."

He closed his eyes. "It hurts," he said. His teeth came down and dug into his lip. He started to moan. His teeth came up from his lip and a yell came out of his mouth. A doctor and a nurse came into the room and they bent over Philip Vogel, who had a hand grenade bounce back at him on his second night in Viet Nam.

In an office at the end of the corridor, Ben Griffin, an officer from the base, sat at a desk and went through some forms.

"We got a plane coming in from Viet Nam tomorrow," he said quietly. "This one is carrying coffins."

QUESTIONS ON CONTENT AND TECHNIQUE

1. Breslin paints a stark picture of reality in his article. Indicate some images that clearly impress the reader.
2. What do you think is Breslin's attitude toward the Vietnam War?
3. How is the story of Vogel's injury unusual, how do you learn of it, and of what significance is it?
4. For what purpose does the writer use the orderly, the nurse, and a girlfriend?

WRITING ASSIGNMENTS

Narration

1. The war changed Vogel's life. Narrate some experience that changed yours.
2. Relate when you or a member of your family had a physical injury.

Philosophical Values

1. Tell about your visit to a hospital, a welfare group, a homeless shelter, or an orphanage, and share your impressions vividly with your readers in order to persuade them to your point of view.
2. Philip Vogel is welcomed to your hometown and asked to give a speech. What will he say?

Chapter 3

Characterization

The "BIZARRO" cartoon by Dan Piraro is reprinted by permission of Chronicle Features, San Francisco.

Readers of a story about a beachcomber will be more interested in why someone becomes a beachcomber than in the information the writer can provide. Yet the writer needs to blend both information and character study to develop a character without becoming plodding or boring.

For example, in Berkley Hudson's piece on retired bronco rider Floyd Stillings, you can see how the writer uses sensual images to describe his subject: "hands, as tanned as the leather of a fine saddle"; "a healthy head of white hair and a curl that falls onto a forehead lined like cracked sod"; "a viselike grip." By showing us Stillings as a character study, the writer also presents us with a succinct biography from his childhood to his retirement.

In the same way, Bella English depicts the treasure hunter hooked on the Boston Red Sox, Anne Driscoll characterizes Mrs. White and her unusual talent agency, and Hattie Clark describes the carver of kachina dolls. In each story, details accumulate to give us a physical picture of each character as well as a psychological one. These individuals come alive for the reader because the writers use characterization effectively.

WHEN YOU WRITE CHARACTERIZATION

- Choose, if possible, a person who has appeal to your audience.
- Prepare questions for the interview and do any homework necessary on background material.
- Describe the individual vividly to give the reader a physical sense of the person.
- Let the interviewee speak in some of his or her own words; paraphrase, but keep the flavor of his or her personality through direct quotes.
- Select, if you can, the setting where the person normally works or feels comfortable, and let it reveal character.
- Focus on a dominant trait or achievement.
- Make the character come alive through blending the description of the person and the setting with memorable dialogue.

Bronco Rider Recollects Years in Saddle

Berkley Hudson

Berkley Hudson is a staff writer for the *Los Angeles Times.*

WORDS TO KNOW

astride with one leg on each side

bronco untamed horse

inducted enrolled

Floyd Stillings reached into his desk drawer to retrieve a small cloth sack resembling a Bull Durham tobacco pouch.

The old man's hands, as tanned as the leather of a fine saddle, carefully lifted out a medallion. In the morning sunlight that filtered into Stillings' apartment in Arcadia, the medal shone like gold.

On the front, with a cowboy atop a bronco, the lettering said, "National Rodeo Hall of Fame." He turned to the back to read this inscription: "Floyd Stillings Honored and Inducted Dec. 19, 1987."

He brought the award home from a banquet in Oklahoma City, home of the National Cowboy Hall of Fame and Western Heritage Center, which since 1965 has honored 112.

"I haven't gotten too hopped up on it yet," Stillings, a champion bronco rider in the 1920s and 1930s, said of the award.

"Hell, I should have been in there years ago. Most people who rodeo spend six, maybe 10 years at it. I spent 21 years. That was a long time. I stopped in March of '42. And that was more than a few years ago."

For the past three decades, Stillings has lived in Southern California. Most of that time, he worked as a trainer, breeder and owner of horses at the Santa Anita racetrack. He still goes there when the horses are running, using the passes he earned as a trainer.

At 83, Stillings lives alone in a tiny apartment on the second floor of his landlord's large home. Sybil, his wife of 35 years, died 13 years ago. He has one main room with bed, desk, couch and lounge chair. In his small kitchen, he uses a hot plate. When he walks up the stairs to his apartment, his aching back forces him to bend over and balance on all fours.

"I'm paying for all those rodeos," in which he broke dozens of bones, he said.

Stillings is a sturdy man with a healthy head of white hair and a curl that falls onto a forehead lined like cracked sod. His eyes are as blue as the sky over Montana, where he journeyed at age 13 after running away from his family in the horse-and-grain country of Pullman, Wash.

From a storage closet, he brought out a stack of scrapbooks that tell part of the story of Floyd Stillings, cowboy.

Why did he ride?

"I loved it. I didn't have to prove nothing." As a child who rode horseback to school between the ages of 6 and 8, he added, "What else could I do?"

"I led a wildcat's life," he said. "You have to be 'bout half bronco to do it."

He opened a scrapbook. Yellowed clippings and faded black-and-white photographs fell from it.

Stillings left home because he and one of his two brothers "fought like stray dogs." In Montana he helped break cavalry horses for the U.S. Army during World War I. "When I left home, I left. I didn't tell nobody where I was going. I thought I was a man. That's when hell started." He had to learn fast because he had to eat.

He turned to a page in the scrapbook with a picture of a crowd gathered under circuslike banners proclaiming: "T. O. Burroughs Wild West. Real Bucking Horses and Long Horned Steers." At the time, in the early 1920s, he was a teen-age rider in the Burroughs show. In a round-topped cowboy hat that would have done Tom Mix proud, he romped across the dirt arenas of the West, once even traveling to Hawaii.

In another 1920s photograph, staring out from under a huge hat and with a scarf swept around her neck, was Louise Hartwig, then Stillings' girlfriend. At one rodeo, he saddled her bronco, left the chute without watching her ride and came back later to find that the horse had bucked her and trampled her.

On two other occasions, he saddled broncos for women who were killed by them. He said his saddling had nothing to do with the deaths, which he blamed simply on bad luck and tough horses.

Even his girlfriend's death, Stillings said, didn't slow his desire to ride. "That just puts a match to the kerosene . . . just makes you that much more determined to ride."

Wedged into the scrapbook was a series of letters written through the years by friends who felt that he should be included in the Rodeo Hall of Fame. One was from Gene Autry, who cited Stillings' work in rodeos Autry ran in the 1930s and early 1940s. The Autry letter, dated 10 years ago, said: "He was always a top cowboy and I respected him very much."

Another letter, from Lloyd W. Taggart, a former employer of Stillings' who was in the construction business in Wyoming, listed Stillings' major achievements. In 1926, he was bull-riding champion in New York's Madison Square Garden. The next year, he won the saddle-bronco championship in Chicago. Two years later, he won the bronco championship at the celebrated Cheyenne Frontier Days. In 1932 and 1933, he won the bronco riding at Madison Square Garden; he made the finals in that event in eight other years. In 1933, he was bronco winner at the Pendleton Roundup in Oregon.

"The Chicago show was the turning point of my life," Stillings said. "I was hard and in good shape, and I was staying sober." By this time, he was earning good money and had a national reputation.

He was following in the path of a man he'd first met and admired at the Pendleton Roundup in 1922, Ray Bell. Today, Bell, a breeder of race horses, also lives in Arcadia.

Bell, who was named to the Rodeo Hall of Fame in 1986, said Stillings was a determined if not a flashy rider. "He's a real 100% Westerner," Bell said. "The kind you'd have met in the 1880s on a covered-wagon train.

"He does get hot awful quick. But he's never said a cross word to me. He means what he says, and he don't exaggerate. He just tells the truth."

Stillings lived as hard as he rode. One year he won $1,000 at the Cheyenne Frontier Days. "You could buy a brand-new Chevrolet for $500," he said. "That one year, I bought three in six months' time."

The first one was totaled in a trip from Denver to Deadwood, S.D. A bronco-rider friend was driving when they crashed into horse-drawn wagons. Later, in Deadwood, he met up with a woman rider named Jiggs. She told him where they could find a keg of whiskey, and off they went in the second car, which he'd bought from money he won in Deadwood. By day's end, they'd finished off the whiskey and the car. He won again in Soda Springs, Ida., enough to buy the third car.

Stillings interrupted his story to explain another photograph, which showed his spurs sticking straight into the side of the horse. "When I made up my mind to ride your horse, your horse was rode," he said. "If you spurred the son of a bitch hard enough, he'd weaken."

In his youth, Stillings said, he was very strong. Even today, his handshake lets you know that for a man of any age, he has a viselike grip. To illustrate, he crooked the middle finger of one hand and then the other. "I could chin myself with that finger right there, with a handkerchief wrapped around it."

What of the horse being forced and spurred?

"Forget the horse," he said. "You ride the horse till he quits bucking."

From the closet, Stillings brought out a pair of thick steel spurs wrapped in leather. "They're cut to hold the stirrup." He cradled them in his hands, shifting them back and forth, just looking at them in silence.

"Hell, I've had a horse buck me off with both my arms on the ground and both feet still in the stirrups," he said. To explain, he retrieved what he called "boot-shoes," custom-made for him. Rubbing his hands on the still-soft leather of the ankle-high boots, he explained that the odd cut of the shoes held them fast in the stirrups. And if a cowboy really wanted to make sure that his boot stayed put, Stillings said, he would melt bubble gum into the crevice where the heel met the stirrup.

Reaching under his bed, Stillings pushed aside the control switch for his electric blanket. He jerked out what looked like a thick roll of leather that snapped as he unfurled it. "I rode many a bucking horse with these." They were his chaps. He studied them and then, discovering a dark spot on the leather, said: "There's still blood on them. That's old, dried blood."

Stillings said he could tell more stories, of beautiful silver belt buckles won and then stolen, of championship money paid in gold that he lost when a Wyoming bank shut down during the Depression, of working as a cowboy extra in the movies, of roughnecking on oil rigs, of riding from rodeo to rodeo throughout the country, across Australia, Japan and England, and of the thousands who cheered him in Madison Square Garden.

He could tell these stories, he said, because he'd lived them. "There was a lot of rough trips in them journeys. It wasn't all holidays." He looked as if he might cry when he said this. He didn't. He just paused in silence and put away the scrapbooks.

Now, he said, he just wanted to go to the track and watch the horses race.

QUESTIONS ON CONTENT AND TECHNIQUE

1. How does Hudson use comparison to describe the old cowboy?
2. How many of the senses does the author use? Explain how they develop his image.
3. What is the dominant impression of the cowboy's apartment?
4. Describe Stillings in one word. Select a detail and discuss why it is particularly effective in showing that certain trait of his.

WRITING ASSIGNMENTS

Characterization

1. Talk to a person who has been involved in a dangerous or rugged occupation.
2. Choose someone over 40. Let him or her tell about a youthful hobby or job.

Memories and Reflections

1. Find an early photograph of an elderly person in your family. Write of his or her recollection of the event when the picture was taken.
2. Discuss someone you know who has many of the qualities of this old-time cowboy.

A Nickel Here, a Nickel There

Bella English

Bella English writes a column for the *Boston Globe*.

WORDS TO KNOW

chagrin embarrassment

dumpster any person or vehicle that picks up trash

empirical based on observation

entourage followers of a person

troves collections of objects found

HINGHAM—"We won't do too well today," says Ernie Franks, gesturing down the street. "The dumpster man just passed us."

I have held him up by getting lost, but geez, it's still only a few minutes past seven. Ernie's been up for ages, and by now he's usually half way through his two-hour constitutional.

It's more than just a walk. It's a treasure hunt. Every day, with two weeks off for good behavior, Ernie collects bottles to support his lifelong habit, the Boston Red Sox.

The nickels from the beer cans and Coke bottles enable Ernie to spend two weeks at the Sox training camp in Winter Haven, Fla. He leaves next week, and has $800 so far.

"The flight and hotel room costs $784, then I need extra for meals," he says, plucking a Mountain Dew bottle from the side of the road. If he makes $1,000, that'll be 20,000 cans.

Ernie, 72, is the kind of fan who can tell you who played which base on the '51 team, who answers without hesitation when you ask about the most spectacular play he ever witnessed: "Willie Mays making a catch off Vic Wertz in the '54 Series."

Over the years, he has seen 55 World Series games. This will be his 14th year at spring training, and he hasn't missed opening day at Fenway in decades. Why, Ernie even travels to see the Sox' Pawtucket farm team.

He's a familiar figure in town, making his way down Main Street with a leash restraining a wriggling dog in one hand and a broomstick-turned-cane in the other. His cat trails behind.

The sky is slate, with patches of blue just beginning to break through. School buses and trucks pass and blow their horns. Students recognize his limp arm and say hello. Joggers nod.

"The gentleman in that house there," he says, waving his cane at a stately Colonial, "saves bags of cans for me." Lots of people do, dropping them off on his porch. Once, a man brought over several huge bags, but left them at the wrong house, much to the chagrin of Ernie—and the woman whose porch the bags were left upon.

Ernie and his four-legged entourage turn in at Hingham High School. He looks in the dumpster. "Nothing. He beat us to it."

But outside a door sits a box containing several soft drink cans. "The janitors leave 'em for me," he says, depositing 10 cans in a plastic garbage bag.

Ernie, retired after 48 years as a longshoreman, goes to Winter Haven with the Bosox Club. They stay at the Howard Johnson's and their routine varies little. Breakfast, over to the park to watch the Sox practice, lunch, over to the park to watch the Sox play. Swimming? Sunning? God forbid!

Ernie grew up in South Boston, where he used to pick up two half-pint bottles for a penny. In later years, he'd recycle aluminum cans for 22 cents a pound. No one was as happy as Ernie Franks when the bottle bill passed.

He has watched baseball change from when professionals played more for fun than money to today, when players strike over six-figure salaries. "You know that new rookie, Benzinger?" he asks. "He gets $4 for every autograph he signs at official appearances." There is bewilderment on his face and in his voice. Four dollars, after all, is 80 cans.

In the high-school parking lot, Ernie walks up and down each row of cars. Sometimes, he finds coins in the gravel, usually pennies. Pieces of brass and copper he takes to the junk man.

"Another thing I do is fish the telephones," he says, pointing to a pay phone across the street. Clearly, Ernie Franks is a man you'd want to take on a scavenger hunt.

After years of empirical research, Ernie knows the treasure troves: schools because "kids are lazy. They drink Cokes and throw away the bottles." Athletic fields and tennis courts because lots of soda is consumed. Gas stations because they always have pop machines.

He makes his way down the quiet streets over to a Sunoco station. "You got anything for me today?" he calls to an attendant. The young man returns with seven bottles and cans.

Outside Pete's Barbershop is a box containing several Pepsi bottles and a can of "Jolt," which Ernie describes as "something new."

Back home, Ernie hauls out a stack of old baseball programs, yellow newspaper clips and ticket stubs. There's a Polaroid picture of him with Ted Williams.

Ernie will make another round at 2:30, and maybe a third at 6 P.M. After all, time is running short, and the more bottles he collects in Hingham, the better he eats in Winter Haven.

QUESTIONS ON CONTENT AND TECHNIQUE

1. What is the dominant impression of Ernie throughout the interview?
2. How does Ernie earn his spending money?
3. What technique has the writer used in the introduction to interest the reader?
4. Select several lines that show how important baseball is to Ernie.

WRITING ASSIGNMENTS

Characterization

1. Some people, like the dumpster man, devote their lives to simple matters. Talk to such a person and write your essay giving detailed descriptions of his or her physical appearance, body language, or tone of voice.
2. Ernie is a baseball fan. Find someone who is an avid sports fan and let your reader share with the fan's excitement by writing about his or her activities.

Work and Play

1. Choose someone like Ernie and discuss his or her daily routine. Be sure to create a dominant feeling in the reader by your portrayal.
2. Have you ever saved bottle caps, coupons, pennies, or box tops for a prize or reward? Relate the excitement, the routine, and the result.

A Lonely Believer in Sasquatches

David Foster

David Foster of the Associated Press tells of the believer Paul Freeman.

WORDS TO KNOW

carcass dead body

dermal relating to skin

scat animal droppings

skittish easily frightened

Walla Walla—Even a Bigfoot believer like Paul Freeman concedes the supermarket tabloids get carried away: "HUGE BIGFOOT MONSTER TERRORIZES THE ROCKIES! It stunk like a sewer, roared like a lion and clutched the leg of an animal in its hand."

"BIGFOOT ATTACKED US! Blood-Crazed Creature Savages Camera Crew and Pounds 2-Ton Truck Into Junkyard Scrap."

Freeman smiles at the outlandish stories, which he collects in a cardboard box. "There are some crazy people out there," he says.

Freeman himself has been called the craziest of all.

But he knows otherwise. He says he has seen Bigfoot. Four times. He swears it's true, and he is out to convince a doubting world that the legendary ape-monsters, perhaps a thousand strong, really do roam the dark woods of the Pacific Northwest.

"I know they are there, and I know what I see," Freeman says. "Nothing has to be proven to me. But I'd like to prove it to the public, so they'll say Freeman's not really a kook."

Bigfoot—or Sasquatch, as the Indians called the beast—is one of the Northwest's enduring legends. More than 750 sightings of the creatures or their oversize footprints have been reported over the past century, mostly in the evergreen forests stretching from Northern California to British Columbia.

Yet no Bigfoot has ever been killed or captured. No carcass or bones have ever been found.

A few purported Bigfoot photographs exist, including a picture taken in October by Freeman's son, but they always seem to be out of focus, too dark, or too far away. What looks like Sasquatch could be a misshapen tree stump or someone in a monkey suit.

Skeptics point to hoaxes, like the time a Washington man created a whole Bigfoot family by stomping around with three whopping pairs of feet he had carved of wood.

But if you want to believe, talk to Paul Freeman.

Drive with him eastward from Walla Walla, where the flatlands of southeastern Washington rise into the Blue Mountains of the Umatilla National Forest. Listen to Freeman's tales of safaris into the forest's 177,000-acre wilderness area. Behold a lonely land of wind-bared ridges and dark, forested canyons.

Bigfoot country, Freeman says: "You can go in there all summer and not see anybody."

Freeman tells of suddenly skittish horses, of normally docile dogs growling fiercely at the darkness. "Your skin gets kind of crawly and the hair stands up on your neck," he says. "You know you're being watched, but you don't know from where."

Freeman, 45, does not seem the type to spook easily. He is beefy, bearded and, at 6-foot-4 and 265 pounds, approaches Sasquatch proportions himself. He's a meat-cutter by trade; an outdoorsman and hunter by nature.

He says he, too, was a skeptic—until June 10, 1982, when he was working as a watershed patroller for the U.S. Forest Service and met up with a shaggy, reddish-brown Bigfoot nearly 8 feet tall.

When word got out, Freeman became an instant celebrity, but the fame was spiked with ridicule.

Freeman quit his Forest Service job and moved away, drifting through a series of jobs. A gnawing need for vindication, he says, drew him back to Walla Walla in 1984.

He has been on the spoor of Bigfoot ever since. He says he is in the woods three days a week and figures he has sunk $50,000 into the search, financing it by driving trucks part time and tapping profits from the sales of a meat-cutting business.

There is a trunk filled with plaster casts of Bigfoot tracks, and hair samples that, according to Freeman, experts cannot identify as man or beast.

Near the kitchen door of his rented home, a map is webbed with lines marking where he and son Duane, 22, have tracked Sasquatches. In the freezer sits a chunk of suspected Bigfoot scat.

Last Oct. 5, Duane snapped three color photos that he and his father say show a creature they sighted 35 miles east of Walla Walla. The best one shows a black, ape-like shape 150 yards away.

Duane says it made a believer out of him, but the fuzzy pictures do less for one who wasn't there. "I was shaking a lot," Duane explains.

Freeman says that Bigfoot was on the small side: about 7 feet tall, maybe 700 pounds. The biggest, he says, top 8 feet and leave 18-inch footprints. Uprooted trees attest to their strength, he says, but unlike the monsters that stalk tabloid headlines, they are gentle and shy.

The secretive animals evade detection by sticking to dark canyons, foraging at night, and even altering their prints to resemble bear tracks, Freeman says.

"Sure, they're that smart," he says.

They eat mushrooms and skunk cabbage, elk calves and salmon, Freeman says. Come winter, they may hole up in caves, which he says would explain their awful stench.

Freeman has received moral support from at least one researcher in the murky world of "cryptozoology," the study of questionable creatures.

Grover Krantz, a Washington State University anthropology professor and veteran Sasquatch seeker, has examined some of Freeman's plaster casts and found them rather convincing, complete with fingerprint-like dermal ridges. But another Bigfoot researcher, Canadian author Rene Dahinden, denounces Freeman as a publicity-seeking huckster.

Freeman says he'd just like to get a good photograph, or maybe some bones. He has heard there are caves deep in the Umatilla's wilderness and says that might be where Sasquatches hide their dead.

"If I could find some bones," he says, "it would pay me back 100 times over what I've spent."

QUESTIONS ON CONTENT AND TECHNIQUE

1. Explain some reasons (according to Foster) for Freeman's belief in Bigfoot.
2. How does Foster balance his controversial article to appeal to both believers and skeptics?
3. In what ways does the author catch the attention of readers in his opening and satisfy them at the closing?
4. How does Freeman's behavior support his beliefs and lend credibility to them?

WRITING ASSIGNMENTS

Characterization

1. Interview someone who holds an unusual point of view or belief.
2. Observe a publicity-seeking huckster and create that image for your reader.

The Natural Environment

1. Explain why so many people are fascinated with creatures like E. T., Sasquatch, the Abominable Snowman, etc.
2. Relate a psychic or scientifically unexplainable experience of yours or that of someone you know.

Maker of Kachina Dolls

Hattie Clark

Hattie Clark is a staff writer for the *Christian Science Monitor.*

WORDS TO KNOW

bedecked adorned

icon religious image

jocular jolly

taciturn not inclined to talk

unwary not careful to guard against danger or deception

Polacca, Ariz.—The sunlight is just right, beaming into the dim shed through an open door. It glows on a row of torsos. They're wooden, of course.

Amid them sits their carver, Fletcher Healing, a Tewa Indian. He's making kachina dolls for shops, boutiques and the tourist trade. For these outlets, Healing sticks strictly to the Tewa clown, a slim but jocular figure painted zebra-style in black and white. For a splash of color, there's a slice of watermelon in his wooden hands. This particular doll is a particularly good seller in the Anglo market.

Healing knows all about Tewa clowns because he grew up in Tewa Village.

Way back in 1700, a group of Tewa, who lived in the Rio Grande area, sought refuge with the Hopi. Their descendants are still on the Hopi First Mesa today. Understandably, the Tewa and Hopi share many cultural patterns, including kachina beliefs.

"This was a hobby I had," says Healing, "to keep me busy."

And that it does. The carver, who is a retired highway maintenance employee with the Arizona Department of Transportation, has found himself another full-time occupation.

How many kachina dolls does he craft a month?

"I can't keep track. I work all day, then sometimes I take a rest," he says. But the orders flow in year-round.

"He gets orders from shops, even in Indiana," says his wife, Julia, a Hopi, who is somewhat puzzled that Hoosierland with its Indy and basketball mania would welcome kachina dolls. Julia Healing was raised in the Hopi village of Sichomovi, near the Tewa settlement, both high on the windswept mesa. The couple now live at the mesa's base in the Hopi village of Polacca.

Kachina dolls aren't playthings like Cabbage Patch and Barbie. In the Anglo market, they're collected by adults who house them in glass cases or sandwich them between Shakespeare, Updike, and the like on their bookshelves.

In recent years, the dolls have become hot commercial items, and carvers churn them out, keeping pace—if not ahead—of the Anglo appetite.

But, Healing will tell you that for the Hopi and Tewa, kachina dolls carry deeper significance than collectible items to spruce up living room decor. They're given to little girls, both as toys and teaching tools. Each doll is carved, painted, and bedecked to reflect a particular kachina spirit within the Hopi religion.

Although the dolls often hang from rafters or on walls in Hopi homes, they're not idols or icons. Rather, they acquaint youngsters with the vast array of kachinas that range from Crow Mother and Black Bear to Squash and Mudhead.

Much of the time, Healing works in the shed behind his house. You can't miss the scene as your car bumps up the dusty road to the mesa above.

"They see me sitting here," he says, referring to the tourists. "I don't go out, though," a phrase that tells he doesn't need to recruit buyers. He sells each doll, about 10 inches tall or so, for about $175.

Healing's hair has silvered, and the sun coppered his hands long ago, a color that contrasts with the black and white he meticulously applies to his dolls. He's taciturn, too, but cordial, letting you watch him work.

"Yes, I carve them by hand," he says, a comment that elevates his figures above the lathe-turned dolls that sometimes slip into the marketplace to trap unwary buyers.

Like other kachina-makers, Healing carves his dolls in sections: legs, arms, torso and head.

In earlier times, kachina dolls were simpler, more static in stance, so they were carved from single pieces of wood. But today's figures come in action-packed postures or lifelike positions, and artisans find it easier to carve them piecemeal.

Some collectors still seek those early dolls of the late 1800s and early 1900s. They view these simple art forms as better representations of supernatural beings, leaving today's refined figures with their detailed noses and toes to buyers who like sleek craftsmanship.

True to tradition, Healing fashions his dolls from the root of the cottonwood tree.

"It's easy to work with and doesn't break," he explains.

In times past, carvers could glean their material from the banks of the Little Colorado, selecting cottonwood driftwood. But these supplies have dwindled as more and more craftsmen fill demands. So, Healing resorts to distant commercial suppliers.

Unlike some male carvers, Healing is not busy making kachina dolls for daughters at ceremonies. The Healings have one adult son and a 6-year-old grandson. "And boys get rattles and bows and arrows, not dolls," says his wife.

Kachinas fit into a complex Hopi system of beliefs.

The Hopis live high on mesas in the rain-hungry lands of northern Arizona.

QUESTIONS ON CONTENT AND TECHNIQUE

1. Identify places where Clark uses colors to enhance her descriptive details. How does this serve her purpose?
2. Mr. Healing mentions that kachinas are used as teaching tools. How do you think they might teach youngsters?
3. Does the writer include enough description for you to visualize the kachina? Explain.

WRITING ASSIGNMENTS

Characterization

1. Interview a person of an ethnic, religious, or racial group about some aspect of his or her culture.

2. Have someone tell you about a treasured art object. Ask the owner such questions as where it was obtained, why it was chosen, and of what significance it is.

Language and The Arts

1. Think of a favorite toy that you had as a child, and discuss its meaning to you.
2. Describe a personal hobby or craft or that of someone else, and show how it reflects personality or culture.

The Telescope Man

Rafael Alvarez

Rafael Alvarez is a reporter for the *Baltimore Sun.*

WORDS TO KNOW

anonymous of unknown origin

astral relating to stars

Pleiades a loose cluster of stars in the constellation Taurus

waned decreased in intensity

Call this guy the Telescope Man.

For some loose change, the chance to make small talk about big dreams, and the sheer and simple thrill of it, Herman Heyn will give you a peek at the heavens.

In this land of sidewalk opportunity there glows a galaxy of ways to persuade pedestrians to drop money in a hat.

Some guys whine Bobby Dylan songs, strumming a battered six-string and croaking their hearts out about the many things that "God said to Abraham. . . ."

Some guys juggle cabbages, some paint their faces and pretend they can't talk, and others shove fire down their throats.

But Herman Heyn—57, part-time math teacher, affable astronomer for the common man, and chaser of many an eccentric hustle—has been averaging $28.48 a night by setting up an 8-inch

Meade telescope on Baltimore street corners, pointing it at the sky, and giving passers-by the chance to see a crater on the moon.

Or Jupiter with a six-day moon beneath it; maybe an anonymous shooting star as it passes through town; the Pleiades and red-giant Betelgeuse, the Orion Nebula, or the Domino Sugar sign if that's the universe you happen to be in the mood for.

"You don't live for the spectacular—that's great when you can get it—you live for day-to-day observing," says Mr. Heyn, a man who surrendered to the spell of starry, starry nights after a grade school science teacher drew the Big Dipper on the blackboard.

And there the dipper hung that night when little Herman stared out of his bedroom window.

"My role," says the Telescope Man, "is helping other people see what's out there. Stuff they would never see on their own.

"One guy in Fells Point told me, 'If I die tomorrow I'll die content that I at least got to see one of Jupiter's moons before I went.'"

And while you can't put a price tag on giving someone a thrill they've never known, there is that hat lying beneath the telescope's tripod and it doesn't take a Copernicus to figure out what it's for.

Mr. Heyn says he doesn't ask for it; but the money has been there each time the Telescope Man and his $1,200 peephole have ventured out of his Waverly row house since last November.

Part scientist, part businessman, part Barnum of the Big Bang, Mr. Heyn has kept a faithful log of his astral gigs as they have been acted out in Charles Village and Fells Point, enthusiastic attempts to "have another source of income and teach people about the stars."

Ellen L. Edwards, a 39-year-old nurse on her way to purchase a Lotto ticket, ambled up to the scope and peered through the lens pointed at the sky high above the Homewood campus of Johns Hopkins University.

"I can see Jupiter and four moons!" she said, setting her sights on the spheres that go by the names of Ganymede, Io, Europa and Callisto. "And a lot of blue clouds or something with stripes across it. What a thrill! I love to look at the sky."

Mr. Heyn hopes many will do so tonight when Venus and Jupiter approach each other for a near cheek-to-cheek meeting—at least that's how it looks from Earth—expected to result in their brightest, most visible pairing in years.

So bright, in fact, that Mr. Heyn could have naked-eyed them as a kid before owning his first lens, a 3-inch diameter Mogey his Dad bought him just after World War II, an instrument powerful enough "to see the rings of Saturn."

A boy and his scope. It was a love affair that dominated young Herman's emotions until he turned 18.

"In high school, what social life was for other people, for me was staying home on a Saturday night reading an astronomy book," said Mr. Heyn, who lives among the clutter of the universe in the shadow of Memorial Stadium. "Mom was always pushing me to go to parties and get dates, but I just wanted to read. When I look in the sky I still see the constellations the way I learned them in those early books."

After graduating from City College, however, he sold his telescope for $180 to finance a trip to California with friends. For the next 18 years, his passion waned.

And then, sitting at the breakfast table one mid-November morning in 1966, Herman Heyn saw a buried newspaper item that made his pulse race. That very night promised the return of the famed "Leonid Meteor Shower," a flying flash of entertainment visible within "the sickle" of the constellation Leo that hits a spectacular peak about every 33 years.

"I had missed it as a child because I was only 3 in 1933 and I remembered being a kid thinking, 'Gee, I hope I'll be alive when it comes back,'" said Mr. Heyn. "But I had totally forgotten about it."

That night, he waited in the dark in the backyard of his Bosworth Avenue home with a 35mm camera propped up against a tree with its shutter open. It was Baltimore. Cloudy and hazy. The view was reportedly great out in Utah, but Mr. Heyn spent several hours without seeing much of anything.

His camera, however, did pick up some star trails, and the experience was enough to set the Telescope Man off again. Combining astronomy with photography, Mr. Heyn's renewed vigor moved him to haul his family up and down the coast—sometimes off the coast—for eclipse vacations. His growing expertise landed a few of his photographs in astronomy books and an Italian encyclopedia.

Today Mr. Heyn designs and markets T-shirts—he's got a magnificent one of Halley's Comet and Mark Twain, whose life began and ended with appearances of the comet—teaches math and high-school equivalency courses for the city of Baltimore; rents a room to a Johns Hopkins University graduate student; works at the Waverly Farmers' Market in the summer; loves folk music and folk dancing; and provides a window to the Milky Way for anyone with enough time to put their eye up to a lens.

He calls himself "Baltimore's Streetcorner Astronomer" and now is struggling with city bureaucrats for a formal permit to peddle the stars wherever he pleases—particularly at Harborplace, with summertime around the corner.

It's all an acknowledged hustle—"Heaven if you're a hustler and hell if you're not," reads the sign above his desk—but for Herman Heyn, the Telescope Man, it sure beats the daily race of rats that ran him ragged for so long.

"I hand-to-mouth it," he says, a smile spreading across his gentle, bearded face. "But I feel great."

QUESTIONS ON CONTENT AND TECHNIQUE

1. What qualifies Herman Heyn as a street-corner astronomer?
2. Describe how you picture the Telescope Man.
3. Herman Heyn has "one foot in heaven and another in hell." Give passages that illustrate each.
4. What does the phrase "part Barnum of the Big Bang" mean?
5. How do you react to the repetition in the fourth and fifth paragraphs?

WRITING ASSIGNMENTS

Characterization

1. Write a character sketch of some circus barker, door-to-door salesperson, or anyone "with a pitch" so that your reader glimpses the inner person.
2. "My role," says the Telescope Man, "is helping other people see what's out there." Choose a person in another field who does this and write your paper on him or her.

Work and Play

1. The Telescope Man has many facets to his life—part scientist, part Barnum. Write an essay illustrating several roles that you also play.
2. Relate a hobby or interest that lured you from school or work.

For Hire: TV Actors That Oink

Anne Driscoll

Anne Driscoll wrote this article for *The New York Times.*

WORDS TO KNOW

episodes occurrences

lark romp, have fun

Ipswich, Mass.—Getting dogs to appear asleep, geese to open their beaks and white doves to fly into darkness are just some of the tricks of Carlene White's trade.

She owns Animal Episodes, a talent and modeling agency that provides animals for commercials, television, film and stage productions.

Mrs. White says she has been training animals since she was 5 years old. At her country home here, she has a 350-pound pig that was trained to sit, stay and come on command; a horse that can wear an airplane costume with a 16-foot wing span; and 32-inch donkeys that pull a miniature beer wagon. She also contracts with the owners of hundreds of other animals, ranging from pet golden retrievers to milk cows, for their appearances in print and on film.

"I started this as a lark 10 or 12 years ago and we've just grown and grown and grown," said Mrs. White, who is 51 years old.

She had been a 4-H leader for 20 years and her club of girls 7 to

14 years old sponsored an annual circus with animal acts that included a pony that rode a seesaw, a Newfoundland shaved to resemble a lion and a pony trained to run into a wall made of cardboard bricks.

Because of her involvement with animals, Mrs. White became a member of a committee to explore the need for a veterinary school in Boston, and the effort led to the establishment of the Tufts Veterinary School. The committee decided to air several television commercials featuring horses, cows and chickens, but the photographer for the project did not know how to find the animals or how to handle them.

"'I can get you the animals,' I told him," Mrs. White recalled. "I spent a week with that photographer and saw that he had trouble working with the animals. I thought, hell, I can manage almost any animal."

Mrs. White says few people, including many advertising directors, understand the challenge of getting animals to perform before a camera, even when the effect is supposed to appear natural. "The public assumes that you can dope them into doing what you want," she said. "They see a cat asleep on the set and figure the cat has been drugged, but that's not true at all. To get a cat asleep, you've got to put them in a nice warm spot and keep them up for a long time ahead of time." She said she has never drugged or hurt an animal to make it pose.

Her own dog, D (short for Dog), a portly part-beagle looking older than her 3 years, closes her eyes on command and keeps them closed. Mrs. White says D made about 20 commercials last year, earning about $100 per week. "She will hold a pose, will tip her head an eighth of an inch at a time," Mrs. White said. "She's fantastic, but she's a mutt. My daughter found her in a gutter in Lexington, Ky., when she was so young she had to bottle-feed her. But she knows exactly what she's doing when she walks into a studio."

Liz Bustin's golden retriever, Bucky, broke into show business through Mrs. White's agency a year ago. Since then he earned enough to send the Bustins to a New Hampshire ski lodge last winter. Many days while Ms. Bustin is busy selling insurance, Bucky is being chauffeured to a studio in Boston to pose for a commercial. He has appeared in anything from a double-page full-color ad in a national magazine to a television commercial for a Boston bank.

"Part of his popularity is due to the fact that goldens are really 'in' right now," Mrs. Bustin said. "They are a very yuppie dog."

Not all the animals Mrs. White works with are as cooperative as

Bucky and D, Mrs. White says. She was once asked to pose 13 geese with their mouths open for a full-page newspaper ad. The geese would not cooperate until she turned up the heat a few degrees in the studio, and the photos could be shot only after the geese began to pant.

Four years ago, when she did a commercial for the Olympics, she needed a shot of 60 white doves flying into a black background. She had 30 people lying on their backs release a dove from each hand into one big, black net.

She has worked with dangerous animals as well, once posing a tiger in a car with a Boston radio personality. And she has been bitten on occasion. "The danger doesn't bother me," she said. "My husband's a doctor."

She has worked with celebrities like Cher and Jack Nicholson in "The Witches of Eastwick," Ed Begley Jr. in "St. Elsewhere" and Peter Graves in a public television production. She says the animals are truly the big stars.

"We had one pig called Piggity, and I could take her to downtown Boston without a leash," Mrs. White recalled. "She would sit, heel, lie down and stay, and it only took 10 days to teach her. I used her for commercials. She grew to be 350 pounds."

QUESTIONS ON CONTENT AND TECHNIQUE

1. What are some advantages for Mrs. White in being an animal trainer?
2. Tell about one behind-the-scene technique that she uses to get the behavior she desires.
3. How does the author awaken interest in the reader in her opening lines? Which do you prefer—her opening or closing? Why?
4. Copy the lines that show a single quote within a quote and explain how for a writer this punctuation is useful.

WRITING ASSIGNMENTS

Characterization

1. Interview an animal lover, and record some anecdotes that might be entertaining.
2. Have a groomer, jockey, guide-dog trainer, zoo keeper, or anyone who works with animals tell you how to manage them.

Work and Play

1. Driscoll mentions that Mrs. White has never drugged or hit an animal to make it pose. Discuss some cruelty to animals that you have observed, giving the reasons, the effects, and possible solutions.
2. Narrate some incident when you attempted to have a pet or animal perform, and it decided differently.

Chapter
4

Example

"Oh, it's just kind of a hobby with me . . . !"

You have enlivened your writing by using description and narration. Now let's take it one step further and expand those techniques with examples.

Besides saying it's a cold day, you can show your reader how one's breath comes out as thick as smoke and one's ears tingle and then grow numb. Or to describe a rock singer, you can give an example of tight leather pants and spiky hair.

Writers use the example mode to show—rather than tell—why something is true by substituting specific details for generalities.

In Enid Nemy's piece on lucky charms, she uses details to show why people believe their special charm is lucky: "He happened to wear a blue and white striped cotton turtleneck sweater while working on what is known in architectural circles as a charrette, the rushed last stage of preparation for a presentation. All went well. The turtleneck became his 'lucky charrette shirt.'"

Another use of example is seen in the Jack Anderson and Dale Van Atta article. These writers do not merely describe Senator Robert Dole as handicapped. Instead they say he "has little use of his right arm, no use of his right hand and not enough feeling in his left hand to tell the difference between a dime and a quarter."

In the selection "Today's History Lesson," Bob Greene does not speak in generalities about the presidents. Rather he mentions that George Washington as a teenager would "write gushy poems about love, intended to be read only by himself."

Roger Ricklefs, in his story on video babies and pets, does not say the images act like babies or pets, but shows how video dogs sit up, roll over, get the ball; and how babies gurgle, coo, and "wave to Grandma."

In every case the writers use specific examples—facts that create images in the reader's mind—to make their stories real and believable.

WHEN YOU WRITE EXAMPLE

- Remember to show important ideas by using examples of description and narration rather than assuming your reader sees or understands the material as you do.
- Don't forget that readers like to be shown not told: The bent-over, unshaven pedlar is preferable to the poor, old man.
- Expand your writing through examples that lead your reader to comprehend the seriousness, complexity, or uniqueness of your ideas by offering a variety of anecdotes, illustrations, and details that build interest.
- Keep in mind that facts buttressed by specific images persuade the reader that the material is lively and believable.

Those Who Swear by a Lucky Charm

Enid Nemy

Enid Nemy is a regular columnist for *The New York Times.*

WORDS TO KNOW

aperitif a before-dinner alcoholic drink

couturier dress designer or maker

mundane lacking concern for the ideal or spiritual, centered on the world

If you were wearing a red, blue and white-striped shirt when you found an ancient temple that other archeologists had been seeking for centuries, you might become inordinately fond of that shirt and even consider it a talisman. Iris Love was wearing such a shirt when she discovered the Temple of Aphrodite in southwest Turkey in 1969 and, quite naturally, she considered it lucky.

After that, she said, whenever she reached a crucial point in one of her digs, she'd put on the shirt, and although it didn't come through all the time, frequently it did work its magic.

"After about 10 years the shirt was in shreds, but I preserved it like a sacred relic," Ms. Love said. "Sometimes I'd just put it on in the morning for a little while, and then take it off."

Ms. Love said she believes sincerely in luck and lucky charms, so sincerely that whenever she travels, she carries what she calls "five pounds' worth of lucky charms" including a Chinese Kwan Yin, a Japanese bronze rabbit, an Egyptian scarab and a Hebrew chai. And she always, traveling or not, wears something blue, "to protect against evil," she said, and because it's lucky, especially when combined with red. That's what she said. And if she can't manage it with her outwear, she does so with underwear.

Not everyone who possesses what they think of as a lucky piece of clothing or jewelry can boast of the spectacular coup achieved by Ms. Love and her shirt. But then again, they're not out to find a centuries-old temple; they're perfectly happy with a slightly more mundane kind of luck.

Ruth Dubonnet, who was married to the late Andre Dubonnet of the aperitif family, still remembers a black lace evening dress she had more than half a century ago. She was the Countess Vallombrosa de Mores then, not Dubonnet, but that's neither here nor there.

What does matter is that the then-Countess and a few of her friends backed a couturier named Mainbocher when he opened his Paris salon. She said she still believes that the evening dress he made her, the first he had done for an individual and which she wore to the opening, "brought good luck to the business."

"After that, I always knew I'd have a wonderful time when I wore it, and I did," she said.

Twenty-five years ago, Paul Segal was studying architecture at Princeton University. He happened to wear a blue and white striped cotton turtleneck sweater while working on what is known in architectural circles as a charrette, the rushed last stage of preparation for a presentation. All went well. The turtleneck became his "lucky charrette shirt," he said, and he put it on whenever anything important was coming up.

Since graduation, it's been in a drawer, but it will never be thrown away. It isn't that he's superstitious, but, said Mr. Segal, a partner in Paul Segal Associates, "I don't believe in pressing my luck either."

When Caroline Jones first saw the sequin jacket sent to her by her personal shopper she thought it was, to put it plainly, weird. It's reddish-rose, a little iridescent, casual but dressy, but the shopper persuaded her to try it. On it went with a black skirt, out she went to a business dinner and by the end of the evening, she had a new client for the advertising agency that bears her name.

"It's not only good looking, it really is lucky," she said. "I've only had it about six months. I've worn it about five times, and I know something good is going to happen every time I have it on. It's part of my life now."

When Barbara Goldsmith starts to write and the words don't come quickly as usual, she puts on a full-of-holes cashmere sweater that she's had since college and that she thinks helped her pass her college exams. "And it helps me write," she says.

Of course, the true lucky object of Ms. Goldsmith, the author of *Johnson vs. Johnson,* a book about the court case involving the pharmaceutical family, is a pre-Columbian idol shaped like an alligator; she bought it for herself years ago.

"It even helped me stop smoking," she said. "I wore it and I kept saying, 'I'm not going to smoke any more and it worked.'"

For Kimberly Farkas, who is active on various charity committees, . . . [good] luck is a ring: a gold band with tiny diamonds given to her years ago by her husband. "If I don't wear it, I carry it with me," she said.

Her husband, Jonathan, a theatrical producer who was involved in Broadway productions like "Liaisons Dangereuses," has a 20-year-old gray umbrella he carries to distant meetings and on all his trips.

"It's not even weatherproof anymore," Ms. Farkas said. "But he feels so strongly about it that he keeps it out of the umbrella stand before we have a party, in case someone picks it up by mistake."

As for Mary Roebling, she says that she knows that "good things happen" every time she wears the diamond-trimmed pearl earrings she bought in Japan at the estate sale of Mikimoto, the jeweler.

The good things happen regularly when she's playing bridge with the chairman emeritus of the National State Bank in Trenton, N.J.

"I know I'll get good hands," she said. And she does.

QUESTIONS ON CONTENT AND TECHNIQUE

1. According to those interviewed, how have some lucky charms helped them?
2. Where does the thesis appear? See the glossary.
3. What are some other factors that aren't mentioned that might bring people "luck" while they are wearing their lucky charms?
4. What do you think is the writer's purpose in this piece?

WRITING ASSIGNMENTS

Example

1. Write an essay listing examples of good-luck charms that people often use. You might interview different people just as Enid Nemy did.
2. A good-luck charm is often kept by someone who is superstitious. Develop an essay using examples of various superstitions.

Philosophical Values

1. You may own favorite items of apparel or jewelry. Describe them and explain why they hold a special place in your wardrobe.
2. Relate an incident where you were lucky.

The Naming of the West

Mike Flanagan

Mike Flanagan wrote this carefully researched piece for the *Denver Post.*

WORDS TO KNOW

entitling naming

lexicon dictionary

lobby try to persuade legislators

The naming of the West was a grand, complicated adventure. Entitling the territories that became the 17 western states was a formidable undertaking that taxed egos and lexicons alike.

California and Texas were never territories; their names were in use long before the settlers arrived. "California" was first used in a 1510 Spanish romance, "Las Serges de Esplandian," which said, "At the right hand of the Indies there is an island called California . . ." Cortez applied the name to the peninsula's southern part in 1533.

The region that became the republic, then the state, of Texas was called "Tejas" as early as 1541. This was the Spanish version of the Caddo Indian word *texia,* meaning "allies."

Oregon is possibly a corruption of the French word for Wisconsin, *Ouisconsin,* from the original Algonquian meaning, "grassy place." The name was first applied to a fictitious river believed to flow westward to the Pacific Ocean. Its initial print appearance was in Britisher Jonathan Carver's 1778 book, "Travels Through the Interior Parts of North America."

New Mexico had been named in 1598 when Spain's Juan de Onate came to colonize. For statehood in 1912, Acoma was preferred over Hamilton, Montezuma and Lincoln simply because it would put the state ahead of Alabama on alphabetical lists.

Created on the same day as the Territory of New Mexico—Sept. 9, 1850—was the Territory of Utah. Brigham Young's Mormons, forced West by religious persecution, had organized the Provisional State of Deseret ("honeybee" in the Book of Mormon) in 1849. Congress members rejected it, partly because they were at odds with the Latter-day Saints over polygamy and partly because it sounded like desert. Utah came from a Navajo word for the Utes and means "higher up, the upper land."

The residents of northern Oregon Territory wanted to call their new territory Columbia. A move to honor the first president caused heated debate in the House, where it was believed that with Washington, D.C., and the counties and towns already bearing the name, a major headache would result. "Washingtonia" was turned down in favor of Washington, which became a territory March 2, 1853.

The territories of Nebraska and Kansas were created May 30, 1854. Nebraska came from either the Omaha word *nibthaska* or the Oto word *nebrathka,* both referring to the "flat water" of the Platte.

Kansas was named for the Kansa Indians seen by Coronado's men in 1541. *Kansa* is said to be Sioux for "people of the south wind," or it may be from the French title for the same tribe, which also formed the root of Arkansas. But the Smithsonian Institute said in 1954 that both are wrong, that the correct name might be "Kanze."

Nevada is Spanish for "snowed upon." The Committee on Territories rejected "Washoe," a native tribe, preferring to compliment the Sierra Nevada mountains, even though the range lies mostly in California. Nevada and Dakota territories were carved out of Utah Territory on March 2, 1861.

Dakota was sacred country to the Dakota or Sioux, the latter a name from their enemies from a Chippewa word for "snake." Dakota meant "alliance of friends."

When western New Mexico Territory petitioned Congress for recognition in 1854, suggestions included Gadsonia and Pimeria. Arizona did not mean "arid zone," but was Spanish for the Pima Indian word "Arishoonak, place of the small spring," a locale across the border near present Nogales.

To further fog the issue, silver was discovered by Spaniards there in 1736, giving credence to the Aztec word *arizuma*, or "silver-bearing." Arizona's territorial status came in 1863.

Naming Colorado after Zebulon Pike proved impractical, simply because worthier Americans had yet to be so honored. Names reviewed by the House and Senate committees included Lafayette, Franklin, Osage, Colona, Yampa, Nemara, San Juan, Tahosa, Arapaho and Lula.

Finally, after a two-year deadlock, they decided on "Idaho," believed to be Shoshone for "gem of the mountains." A fear that the word might not mean that, coupled with a plea from citizens, swayed the vote for "Colorado," Spanish for "red," honoring the river.

That name had not even been considered in the long debate. Worse still, surveys showed that Colorado the river wouldn't come near Colorado the state. Legislators looked to the river's eastern branch and passed an act that read: The name of the Grand River in Colorado is hereby changed to the Colorado River.

In 1863, when the bill to create what became the Territory of Idaho was written, Ohio Congressman James M. Ashley of the Committee on Territories wanted to call it Montana, Latin for "mountainous." That passed the House, but the Senate still liked Idaho. This time the senators got their way.

When that territory was divided the following year, Ashley, a Republican, lobbied to keep it from being named for the first Democratic president, Thomas Jefferson. Again he backed Montana, and won.

"Wyoming," from the Algonquian word *mache-weaming*, ("at the big flats," or "large prairie place") first was applied to Pennsylvania's Wyoming Valley, site of a 1778 massacre immortalized in Thomas Campbell's 1809 poem "Gertrude of Wyoming." To name the 1868 territory Wyoming was another of Ashley's ideas and was accepted over its closest competition, "Cheyenne."

On May 2, 1890, a year after the land run opened the unassigned lands to white settlement, congressional delegates met. When asked by the commissioner of affairs what the new territory should be called, Chocktaw Rev. Allen Wright announced "Oklahoma," a combination from his native tongue of the words *ukla* (person) and *huma* (red). Cherokees, who believed they should have first choice, were offended.

In 1906, citizens voted to name their state Sequoyah, after the Cherokee alphabet inventor, but were overruled by Congress. Oklahoma, the 46th state, entered the union on Nov. 16, 1907, and the great name game was over.

QUESTIONS ON CONTENT AND TECHNIQUE

1. What techniques does Flanagan use to avoid using the term "name or naming" too often?
2. Can you suggest any method of organizing the article other than state by state? Would the clarity be more or less effective?
3. What details does the author generally include in each paragraph?
4. How and why does Flanagan vary his paragraph openings?
5. Observe and comment on how and why Flanagan indicates his sources.

WRITING ASSIGNMENTS

Example

1. Select some place, street, or building in your town or community that has had several names. Give the reason or reasons for the changes.
2. Some people have had several names because of marriage, divorce, or nicknames. With examples, show how this can affect the person.

Language and the Arts

1. Pretend that you are able to name the street or school nearest you. What would you name it? Why? How would the name affect the community?
2. Can you recall an incident or happening in your life where the naming process, the wrong name, or a mispronunciation of a name caused a problem?

The Last Thing You Notice

Jack Anderson and Dale Van Atta

Jack Anderson, a widely read syndicated columnist, is one of America's watchdogs. Dale Van Atta is his associate.

WORDS TO KNOW

despondent depressed

epilepsy nervous disorder marked by convulsive attacks

genesis beginning

hierarchy persons or things arranged in a graded order

hoopla rowdy excitement

impede stand in the way of

surrogate serving in place of someone or something

Lost in the political hoopla this year is something that heartens millions of handicapped Americans—the disabilities of three men whose significant political power has made their handicaps the last thing you notice.

Sen. Daniel Inouye (D-Hawaii) was Senate leader of the Iran-contra investigating committee.

The absence of an arm, lost in World War II action, did not impede Inouye from reaching such heights and, once there, effectively leading the Senate portion of the investigation. If anything, the handicap became such quiet testimony of his own patriotism that it dampened the spit and polish of Ollie North and provided for an eloquent summation by the senator after the colonel had flaunted his medals. Now it is likely that Inouye will be elected the Senate majority leader next year.

The second man is Sen. Robert Dole (R-Kan.). As a result of a World War II battle, Dole has little use of his right arm, and not enough feeling in his left hand to tell the difference between a dime and a quarter.

The third man, Rep. Tony Coelho (D-Calif.), is emerging as a prominent and potent political leader. He is the No. 3 man in the House hierarchy, the majority whip. His "disability"—if the word fits any of the men—is not worn on the outside. He is an epileptic.

At age 22, Coelho was poised to enter the seminary and study for the Roman Catholic priesthood. Then he learned he had epilepsy. The church would not accept epileptic priests.

Friends introduced the despondent Coelho to comedian Bob Hope, who took Coelho under his wing. Hope urged him into politics, and Coelho spent 15 years on the staff of Rep. B. F. Sisk. When Sisk retired, Coelho ran for his seat and won.

Today he serves as a quiet counselor, a surrogate minister, to members of Congress who want to confide their problems. He is also particularly attuned to the causes of the downtrodden.

Far from whining about his invisible "handicap," Coelho credits it with helping him to achieve the success he enjoys. "To a great extent," he told us, "because of my epilepsy, I have a tremendous inner peace. And that reflects in everything I do."

Without any fanfare, he has established his own foundation to help epileptics develop job skills, adjust to their disability and "destroy these negative myths that we have about disabilities in general and epilepsy specifically," Coelho said.

For him it is vital to be a role model. "All of a sudden, people with epilepsy, or loved ones of epileptics, see that if you can make it, then why can't they? This is the key thing that you can do," Coelho said.

Bob Dole once found it difficult to talk about his handicap. It didn't even come up in conversations with his wife. Coelho privately preached to him the virtue of proclaiming it, instead of ignoring it.

Most people "learn to live with a disability. You accept it and you don't talk about it," Coelho said. "If you're open—as I'd been urging Dole to be more open about it—you become a role model."

Dole does inspire others at the rehabilitation centers he visits on the campaign trail when he talks about the years of struggle from total paralysis to the activity he enjoys today. His message is: "Strength through adversity."

Like Coelho, Dole has formed his own foundation for the handicapped. He did that in 1983. The genesis was a meeting with two severely disabled young people in Dodge City, Kan. Both were in wheelchairs and couldn't move much more than their eyes.

Dole recalled, "Back home, I sat in our bedroom and told Elizabeth how deeply moved I had been by this encounter. 'I've been meaning for years to start a foundation for disabled persons,' I said, 'and I haven't done it. This is the time.'" His foundation has raised about $4 million to help the disabled with job training and placement.

These men of different politics—Inouye, Dole and Coelho—have made it a banner for the estimated 36 million disabled Americans.

QUESTIONS ON CONTENT AND TECHNIQUE

1. The term "spit and polish" is used in the article. To what does it refer?
2. Some persons object to the word "handicapped." Can you think of a better term?
3. How do Anderson and Van Atta guide you from one example to another?
4. What is the main idea the writers wish to share with you?
5. The writers could give all the information about each man before moving to the next. Instead they move through the three men and then return to each of them again. Can you see the advantage of this type of organization in an "example" paper? Explain.

WRITING ASSIGNMENTS

Example

1. Write an essay about other persons you know or have heard of who have overcome physical limitations to succeed.
2. Some people choose to devote their lives to helping others. Write an essay, developed by example, on several who have done this for humankind.

Social and Political Issues

1. Discuss an obstacle in your life and how you overcame it.
2. Select several persons in your life who acted as role models, and show exactly how they influenced you.

Lady Luck in the Gold Country

Arthur Ribbel

Arthur Ribbel, a longtime San Diego newspaperman now retired and living in Carlsbad, California, wrote this article for the *San Diego Union*.

WORDS TO KNOW

barley a grain

crevice a narrow crack

ramrod a rod used to load or clean a gun

troy a system of weight based on a pound of twelve ounces

A miner often had a partner in the wild scramble for riches during the epic California gold rush, but the best partner a miner could have was named Luck.

"I'd rather be lucky than smart," was the creed of the Argonauts.

At least that was what many of the pick-and-pan boys who hit metal would have told you, and it was Lady Luck that led some of them to the big nuggets.

It was luck, no doubt, that led Jim Marshall on Jan. 24, 1848, to examine the tailrace of Capt. Sutter's sawmill at Coloma. There he saw glittering metal in the water.

On March 15, 1848, the first newspaper story on the gold discovery was printed in a San Francisco newspaper. But as luck would have it, not many people paid much attention to the story.

Workers at Sutter's mill sought to push their luck by sneaking off their jobs to pry gold nuggets out of rocks with penknives, even after they had pledged to keep secret Marshall's find. And soon the cry went out—Gold! Gold! And before long, the worldwide gold rush was on.

It wasn't long before more than 2,000 miners were in the Sierra foothills wooing Lady Luck. And she made friends with a lot of them while she ignored others. Lady Luck must have been along when the famous Carson Hill gold nugget, weighing 195 pounds, was found, as well as these other great gold nugget finds in the Sierra foothills. They included:

The Monumental Mine nugget, found near Downieville in 1869, weighing 1,898 troy ounces. Almost 100 years later, another such nugget was found near Sierra City in 1960.

The Knapp Ranch nugget, found in 1852 at Columbia, weighed 1,000 troy ounces. The Woods Creek nugget, 900 troy ounces, turned up in the Sonora District.

The big Gold Hill nugget, 1850, was found near Columbia in 1856.

Native California Indians had found gold before the gold rush and brought some of it to the Mission padres. The padres are said to have used it to pay the Mission soldiers.

In early California, a man named Francisco Lopez was searching for some horses at San Francisquito Canyon, about 35 miles northwest of Los Angeles, and stopped to dig up some wild onions for lunch. He found gold nuggets clinging to the roots and started a small gold rush.

There is a yarn from the gold town of Rough and Ready with a different slant on luck. The boys of the town were digging a grave for an unlucky fellow miner, when one spotted something familiar—gold gleaming in the freshly turned earth at the grave site. Before the parson had finished his ceremony, the boys were shoveling and laying their claims around the coffin.

Miner George Knight was chasing his cow by moonlight at Grass Valley when he stubbed his toe on a rocky outcropping. When he picked himself up and looked at it, he saw gold. He forgot about the cow, and set off a rush.

Coulterville had a most unusual "gold rush." Someone had buried a store of gold coins back in the old days and never came back to claim them. Later, a heavy downpour of rain bared some of the coins and the townsfolk set to with shovels, picks and spoons to find the gold pieces. They tore up the whole of Main Street in the rush.

Angels Camp, the home of the famous Jumping Frog contest, also came out with its story of a gold find. A miner had trouble getting the ramrod out of the barrel of his old muzzle-loader rifle, so he fired the gun into the ground. The ramrod blew a hole that dislodged a piece of gold quartz, and there was another lucky find.

In the Julian Hills of San Diego County, a mule was said to be the cause of the discovery of the Stonewall Mine. The gold discovery is generally credited to William Skidmore, who arrived in Julian in 1869, although at least three others were reported also to have found the mine. Skidmore was searching for a stray mule when he stumbled onto a rich gold ledge that led to the lode.

The thrill of gold overwhelmed Edward Buffum in 1848 at Hangtown (later renamed Placerville). He poked with his pocket knife into a crevice filled with gravel. At the bottom was yellow gold in little pieces about the size of barley.

"Oh, how my heart beat," he wrote later. "I sat still and looked at it for some minutes before I counted it."

By luck and by hunger, a famous dish was given to the world by a Hangtown miner. With gold in his fat poke, he asked the cook at a Hangtown restaurant to fry him up some eggs, bacon and oysters. That was Hangtown Fry, or the beginnings of it. That dish made its way into the menus of some of the most famous restaurants in the country.

Salting a mine (planting gold dust to dupe a buyer) backfired on one slicker in the diggings. He stuffed his musket with a few gold nuggets and fired them into the earth and then sold the plot to an unsuspecting newcomer. The claim turned out to be one of the richest for the lucky buyer.

Another such yarn comes from Mokelumne Hill. A miner, new to the scene, politely asked where was a good place to start digging for gold. The boys thought they would pull a joke on the tenderfoot, so they pointed to a nearby hill that had been "combed and picked dry."

The newcomer pitched in and dug. He hit pay dirt to the dismay of his "benefactors," and filled his poke with gold from the "dry hill."

Gold dust was the usual medium of exchange in the Gold Country. A pinch of dust between the thumb and forefinger was called $1 worth. A teaspoonful passed for 1 ounce at $16. A wine glass-full was $100 and a tumbler-full was $1,000. Sometimes, greedy merchants would wet their thick thumbs and forefingers to pull a larger pinch of gold from a poke.

Even today, the zeal for gold runs high as amateur miners pan for the precious metal along gold country streams and banks.

Is there anything to discourage a rookie miner from the fantasy that a big nugget might be waiting just around the bend or over the next hill? Not while Lady Luck is still around.

QUESTIONS ON CONTENT AND TECHNIQUE

1. What is the main idea that the examples throughout the article support?
2. Where could the author have obtained his information? Give several possible sources.
3. How does Ribbel characterize Luck in the first paragraph?
4. Which anecdote was most surprising to you and why? See the glossary if necessary.

WRITING ASSIGNMENTS

Example

1. Illustrate through examples the different ways that people achieve success.
2. "Workers at Sutter's mill sought to push their luck." Write an essay giving examples of when you "pushed your luck" and what happened.

Social and Political Issues

1. Narrate an event in which luck played a role in your life.
2. Suppose you won a state lottery. What would you do with your winnings? Would it change your life and the attitudes of others about you?

Copy Editors

Frank Wetzel

Frank Wetzel is the ombudsman for the *Seattle Times*.

WORDS TO KNOW

egregious notably bad

impeccable faultless

insidious treacherous

Copy editors are the unrecognized heroes of newspapers. Unlike reporters, they do not witness history from front-row seats.

Instead, they work the worst hours in the newsroom, get the least public recognition, and draw the most abuse. They are the grunts of journalism, the safety net under the trapeze act.

Just as God's eye is on every sparrow, so readers notice a newspaper's every misspelled word, grammatical mistake, factual error. Each slip in print is a copy editor's fault.

Not solely, of course, because someone else made the mistake initially. But copy editors are supposed to be impeccable in grammar, unerring in accuracy, indelible in memory. Those who live on Bainbridge Island are expected to walk all the way to work.

Still, copy editors occasionally boot one. Even if they possessed all the virtues noted above (they don't; they're merely human), some errors would still slip past because of the press and stress of

Reprinted by permission of the *Seattle Times*. [The title is ours.]

demanding deadlines. (An egregious error probably will appear in today's paper, simply because mistakes are being discussed.)

Trouble is, most readers don't realize how many mistakes copy editors catch. That's like watching a football game on television without instant replay, which shows the touchdown was scored really because of a key block at the line of scrimmage.

Anyway, a couple of weeks ago I asked Mike Stanton, the general news editor, and through him Karen Cater, chief of the copy desks, to keep tabs on the errors picked off by copy editors.

The Times' news desk handles local, national and international news with 32 full-time and 3 part-time editors. In addition, other copy editors work for specific sections: 11 in Sports, 2 in Business, 2 in Editorial, and 7 in News-features.

With those numbers, you would suppose that if editors couldn't block an error they could smother it. But remember, they operate almost around the clock, every day of the year.

Copy editors also lay out the pages and write the headlines, summing up in a half-dozen words what it takes reporters hundreds to say. Vague, ambiguous headlines cause more mischief than anything else in the paper. When done well, however, headline writing is a skill that ranks with composition of haiku.

Here are a few simple examples of captured mistakes collected recently by Cater. The incorrect word is in **boldface**:

> The tally includes the cost of replacing the missile's huge first stage, which was (**totally**) destroyed . . . (redundant).

> "Drinking should be responsible and moderate," Rubin said. "In fact, one or two drinks a day probably has some moderate protective (**affect**) effect against heart attacks."

> Says Christman: "We serve the public in all endeavors, hale and (**hardy**) hearty, to keep them from having an accident."

> The laws of economics (**suggests**) suggest that someone must be making a killing on this.

In sports, where writers tend to be swashbucklers, the copy desk keep a list of "hard wurds" that reporters have misspelled:

Lasers, not lazers. Foresaw, not forsaw. Equaled, not equalled. Catalog, not catalogue. Guttural, not gutteral. Tendency, not tendancy. Rarefied, not rarified. Allegiance, not alligiance.

Copy editors sometimes catch errors in geography, too. For example, a story started: "A Taiwanese 'ghost ship' that drifted into Washington waters this month contained a substantial amount of decomposed salmon." Trouble was, the ship was nowhere near "Washington waters"; it wasn't even within the U.S. 200-mile zone. The story was edited to say the ship was sighted 400 miles off the Washington coast.

Cater notes that a copy editor with a good memory saved The Times from a serious misstatement. A story said Tyrone Briggs had been convicted of two rapes. It was corrected to say that Briggs had been convicted of several other felonies, including attempted rape.

Another story said the Children's Initiative directed the legislature to raise $360 million over two years. In fact, however, the initiative directs the legislature to raise $720 million. The story was corrected.

A story about Curt Smitch, nominated as director of the state Wildlife Department, said flatly that he was arrogant. It was edited to attribute the accusation to his critics.

Copy editors scan national articles for local angles that will help Seattle-area readers make sense of stories. At a copy editor's request, a reporter found out on deadline that a Supreme Court ruling in a Wisconsin child-abuse case probably didn't apply to Eli Creekmore's death here. Local angles were also inserted into stories about the U.S. trade deficit, Salman Rushdie's novel, and gun control.

These word cops must be ever vigilant. Even innocuous, mundane errors are insidious and gnaw at a newspaper's credibility. Copy editors' work isn't romantic, dramatic, glamorous or flashy—only essential.

QUESTIONS ON CONTENT AND TECHNIQUE

1. Where does Frank Wetzel show glimpses of tongue-in-cheek humor? How effective is it?
2. In listing the duties of a copy editor, what does the reporter teach the reader?
3. An error like a minnow can slip by the shoals of what three persons.
4. Where in the piece is a phrase that might make a good title?

WRITING ASSIGNMENTS

Example

1. "Copy editors are the unrecognized heroes of newspapers." Write on the following: ______________ are the unrecognized heroes of ______________. Use graphic examples to prove your thesis statement.

2. Write an essay on several occupations whose major importance is catching errors. Give multiple examples.

Work and Play

1. Most of us have been embarrassed at some time or another by being caught in a silly mistake. Can you recall such a situation in your life?
2. Part of a copy editor's task is to check facts. Have you ever heard or seen someone get the "facts" wrong? How did you react? What was the result?

Read and Weep

Janet Sutter

Janet Sutter wrote this article for the *San Diego Union.*

WORDS TO KNOW

ban prohibit

expurgated censored

obscene indecent

The freedom to read is always something to celebrate. And that's what they're doing downtown at the main San Diego Public Library. As a head start on Banned Books Week, there's a display of books that haven't always found friendly acceptance. Many are familiar titles, others are not, but no matter what the century, what the decade, books are always being questioned or actually banned.

Some of the books on display:

William Faulkner's "As I Lay Dying" was banned by the Graves County School District in Mayfield, Ky., in 1986 because it contained "offensive and obscene passages referring to abortion and used God's name in vain."

In 1985, Mark Twain's "The Adventures of Tom Sawyer" was removed from London school libraries by education officials who found it "racist" and "sexist."

In 1982, "Anne Frank: The Diary of a Young Girl" was challenged in Wise County, Va., by parents who complained about sexually offensive passages. In 1983, four members of the Alabama State Textbook Commission called for the rejection of the book because it's a "real downer."

"Bury My Heart at Wounded Knee" was removed in Wild Rose, Wis., in 1974. "If there's a possibility that something might be controversial," reasoned a district library administrator, "then why not eliminate it?"

Roald Dahl's book "The Witches" was challenged in 1987 as part of the Amana, Iowa, first-grade curriculum because the book was "too sophisticated and did not teach moral values."

"A Farewell to Arms" by Ernest Hemingway was banned in Italy in 1939 "because of its painfully accurate account of the Italian retreat from Caporetto."

Chaucer's "The Canterbury Tales" was expurgated almost from its first appearance in America and was still being subjected to revisions as late as 1928.

"Alice's Adventures in Wonderland" by Lewis Carroll was banned in China in 1931 because "Animals should not use human language," and that it "was disastrous to put animals and human beings on the same level."

Stacks of classics have been on someone's book-banning list, including "Hamlet," "King Lear," "Adventures of Robinson Crusoe" and "Wuthering Heights."

It's a long list. Read it and weep.

QUESTIONS ON CONTENT AND TECHNIQUE

1. What is the most common reason for book banning?
2. Have you read any of these banned books? Which ones? Do you agree or disagree with the reason for its removal?
3. How could the writer organize the article differently to facilitate a transition from one group of examples to another?
4. The concluding paragraph contains only two sentences. How effective is it?

WRITING ASSIGNMENTS

Example

1. Write an essay giving examples of three books anyone should read.
2. Sutter mentions that a book was banned because it was a "real downer." Give several examples of books or films that meet that definition.

Education

1. Does a community have a right to choose what its youth can read? Write your point of view.
2. Studs Terkel defended his book *Working* before a high-school board of trustees. If you were an author whose book was banned, what argument would you use?

Today's History Lesson

Bob Greene

Bob Greene is a well-known syndicated columnist long associated with the *Chicago Tribune.*

WORDS TO KNOW

constitution physical structure or health

disconcerting disturbing

glean gather

insomnia inability to sleep

profane irreverent, vulgar

Today's history lesson consists of little-known facts about some of our earlier presidents, gleaned while I was going through books trying to find out what color eyes they had. The facts you are about to read come from respected historical texts.

George Washington, as a teen-ager, was extremely awkward and tongue-tied when approaching girls for dates. Often, instead of talking to girls, he would go to his room and write gushy poems about love, intended to be read only by himself. He also hated swearing. In 1776, as general of the Army of the United Colonies, he issued an order to his troops: "The General is sorry to be informed that the foolish and wicked practice of profane cursing and swearing, a vice heretofore little known in an American army, is growing into fashion." He said this should stop immediately.

John Adams was always saying that he was sick. "My constitution is a glass bubble," he complained. The slightest draft gave him a cold; he said that the air in Boston gave him chest pains; he told friends that he had headaches, heartburn and general weakness. By the time he became president, most of his teeth had fallen out.

James Madison—5 feet 4, 100 pounds—was so shy and reserved that he was utterly incapable of making small talk with fellow politicians. His voice was so reedy and soft that even when he was making formal speeches, people beyond the first rows could not hear a word.

John Quincy Adams apparently was no barrel of laughs. His voice was high and shrill, and he was always complaining of various aches and pains. He told people that he suffered from insomnia, indigestion, nervous anxiety and eye discomfort. He said that at times he had "an imaginary wish that [life] were terminated."

As a child and teen-ager, Andrew Jackson (yeah, that's right—Old Hickory) had the disconcerting habit of slobbering. By the time he became president, the slobbering had stopped—but had been replaced by a feeling of discomfort near his heart. This was readily explainable: he had been shot by a man named Charles Dickinson during a duel in 1806, and the bullet remained lodged in his chest.

See . . . You're getting interested in this stuff, almost in spite of yourself, aren't you? And there are so many more presidents to go. . . .

QUESTIONS ON CONTENT AND TECHNIQUE

1. What is the effect of the examples on you, the reader?
2. Greene uses several techniques to develop his examples. What are they?
3. How do you react to the little-known facts? What if our current president were written about in such a manner?
4. Do you know any unusual facts about former presidents? Give one if possible.

WRITING ASSIGNMENTS

Example

1. Every nation has historical leaders that it considers heroes. Write an essay using three examples of American leaders today that you admire.

2. Write an essay illustrating the three traits you find most important in a presidential candidate, for example, good communication skills, honesty, and a sense of humor.

Social and Political Issues

1. Nominate a patriot of the year and explain your choice.
2. Assume the role of president. Write a speech telling Americans what the major issue of the United States is today.

And Beta Makes 3: Video Baby

Roger Ricklefs

Roger Ricklefs is a staff reporter of *The Wall Street Journal.*

WORDS TO KNOW

celluloid a colorless synthetic used for toys

exotic foreign, strange, exciting

surrogate a person substituted for another

You're a creature of your times. You want a baby. But you don't want diapers. You don't want midnight feedings.

Technology saves the day. For $19.95, and just 13 minutes out of your busy day, you can have "the full, rich experience of parenthood without the mess and inconvenience of the real thing." It's called Video Baby.

Let's slip it into the VCR and see. Why, it's a girl! A cuddly, blue-eyed little girl. Look at those little fingers. Isn't she adorable?

The soothing voice of a narrator is heard, inviting you to name this little cherub. "You'll know immediately if you've chosen a name your baby likes," the narrator says. "Call your Video Baby by name now." There is a brief pause, while the proud parents say "Melissa" or "Penelope." Then the baby smiles glowingly.

"This is tailor-made for yuppies," says Peter Wild, the chairman of Creative Programming Inc., which has just brought the video infant into the world. "The enjoyment without the commitment."

He seems to know what he is talking about. The shelves of video shops are sprouting with tapes for people who will take their gratification electronically, just so long as it is instant.

Tired of lugging firewood and fiddling with dampers? One tape offers the yuletide warmth of a flickering fire, with Christmas carols in the background. And never any ashes to scoop.

For those who find even a fishbowl too taxing, one company offers Tropical Fish Tank. Turn it on and your television screen becomes an electronic aquarium full of exotic fish.

Creative Programming has several other products for the times. For instance, tradition has it that the American dad sooner or later takes his kid fishing, but millions of modern fathers have never baited a hook. So the company has a home video, called "Look Mom, I'm Fishing," that shows "how to teach your kids to fish even if you don't know how."

Mr. Wild explains: "Everyone gathers around the old VCR and learns. Isn't that how folklore is passed down these days?"

Besides Video Baby, Mr. Wild's company has just brought out Video Cat. It completes a family started last year with the company's Video Dog. The baby and the cat are new, but the dog has thousands of masters now.

Who adopts these celluloid surrogates? "I bought Video Dog for my boyfriend because he lost his own dog in a divorce," says Sara Papenfuss, a camera-store manager in Oshkosh, Wis. "We watch the tape every day. Most of my friends find it pretty stupid, but they aren't dog lovers."

Norma Pollack of Brooklyn, N.Y., says her single daughter in Manhattan first tried a real dog, but "she returned it after one week because she realized it was a living thing. It had to be fed." Mrs. Pollack gave her Video Dog, but the daughter rejected it. Mrs. Pollack has taken it in.

Anthony Pecoraro once had a real dog, and his daughter got him one of the maintenance-free kind to enjoy during his retirement. "You become attached to the dog on the tape," says Mr. Pecoraro, of Elmwood Park, N.J. "Just the way it lies on the couch reminds me of my own dog."

Except it is self-walking. You simply sit down in a comfortable chair, press the play button on your videocassette recorder and watch your dog walk. If you want it to trot along at your side, press fast forward.

Video Dog reliably fetches The Wall Street Journal. At the owner's command, it will unfailingly "sit up," "get the ball" and "roll over."

You have to name it yourself, but for the truly passive, the owner's manual provides some suggestions. Electra is a good name, it says, or Vido (rhymes with Fido).

As one might expect, the Video Cats are less eager to please. There are two of them on the tape. They play with a ball of string and gaze greedily at a goldfish bowl, but perform no tricks at all.

When you yell the Video Dog's name, the friendly mutt romps toward the viewer; when you call to Video Cats, they just look at you. "The main function of any cat is being petted," the narrator explains weakly.

Video Baby does as many tricks as she can, given her tender age. When cues flash on the screen, the adoptive parents repeat in order phrases like "Let's play peekaboo," "Wave to Grandma," "Smile for Daddy," and "Clap hands for Grandpa." Each time, the little darling happily complies.

She is neat, too. As the child systematically throws all her toys out of the crib, the cheery narrator says: "Fortunately for you, Video Babies always pick up their toys." The action then shifts into reverse, and all the toys fly back into the crib.

Best of all, for anxious parents already worried about French lessons, SATs and private school, Video Baby comes with an assured future. When the narrator mentions various career options, the video child reacts. She seems to smile an especially eager smile when he suggests "investment banker." How was Video Baby to know stocks would crash before she could be marketed?

QUESTIONS ON CONTENT AND TECHNIQUE

1. How do you react to the idea of video babies and video dogs?
2. How does Ricklefs help you visualize Video Baby?
3. The creator of these videos suggests that the VCR is the vehicle for passing down folklore. Discuss this issue.
4. What is the author's attitude toward video babies and video dogs?

WRITING ASSIGNMENTS

Example

1. Give examples of TV commercials you feel are delightful or offensive.

2. Write an essay on examples of electronic inventions that have made life easier or more difficult for all of us.

Science and Technology

1. Explain what changes you have noticed in American society that have made the creation of Video Baby appealing.
2. Technology is replacing human beings in the workplace and in the home. Discuss your response to any one of the following innovations: automatic teller, telephone answering machine, computer dating, dial-a-prayer.

Chapter 5

Process

a dog and his boy by Rick Stromoski

"I say we read the directions before we get any deeper."

Scientists wish to convince their colleagues that their experiments are valid. Manufacturers must include instructions with their appliances so that users can assemble and operate them properly. Students need to demonstrate to their professors that they have performed every part of a lab problem correctly. In each of these examples, papers will be written that carefully and completely describe every step in the process involved.

In Teresa M. Hanafin's piece "How to Blow Up a Building" she also leads the reader through every step of a process and shows how experts effectively raze a 351,000 square-foot building. Robert Smaus, in a similar fashion, tells us how to get rid of snails from a garden, and Allan Parachini describes why hair turns gray.

Notice how in each selection the writer uses pedantic prose. There are no rhetorical flights, no flashy metaphors, no similes. All those figures of speech are sacrificed for clarity so that the reader can follow and understand the information presented.

In the newspaper article by Ernest Hemingway on how to camp out successfully, he expertly weaves all the elements of process writing. This famous novelist had a reputation for terse writing, but in his fiction, this terseness amounted to stark beauty. For example, when you read his short story "Big Two-Hearted River," which covers much of the territory of "When You Camp Out, Do It Right," you can see the difference. In the short story he is playing on the reader's emotions, whereas in the newspaper article he uses a different voice to give practical advice.

Of course, the style of writing need not always be superserious. Andy Rooney's essay about putting off a job is in the best Rooney tradition of poking fun. And by the time you finish reading it, you know exactly the steps involved.

WHEN YOU WRITE PROCESS

- Motivate your readers to want to learn or know the process or operation by piquing their curiosity, selecting an unusual focus, suggesting rewards for completing the task, or entertaining them with bits of humor or specific examples or anecdotes.
- Show the preparation or background necessary for your readers to understand and be able to do the process.
- Clearly write every step necessary to perform the operation.
- Remind your readers in your conclusion of the pleasure, advantage, or necessity of learning this activity or task.

How to Put Off Doing a Job

Andrew Rooney

In this newspaper essay, Andrew Rooney tongue-in-cheek tells his readers how to procrastinate.

WORDS TO KNOW

interim time between

February is one of the most difficult times of the year to put off doing some of the things you've been meaning to do. There's no vacation coming up, there are no long weekends scheduled in the immediate future; it's just this long, grim February. Don't tell me it's a short month. February is the longest by a week.

Because I have so many jobs that I don't like to do, I've been reviewing the notebook I keep with notes in it for how to put off doing a job. Let's see now, what could I use today?

—Go to the store to get something. This is one of my most dependable putter-offers. If I start a job and find I need some simple tool or a piece of hardware, I stop right there. I put on some better clothes, get in the car and drive to the store. If that store doesn't have what I'm looking for, I go to another. Often I'm attracted to some item that has nothing whatsoever to do with the job I was about to start and I buy that instead. For instance, if I go to the hardware store to buy a new snow shovel so I can clean out the driveway, but then I see a can of adhesive spray that will keep rugs in place on the floor, I'm apt to buy the adhesive spray. That ends the idea I had to shovel out the driveway.

—Tidy up the work area before starting a job. This has been useful to me over the years as a way of not getting started. Things are such a mess in my workshop, on my desk, in the kitchen and in the trunk of the car that I decide I've got to go through some of the junk before starting to work.

—Make those phone calls. There's no sense trying to do a job if you have other things on your mind, so get them out of the way first. This is a very effective way of not getting down to work. Call friends you've been meaning to call, or the distant relative you've been out of touch with. Even if someone is in California, Texas or Chicago and you're in Florida, call. Paying for a long-distance call is still easier and less unpleasant than actually getting down to work.

—Study the problem. It's foolish to jump right into a job before you've thought it through. You might be doing the wrong thing. There might be an easier way to accomplish what you want to do, so think it over carefully from every angle. Perhaps someone has written a how-to book about the job you have in front of you. Buy the book and then sit down and read it. Ask friends who have had the same job for advice about the best way to do it.

Once you've studied the problem from every angle, don't make a quick decision. Sleep on it.

—Take a coffee break. Although the term "coffee break" assumes that you are drinking coffee in an interim period between stretches of solid work, this is not necessarily so. Don't be bound by old ideas about when it's proper to take a coffee break. If taking it before you get started is going to help keep you from doing the work, by all means take your coffee first.

—As a last resort before going to work, think this thing over. Is this really what you want to do with your life? Philosophize. Nothing is better for putting off doing something than philosophizing. Are you a machine, trapped in the same dull, day-after-day routine that everyone else is in? Or are you a person who makes up his or her own mind about things? Are you going to do these jobs because that's what's expected of you, or are you going to break the mold and live the way you feel like living?

Try these as ways for not getting down to work.

QUESTIONS ON CONTENT AND TECHNIQUE

1. What is Rooney's attitude toward work around the house?

2. What transitions might be added to show the step-by-step instructions of how to put off doing things?
3. How is his article a reversal of the normal process? Is it effective in showing the roots of procrastination?

WRITING ASSIGNMENTS

Process

1. Write a humorous process of how not to do, make, or operate something.
2. Develop a process of how to deal with your angry wife, parent, mother-in-law, or employer who is pressuring you to do something.

Work and Play

1. Think of a household task that is difficult or time-consuming and write the reasons why.
2. Write about a task that you put off doing and the consequences.

Snail Wars: The Gardener Strikes Back

Robert Smaus

Robert Smaus wrote this article on gardening for the *Los Angeles Times*.

WORDS TO KNOW

abutilon flowering tropical plant

carnage slaughter

Maginot Line defense fortifications in France built before World War II

maggot wormlike larva

mercenaries hired soldiers

outflank bypass

scavengers animals that feed on decayed matter

Frankly, I lost the battle with snails this past spring and summer. Now that cooler weather is upon us, I intend to rethink my strategy so that when the snails become active again in spring, I am ready.

I am investigating the newest arms technology and have ordered several packages of Snail Barr. This is a barrier of copper strips, with lips you bend over, and they are supposedly uncrossable.

"They work because the snails and slugs receive a mild shock that deters them from proceeding when their skin comes in contact with copper." That is the explanation given by the Natural Gardening Company. Since no batteries are included, I assume the shock is delivered by natural ground currents.

These strips can be attached to the trunks of trees, which should keep the snails out of the nearby lemon tree and large abutilon, as long as no branch touches the ground to provide the snails with a ladder to scale my fortification. The strips can also be connected end to end to make a Maginot Line around tender seedlings, which I hope will not be as easy to outflank. About $11 will buy you 20 feet of barrier; about $43 will provide you with 100 feet, enough to encircle an entire vegetables bed.

With these defense works installed, I plan to enlist mercenaries. These are the famed predator snails, or decollate snails. When I first heard of these snails, I was very skeptical because it sounded too good to be true, but now that I know more of their mercenary habits I am prepared to hire on a few hundred, though my initial suspicions turned out to be true.

The latest word on these snails is that they do not seek out ordinary garden snails and destroy them with single-mindedness. They simply occupy the same niche in the garden. That is, they replace the garden snails in the local ecology. If they ate the same things, or as much, they would be no better than the garden snails, but because they are scavengers, they eat all sorts of things and do much less damage to your plants, though they have been known to eat a tender seedling or two.

With this knowledge, I plan to keep them outside the copper Maginot Line, and I have an ace in the hole should they rebel—ordinary snail bait is even more effective on the decollate snail than on the garden snail.

Of course, while they are becoming established, I will have to cease using snail baits, but then I plan to set traps.

The University of California favors this method of snail eradication, and Ted Fisher of UC–Riverside gets the credit for inventing it. One builds these traps from ordinary 1-by-12-inch boards, about 15 inches long. At each end, nail a runner of 1-by-2-inch lumber, on edge. These hold the board just above the ground. Now comes the difficult part for the squeamish. Rub a few crushed snails on the underside of the board. This carnage will attract other snails.

Set the board in a shady, damp area near where snails are feeding. Every five or six days, pick up the board to see what you have lured underneath, and crush them, but do so thoroughly because fly maggots grow inside decaying snail shells.

Between the decollate snails, the copper defense works, and the sneaky traps, I think I can avoid the use of poisonous baits, which will mean that I am not only winning the war against snails but am abiding by the Geneva Convention.

QUESTIONS ON CONTENT AND TECHNIQUE

1. Where and why does Smaus summarize the methods of snail control?
2. Select several phrases that involve warlike images.
3. What clichés does the writer use in paragraphs 5 and 6? Rewrite them.
4. What are the two sources that he credits?
5. What are some particularly effective details that he employs?

WRITING ASSIGNMENTS

Process

1. Write a process paper pertaining to a strategy, that is, the winning or losing of an historical battle, preparing for a test, planning to win a sports contest.
2. Write how you were able to get rid of a pest: animal, vegetable, or human.

Natural Environment

1. Smaus opens with "Frankly, I lost the battle . . . " Then he writes of a new strategy. Perhaps you would like to write on a battle you lost that taught you a valuable lesson.
2. The author suggests alternatives to the use of poisonous sprays. Describe an incidence where concern for the environment caused you to select an alternative (for example, recycling aluminum cans rather than trashing them).

Teaching the Lesson of Nonviolence

Larry Tye

Larry Tye is on the staff of the *Boston Globe.*

WORDS TO KNOW

suspension temporary removal from job or function

Deborah Prothrow-Stith still clearly recalls the night 10 years ago when, as a medical student at Boston City Hospital, she was stitching a knife wound over a young man's eye: "On his way out he turned and said, 'Don't go to bed. The person who did this to me is going to be in this emergency room in about an hour, and you'll get all the practice you need.'"

"What struck me is that if that young fellow had made a suicide attempt and said, 'Don't go to bed. I'm going to take pills when I get home,' we'd have responded very differently," she said. "We would not have let him go."

But neither Boston City Hospital nor anyone else knew much about handling violent youths then, she added.

Today, things are different, said Prothrow-Stith, the state commissioner of public health. An army of health professionals, teachers, police, social workers and parents are battling youthful violence with a passion reminiscent of campaigns against drunken driving

Reprinted courtesy of the *Boston Globe.*

and smoking. And they are arguing their case in classrooms, health clinics, churches, boys and girls clubs, on television and in any other forum they can find.

While these efforts are in their infancy, she added yesterday, the recent fatal shooting of Darlene Tiffany Moore, 11, and the fatal shooting Wednesday night of Michel Alexandre, 16, underscore the need for "real changes in our attitudes and our behavior. . . . We are on the verge of some very dramatic changes."

Schools are the first vehicle for that change. Using a two-week curriculum developed by Prothrow-Stith and others, teachers help students think about anger and how they vent it.

To start with, they consider how big a problem violence is in America: The homicide rate here is five times higher than in Canada, 13 times England and Wales' and 50 times New Zealand's. And in the United States, the assailant and victim are acquainted in 55 percent of violent crimes; they are related in 20 percent.

The issue is brought closer to home when students are told that violence is the second-leading cause of death among young people 15 to 24 years old—and the leading cause among blacks in that age group. But teachers emphasize that violence is tied more to poverty than to race, said BCH's Renee Wilson, who has helped design and run the teaching program.

Youths are asked to think about how they handle anger. And they actually stage a fight, playing the antagonists and the crowd, and then discussing their reactions as they watch on videotape.

"We don't encourage kids to intervene in fights but to prevent them," Wilson said. "The first step is not when the first punch is thrown, but when the decision is made to confront each other."

Boston-area pilot classes in violence prevention began in 1986 with 450 10th-grade students in six high schools, and they are now being tried in cities from Los Angeles to Philadelphia. About two dozen schools here still are running some version of the training, but most are waiting for an analysis due this winter of the pilot classes.

Even before the review is complete, however, evidence is mounting that the classes work. At the Jeremiah E. Burke High School in Roxbury, violent suspensions have been reduced by two-thirds, apparently in part because of three years of such training, said Prothrow-Stith.

And at Cathedral High School in Dorchester, several students used to face expulsion every month—but now, after more than three years of classes and other programs on violence, the number of expulsion hearings is down to several a year, said Anne Bishop, the school's health coordinator. "The atmosphere is clear to students that fighting is not acceptable," she added.

Boston police also are trying to help youths avoid violent behavior. Ten officers are beginning their third year of visiting elementary schools to talk about drug and alcohol problems—and now they are including instruction in "how to turn away from violence," said patrolman William Gavin, one of the instructors.

Youths also are being counseled in nonviolence at boys and girls clubs, churches, health centers, housing projects and other community agencies. Programs such as those in the classroom are running, with help from BCH specialists, at 35 community agencies in Roxbury and South Boston, which have had particularly serious troubles with youth violence.

That training already has paid off, said 15-year-old Jenise Maynard of South Boston, who participated in a program at the Boys Club. "One of my friends wanted to fight me and I said, 'Wait a minute,'" she recalled. "I sat down and thought about it and said, 'There's no reason to fight.' She called me like chicken and all that, and I just walked away."

Before attending the class, Maynard added, she would have fought her friend.

The campaign against violence has a mass media component, too. Two public service advertisements on Boston television stations depict adolescents dying, apparently of wounds suffered at the hands of other youths. One ad ends with the warning. "Fighting is a lousy way to lose a friend"; the other concludes, "Friends for life don't let friends fight."

Finally, parents and community leaders are becoming involved, meeting regularly with police and public health officials to search for ways to battle drugs, alcohol, gangs and, most important, the violence they breed. Commissioner Prothrow-Stith said it will take time to see results, but she insisted that the antiviolence movement has the same high level of commitment as Mothers Against Drunk Driving.

QUESTIONS ON CONTENT AND TECHNIQUE

1. Larry Tye reports how a community is teaching the lesson of nonviolence. However, his article could be a blueprint for action of a community against any problem. Briefly what are the steps involved?
2. There are several examples of single quotes used within double quotes. Locate and explain their usage.

3. Select several comparisons that enrich the piece.
4. What are the major sources for his article?

WRITING ASSIGNMENTS

Process

1. How would you recruit a new member to any campus or community organization to which you belong?
2. Step by step explain how a specific group like Mothers Against Drunk Driving (MADD) have changed public opinion on an issue.

Crime and Society

1. Prepare an argument for or against this statement: Guns, violent films on TV, and lack of employment teach violence indirectly.
2. "The person who did this to me is going to be in this emergency room in about an hour. . . ." What convincing reasons could you give this young man to prevent his revenge?

When You Camp Out, Do It Right!

Ernest Hemingway

After high school, Ernest Hemingway wrote for the *Kansas City Star.* This essay was written for the *Toronto Star.* Later in his career he won both the Pulitzer and the Nobel prizes for his novels.

WORDS TO KNOW

abiding long-lasting

assimilate absorb as nourishment

dyspepsia indigestion

proprietary relating to ownership

tyro beginner

Thousands of people will go into the bush this summer to cut the high cost of living. A man who gets his two weeks' salary while he is on vacation should be able to put those two weeks in fishing and camping and be able to save one week's salary clear. He ought to be able to sleep comfortably every night, to eat well every day and to return to the city rested and in good condition.

But if he goes into the woods with a frying pan, an ignorance of black flies and mosquitoes, and a great and abiding lack of knowledge about cookery the chances are that his return will be very different. He will come back with enough mosquito bites to make the back of his neck look like a relief map of the Caucasus. His digestion will be wrecked after a valiant battle to assimilate half-cooked or charred grub. And he won't have had a decent night's sleep while he has been gone.

He will solemnly raise his right hand and inform you that he has joined the grand army of never-agains. The call of the wild may be all right, but it's a dog's life. He's heard the call of the tame with both ears. Waiter, bring him an order of milk toast.

In the first place he overlooked the insects. Black flies, no-see-ums, deer flies, gnats, and mosquitoes were instituted by the devil to force people to live in cities where he could get at them better. If it weren't for them everybody would live in the bush and he would be out of work. It was a rather successful invention.

But there are lots of dopes that will counteract the pests. The simplest perhaps is oil of citronella. Two bits' worth of this purchased at any pharmacist's will be enough to last for two weeks in the worst fly and mosquito-ridden country.

Rub a little on the back of your neck, your forehead and your wrists before you start fishing, and the blacks and skeeters will shun you. The odor of citronella is not offensive to people. It smells like gun oil. But the bugs do hate it.

Oil of pennyroyal and eucalyptol are also much hated by mosquitoes, and with citronella they form the basis for many proprietary preparations. But it is cheaper and better to buy the straight citronella. Put a little on the mosquito netting that covers the front of your pup tent or canoe tent at night, and you won't be bothered.

To be really rested and get any benefit out of a vacation a man must get a good night's sleep every night. The first requisite for this is to have plenty of cover. It is twice as cold as you expect it will be in the bush four nights out of five, and a good plan is to take just double the bedding that you think you will need. An old quilt that you can wrap up in is as warm as two blankets.

Nearly all outdoor writers rhapsodize over the browse bed. It is all right for the man who knows how to make one and has plenty of time. But in a succession of one-night camps on a canoe trip all you need is level ground for your tent floor and you will sleep all right if you have plenty of covers under you. Take twice as much cover as you think that you will need, and then put two-thirds of it under. You will sleep warm and get your rest.

When it is clear weather you don't need to pitch your tent if you are only stopping for the night. Drive four stakes at the head of your made-up bed and drape your mosquito bar over that, then you can sleep like a log and laugh at the mosquitoes.

Outside of insects and bum sleeping the rock that wrecks most camping trips is cooking. The average tyro's idea of cooking is to fry everything and fry it good and plenty. Now, a frying pan is a most necessary thing to any trip, but you also need the old stew kettle and the folding reflector baker.

A pan of fried trout can't be bettered and they don't cost any more than ever. But there is a good and bad way of frying them.

The beginner puts his trout and his bacon in and over a brightly burning fire the bacon curls up and dries into a dry tasteless cinder and the trout is burned outside while it is still raw inside. He eats them and it is all right if he is only out for the day and going home to a good meal at night. But if he is going to face more trout and bacon the next morning and other equally well-cooked dishes for the remainder of two weeks he is on the pathway to nervous dyspepsia.

The proper way is to cook over coals. Have several cans of Crisco or Cotosuet or one of the vegetable shortenings along that are as good as lard and excellent for all kinds of shortening. Put the bacon in and when it is about half cooked lay the trout in the hot grease, dipping them in corn meal first. Then put the bacon on top of the trout and it will baste them as it slowly cooks.

The coffee can be boiling at the same time and in a smaller skillet pancakes being made that are satisfying the other campers while they are waiting for the trout.

With the prepared pancake flours you take a cupful of pancake flour and add a cup of water. Mix the water and flour and as soon as the lumps are out it is ready for cooking. Have the skillet hot and keep it well greased. Drop the batter in and as soon as it is done on one side loosen it in the skillet and flip it over. Apple butter, syrup or cinnamon and sugar go well with the cakes.

While the crowd have taken the edge from their appetites with flapjacks the trout have been cooked and they and the bacon are ready to serve. The trout are crisp outside and firm and pink inside and the bacon is well done—but not too done. If there is anything better than that combination the writer has yet to taste it in a lifetime devoted largely and studiously to eating.

The stew kettle will cook your dried apricots when they have resumed their predried plumpness after a night of soaking, it will serve to concoct a mulligan in, and it will cook macaroni. When you are not using it, it should be boiling water for the dishes.

In the baker, mere man comes into his own, for he can make a pie that to his bush appetite will have it all over the product that mother used to make, like a tent. Men have always believed that there was something mysterious and difficult about making a pie. Here is a great secret. There is nothing to it. We've been kidded for years. Any man of average office intelligence can make at least as good a pie as his wife.

All there is to a pie is a cup and a half of flour, one-half teaspoon of salt, one-half cup of lard and cold water. That will make pie crust that will bring tears of joy into your camping partner's eyes.

Mix the salt with the flour, work the lard into the flour, make it up into a good workmanlike dough with cold water. Spread some flour on the back of a box or something flat, and pat the dough around a while. Then roll it out with whatever kind of round bottle you prefer. Put a little more lard on the surface of the sheet of dough and then slosh a little flour on and roll it up and then roll it out again with the bottle.

Cut out a piece of the rolled out dough big enough to line a pie tin. I like the kind with holes in the bottom. Then put in your dried apples that have soaked all night and been sweetened, or your apricots, or your blueberries, and then take another sheet of dough and drape it gracefully over the top, soldering it down at the edges with your fingers. Cut a couple of slits in the top dough sheet and prick it a few times with a fork in an artistic manner.

Put it in the baker with a good slow fire for forty-five minutes and then take it out and if your pals are Frenchmen they will kiss you. The penalty for knowing how to cook is that the others will make you do all the cooking.

It is all right to talk about roughing it in the woods. But the real woodsman is the man who can be really comfortable in the bush.

QUESTIONS ON CONTENT AND TECHNIQUE

1. What does Hemingway's title suggest?
2. Hemingway actually gives several processes within his camping instructions. Identify them.
3. How does Hemingway insert humor in his comparison? Give several examples of each.
4. Reread the section on cooking and illustrate how he uses four or five senses in some of his descriptions.

WRITING ASSIGNMENTS

Process

1. This article was written in the 1920s. Update his process with more modern camping methods and materials.
2. In an essay, show the reader step-by-step a process found in nature: a butterfly's life cycle, a bird hatching, a bee pollinating flowers. You may use your own experience or check a science text or an encyclopedia.
3. Instruct someone in the preparation of a food that takes some skill: making candied apples, baking bread, decorating a wedding cake, etc.

The Natural Environment

1. Nature often teaches us in harsh ways. Explain one lesson that it has taught you.
2. Give several ways that the wilderness areas and public parks have been damaged by some visitors.

How to Blow Up a Building

Teresa M. Hanafin

Teresa M. Hanafin is a staff member of the *Boston Globe*.

WORDS TO KNOW

implode burst inward

latent potential

linear-shaped long and narrow

macabre gruesome

primal primitive

J. Mark Loizeaux has a rather macabre sense of what constitutes splendor.

As the man charged with imploding the Travelers Insurance Co. building at 125 High St. at 8:30 tomorrow morning, the sight of the 16-story tower crumpling with a thunderous roar into a monstrous heap of crushed blue and white brick and smashed steel will be a thing of beauty.

Not that Loizeaux, president of Controlled Demolition Inc. of Maryland, is a particularly violent man because he implodes buildings for a living. It's just that being able to destroy something so big satisfies some sort of latent primal urge.

Just ask Peter Small, president of Spaulding & Slye, the commercial development company that is part of the limited partnership

Reprinted courtesy of the *Boston Globe*.

building a new office-retail complex on the site: "It's not often you get to do something really destructive," he says. "It's more fun than I've had in a long time."

Don't let the joviality fool you: Taking down a building of this size, 351,000 square feet, is no easy task, given the fact that the area is congested—the Central Artery and several office towers are within spitting distance—and that the building is held up by 56 bolted structural steel columns.

The 171,000-square-foot Hotel Madison at North Station, which Loizeaux's company imploded in spectacular fashion in 1983, also had steel columns, although fewer because it was smaller.

Like the Madison, the Travelers will be brought down using what Loizeaux calls a "cut-and-kick" method of demolition.

Special copper-sheathed, linear-shaped charges—the same explosive used in the space program to jettison fuel tanks off the shuttles—will be strapped with wire diagonally on the steel columns in the basement and on the first, second, fourth, sixth, eighth and 12th floors.

The explosives, which will detonate with a velocity of 27,000 feet per second, will exert 3 million pounds of pressure per square inch—enough, Loizeaux says, to slice through the steel.

Milliseconds after each set of explosives goes off, exploding gelatin dynamite also placed on selected columns throughout the building will move the steel columns off-center so they collapse, rather than tip over.

More than 300 pounds of explosive will be placed in 600 locations in the building, 70 percent of it on the first and second floors. The explosive and dynamite will be detonated by electric blasting caps.

The time-delay charges will go off sequentially, with the initial blasting occurring on the east side of the building facing the Central Artery and Atlantic Avenue.

The entire sequence will take 7½ seconds to go off; from the first blast, it should take about 11 seconds for the building to collapse, according to Douglas K. Loizeaux, CDI vice president and Mark Loizeaux's brother.

The first five stories will end up compressed into the basement; the rest of the building will make a pile of rubble about 30 feet high in the center, Douglas Loizeaux said.

The blasting will go forth even if it is raining or snowing moderately, but there are some circumstances that will delay or cancel the blast: extremely high winds, which could carry the resultant dust all over the city; an electrical storm, which could interfere with radio transmissions and the electrical charges; cloud cover below 2,000 feet, which could amplify the concussion by causing the enormous pressure generated by the blast to bound back down to earth, and the presence of anyone within the two-block restricted area.

Depending on the speed and direction of the wind, the noise of the collapse may be heard for about a half-mile.

There is, of course, the possibility that something will go wrong, that some split-second timing will be off, or that some steel columns will not be cut adequately.

If so, it's anyone's guess what will happen. It is unlikely that any people will be harmed because no one will be within two blocks, Loizeaux said.

City and state officials who had to issue permits for the demolition, as well as engineers in the area interviewed yesterday, say they are confident that CDI's experience at this sort of thing will preclude any major disasters.

The building's neighbors certainly hope so: To the north sits the Oliver Street fire station and International Place; to the west, the State Street Bank building and 125 High St.; and to the south, the Richardson Block, a set of 19th-century buildings that have survived the downtown development frenzy because of their historic significance.

And then there's the Central Artery, which could be depressed in one fell swoop—certainly saving state transportation officials a lot of money, but putting a bit of a crimp in commuting patterns.

Officials with CDI and the development partnership say they are carrying hundreds of dollars worth of insurance, but naturally don't expect to need it.

QUESTIONS ON CONTENT AND TECHNIQUE

1. Locate a series in the article. How is it punctuated?
2. What does the term "one fell swoop" mean?
3. How does Hanafin make a highly technical process enjoyable to read about?
4. What other information does the author weave into the basic process itself?

WRITING ASSIGNMENTS

Process

1. Think of a process used in your job or daily life that your classmates may not know about. Explain it clearly step-by-step.
2. Using all the elements of a good process essay, explain how a certain technical or scientific procedure occurs.

Work and Play

1. Explain a dangerous, difficult, or unusual process that you have observed, that is, dynamiting a mine, rescuing a person from a building, doing a ventriloquist act.
2. Tell how the destruction of an old building did or would improve your community.

'Tis the Season for Thieves

Randolph E. Schmid

Randolph E. Schmid is an Associated Press writer.

WORDS TO KNOW

pilferage stealing in small quantities

reiterating repeating

While millions of children look forward to a jolly old elf coming down the chimney at this time of year, there's another group that likes to visit the homes of strangers: burglars.

Police report that only the summer vacation season outdoes the Christmas-New Year holidays for burglaries. Other crimes also increase as pickpockets and thieves prey on travelers and shoppers.

Being away from home for a holiday trip, or just to visit friends for a few hours, can be an invitation to burglars. One way to discourage them is to make the house look like someone is home, say officials of ADT Security Systems.

Leave lights on in several rooms, for example. And if you will be gone for a while, attach timers to the lights to turn them on and off at varying intervals.

Leaving a radio playing, tuned to an all-talk station, can also help, by making it sound like people are inside.

And leave drapes and shades in their normal household pattern, ADT officials say.

Before leaving, turn down the volume of the telephone bells. Constant ringing advertises absence to someone outside.

If going away for an extended trip, ADT says, leave a car parked in the driveway and make arrangements to have someone shovel the snow if that is needed. Also, cancel all deliveries—such as milk and newspapers—and have a friend collect your mail and put out some trash at your home on garbage collection day.

The Chubb Group of Insurance Companies reports that many claims in this season involve small pilferage. Officials there urge putting small valuables out of sight when having parties. Doing so before caterers arrive can be a good idea.

Fire claims also jump at Christmas, the company says, reiterating the reminder to make sure the Christmas tree is watered and that the lights are not left on. This may be a good time to check the battery in the smoke detector.

Whether traveling or shopping, never leave visible gifts in an unattended car. Bring them into the motel room with you. At a shopping center at least lock parcels in the trunk.

While traveling, remain constantly wary, say security officials of the American Express Co.

Thieves operating at airports, train stations and other crowded areas usually operate in groups of two to four, they report. One crook seeks to distract the victim while an accomplice steals a wallet, purse, or baggage.

Ploys can include a seemingly spilled purse, a handful of dropped coins or other maneuvers.

In some areas pickpockets have even been known to put up signs saying "Beware of pickpockets." Then they watch people to see which pocket they pat after noticing the sign. That way the crook knows where the valuables are on the potential victim.

Never leave baggage unattended, American Express says, because many thefts are simply crimes of opportunity when someone puts their luggage down to buy a newspaper or other item. Baggage carts should be pushed ahead, where they can be seen, not pulled along behind and out of sight.

Men should not carry their wallet in a back pocket, it is among the easiest to steal from. And women should carry handbags with the flap turned toward the body and carried against the hip or in front where it can be seen. The handbag should never be allowed to slide to the back, where it is out of her sight.

Dressing down can help too, to avoid attracting the attention of crooks looking for affluent victims. And don't carry all valuables together.

QUESTIONS ON CONTENT AND TECHNIQUE

1. Write an ending that frames the article. Returning to the opening, see what clue you might use to close the piece.
2. Although this article uses the timely lead of the Christmas season, how could it be adapted for another season? Are the tips for travelers specific for yuletide?
3. If your task were to expand this article, what sources, techniques, and support data would you use?
4. What paragraph does not relate to theft?
5. How could paragraphs 4 through 7 be combined to remove repetition of the word "leave"?

WRITING ASSIGNMENTS

Process

1. Most of us associate theft with the physical removal of an object or objects, but we all also have had our time stolen by someone or something. Explain how a thief stole your time.
2. If you work or have worked in a business or public agency where special precautions have been taken against any crime, discuss the step-by-step procedure used to maintain security.

Crime and Society

1. Tell of an incident in your life where you had something stolen or vandalized. Relate its significance and the effect on you.
2. Randolph Schmid instructs you how to protect yourself against theft. Write a process of how you could protect yourself against some fear or situation.

Why We Turn Gray

Allan Parachini

Allan Parachini is a staff writer for the *Los Angeles Times.*

WORDS TO KNOW

albino one who lacks skin pigment

culminate rise to the highest point

discernable observable

pigment coloring matter

quantifiable measurable

You squint into the mirror in the morning, your eyes trying to adjust to the harsh bathroom light. Hesitantly, you take a brush to your hair. And, there it is.

Around one or both temples, perhaps radiating up the side of your head. If you're male, you might see it at the top of your sideburns.

Gray hair.

No one has gotten to the root of the problem yet, for the process of graying is an aspect of body behavior that has never been thoroughly studied by medical researchers. Nevertheless, graying is known to be a function of a complex system of body chemistry which, among other things, appears to be influenced by many of the factors identified by traditional folk culture. For instance:

- Stress and worry evidently can influence the rate at which people gray.
- There is something to the notion that people gray "overnight," but it isn't because the hairs turn color rapidly. It is just that dark hairs fall out, leaving only white ones behind—but it usually occurs over a period of a few weeks, almost never literally overnight.
- Graying patterns in all likelihood are inherited.
- Men and women gray in slightly different patterns. Women gray slightly faster than men.
- Light-haired people don't gray more slowly than dark-haired people; it just appears that way because apparent grayness is often created by the contrast between white hairs and darker ones. In light-haired people, the contrast is less pronounced.
- Premature graying is a quantifiable phenomenon, affecting a quarter of all people by the time they are 25. Production of the first gray hairs on the head commonly begins as early as age 15.

The process starts deep in the outer layer of the skin, the epidermis, almost to the inner layer of the skin, the dermis. Each of the 100,000 hairs on the head is controlled by a hair bulb, below the follicle at the deepest part of the root system. It is through the hair bulb that a variety of complex substances are channeled, creating each hair, mainly composed of a biochemical substance called keratin.

In the hair roots and in the epidermis, millions of protein-producing pigment cells, called melanocytes, produce chemicals that determine the coloring of hair and skin. Albinos usually have a normal number of melanocytes, but they lack the chemical means to trigger pigment production. In some people, only a small area of skin lacks functionless melanocytes, producing white spots or streaks in an otherwise dark head of hair.

For an albino, said Dr. James Nordlund, chairman of the department of dermatology at the University of Cincinnati College of Medicine, "it's like a car without a carburetor. There's plenty of fuel (in the form of the cells) but it is not able to convert it into color."

The melanocytes, in turn, are responsible for chemistry that colors the hair that takes shape in the follicle and grows long enough, eventually, to be seen. Once hair has been pigmented by the melanocyte's action, the color cannot be changed because the pigmentation is not just a coating to the keratin body of the hair; it is infused.

The pigmentation chemical, melanin, has two basic components—sort of like the pigments used at custom-mix paint stores. The two basic colors predispose a hair to be dark or light or some hue in-between, depending on the proportion of each pigment that is genetically introduced into the hair-making process.

Coloration is influenced by racial and ethnic factors, but virtually no research has been done on the existence or nonexistence of such influences in graying. Because gray is largely determined by white-dark contrast, genetically dark-haired races or groups would be expected to show more discernable graying than races and ethnic groups with a broader range of light hair colors.

The color chemistry changes with age so that even a person who has not yet grayed may find his or her natural hair coloring changing with advancing age. Many people experience a darkening in their coloring—directly attributable to the maturing function of the melanocytes and the varying production of melanin.

With time, said Dr. Coleman Jacobson, of the Baylor Hair Research and Treatment Center in Dallas, the melanocytes deteriorate and their pigment-producing chemistry begins to shut down. It is a gradual process and, for the period that the melanocyte is still functioning at reduced capacity, the bulb may produce a hair that is gray, or incompletely colored.

As time goes on, though, the melanocyte stops working completely and the hair bulb turns out a completely white product.

The shutdown of the pigment cells usually occurs gradually. About 100 hairs a day are lost just from natural attrition. With age, the older dark hairs fall out, leaving a greater proportion of newly created white hairs. As white hairs gain the majority, the grayness appears to increase. Thus, grayness is an optical illusion created by the mixture of the remaining dark hairs and the newer white hairs.

By 65, everyone has a significant amount of gray hair, even if they continue to appear dark-haired. The 40s and 50s are the ages of intense acceleration of graying for most people.

The phenomenon of turning white in a very short period of time—a matter of days or weeks—does not occur because the dark hair actually turns color, Dr. Aaron Lerner [professor of dermatology at Yale Medical School] and other experts said. Turning white can be due to spontaneous loss of remaining dark hairs on the head of a person who has already produced a large volume of white hairs. Since the dark hairs are older, they would be lost first, leaving only the colorless white strands in place.

The head grays first at the temples and on the sides, then on the top. Hair cutters say women's rear hairlines gray earlier than men's.

Women's facial hair—fine, soft strands of a type dissimilar to head and body hair—does not gray but men's beard hair does, though not by any predictable pattern. Many men notice their chins turn white before the sides of their faces; yet others find cheeks go before chins. As for the rest of the body, there is no set pattern.

And finally, the bad news. The process cannot be arrested, despite the dyes and hair colors, and probably can't be slowed. It's physiologically harmless, yet most people don't like it.

Said James Nordlund, summing up: "It's just a sign we're getting older."

Added Coleman Jacobson, "I think that, if people live long enough, they will all turn gray and they will all turn white."

QUESTIONS ON CONTENT AND TECHNIQUE

1. What is the effect on the reader of the "you" in the introduction?
2. Is Parachini's purpose to entertain, inform, or persuade?
3. How does the author help the reader with highly technical terms?
4. What guides the reader from one part of the process to another?

WRITING ASSIGNMENTS

Process

1. Along with an attractive appearance, many people are concerned with physical fitness. Describe a step-by-step process for improving health, such as losing weight, giving up smoking.
2. Often a child will innocently ask questions that adults find extremely difficult to explain: for example, why the sky is blue; or why the grass is green. Answer such a question with a process essay giving the scientific explanation of some common phenomenon.

Science and Technology

1. What has modern technology done to change the attitudes of society toward persons over 60 in any of these areas: fashion, health, cosmetic surgery, occupations, social activities?
2. Often it is said that science, history, and mathematics develop critical thinking and dispel myths. Agree or disagree with this statement. Illustrate with specific examples.

Becoming a Standup Comic

Murry Frymer

Murry Frymer wrote this process article for the Knight-Ridder News Service and it appeared in the *Denver Post*.

WORDS TO KNOW

impediment speech defect

lucrative profitable

profane irreverent, vulgar

ribald coarse or vulgar

Perhaps you've had this experience:

You're standing at the water cooler in the office telling some hilarious stories. All the secretaries gather 'round in glee.

"Hey, you ought to be a standup comic, Lou!" says one.

You mull that as you drive home on the freeway. Surely, that secretary is right. (And her name isn't Shirley, you add. Hey, you're even telling jokes to yourself!)

Well, how do you get to be a standup comic? How do you put together an act? Do you have to be ready for prime time, or can you start small? Should you give up your 9-to-5 job?

I have put together some answers. First of all, don't quit that 9-to-5 job. If it's like most, it is a great source of material: boss jokes, secretary jokes, food money.

Second, stare into the mirror and ask yourself these questions:

Have you ever been told you are funny by someone who isn't a friend? Did you owe him/her money?

Have you ever been funny sober?

Does your wife (husband) think you are funny? Is he or she disparaging when he or she says it?

Have you ever put a lamp shade on your head and sashayed around the living room doing an imitation of Madonna?

If you can answer yes to any of these questions, we can proceed. Even if you can't answer yes to any of these questions, please proceed. I've worked hard and long on this article.

OK, let us assume it is clear that you ought to be a standup comic. Once the decision is made, there are other concerns, which I will mention briefly.

You should not be the type who is easily hurt. While you are trying to make the world happy, there are people out there who may be trying to make you miserable. They may even sound like they will hurt you seriously. Don't worry. Be happy.

You may have a speech impediment. That can, of course, work either for you or against you. It depends on the impediment. Stuttering can be funny, but only if you really are a stutterer. ("A Fish Called Wanda" walked a thin line. But burlesque and standup have different rules.)

Other impediments, such as lisping and a thick Jewish accent have made lucrative careers for some people. One guy's impediment is another guy's shtick.

If you are not ethnic, or black, or a woman, or funny-looking, or unkempt; in fact, if you are a good-looking blond Adonis, you are facing an uphill battle. All the lesser-looking folk you face in the audience will begin by hating you.

OK, with those concerns out of the way, let us get on to the material.

After scouting more than 500 comedians in the last couple of days, I can sum up funny material as follows:

Funny material deals with parents or spouses, is profane, deals with human weaknesses, includes one impression of Ronald Reagan, involves chatting with the audience and usually has a winner or two about drugs, drink and Elvis Presley.

Impressions, of course, are always good. But don't do impressions of your Uncle Harvey or the prime minister of Ecuador. The recognition factor will be weak.

Food jokes are food if you are fat or anorexic.

Bald jokes are good if there is a bald man in the front row you can poke fun at. But make sure he is not the critic from the local newspaper.

Sex jokes are a mixed bag. If your sex jokes are very dirty, never tell them in front of a mixed crowd. A crowd of all elderly women, though, is OK.

Many comics have had full, successful careers without telling a dirty joke. Jack Benny, for example. However, if Benny ever had guessed how much money Eddie Murphy could make spewing filthy material, he might have hocked his violin for a ribald routine.

Benny actually is a good case lesson. He never had any funny material. He reacted to the funny material other comics had. This is a terrific career gimmick. But it doesn't work for the new comic.

George Burns is another case lesson. For 30 years he stood on a stage reading to Gracie Allen. When she died, he had to find a new act alone. So he told stories about what Gracie had once said. Then he reacted. It has worked.

Some final tips.

What to do if you're bombing:

Check to see if there is an audience. Sometimes, with a bright spotlight in your face, you may not realize that no one showed up or the club went out of business.

If there is an audience, make sure that you and it are on the same wavelength. You can't make Polish jokes in Warsaw. Don't try to kid the VFW about Pearl Harbor Day being in September.

For the first few months, don't play in front of the same audience twice. After you're a hit, you can tell the same audience the same jokes and they will love them. The jokes will have become classics. (Henny Youngman and "Take my wife, please" are both over 80.)

The final rule is supreme confidence. Just because nobody ever laughs at you is no reason to believe you are not a successful comedian. You are simply suffering from the lack of a hip audience.

QUESTIONS ON CONTENT AND TECHNIQUE

1. What is the writer's tone? See the glossary if necessary.
2. List the major steps involved in becoming a standup comic.
3. What does the phrase "bombing" in the context of the article mean?
4. How does Frymer create variety in his sentence structure?
5. Identify the fundamental trait that all comics must possess.
6. Is the purpose of the article to entertain, inform, or convince? Defend your answer.

WRITING ASSIGNMENTS

Process

1. Tell step-by-step how to play a practical joke on someone.
2. You may be thinking of another career. Write your process for obtaining your goal, patterning it after this article.

Work and Play

1. Write about your favorite comedian, the characteristics that make him or her popular, and the "gimmick."
2. Relate an incident where an ethnic, religious, or sexist joke offended you. How did you react? Would you respond the same way now?

Panic Won't Help When Crunch Is On

Niki Scott

Niki Scott wrote this feature which appeared in the *Baltimore Sun*.

WORDS TO KNOW

brochure pamphlet

ironclad strict or exacting

It was a complicated project—one with 50 pieces and an ironclad deadline. But it was important to her company—could earn her a promotion. She volunteered.

"I knew the deadline was tight, but I honestly thought I could do it," she said, her voice shaking. "This is my big chance! Now it's gone."

She's usually calm and competent. This time she was neither. It happens to all of us at one time or another. We panic and stop thinking, stop taking things one at a time, stop considering all our options, stop having faith in ourselves.

"Everything that could possibly go wrong has," she said. "My assistant is in the hospital, our computer broke down, the air conditioning went out yesterday—and I had to send everyone home early. And the printing plant just called to say our brochures won't be ready on time.

"The repairman says he can't get to our computers for three days. What can I do without a computer? It's no use.

"I've had it. I'll never pull this together in time. I'm just going to have to tell my boss that I blew it. He won't fire me, but he sure won't feel inclined to promote me any time soon, either. What a mess," she added miserably.

But had she asked her computer company for a rental machine? Or checked about leasing one from another company? Or tried to beg, borrow, or steal one from another department?

No.

Had she negotiated with the computer repair people—explained the importance of the project and its ironclad deadline—while reminding them, perhaps, that her company is a valuable client?

Had she also checked other computer repair companies in the area and, if necessary, offered to pay more for immediate service?

No.

Had she considered hiring a temporary assistant while hers is in the hospital? Had she considered explaining the situation to her workers, asking them to work late to meet this deadline?

Had she reconsidered the deadline? Checked to see if it could be moved back a week?

"I didn't think of any of those things. I was too busy scaring myself to death," she chuckled. "I panicked—pure and simple."

If you are in the middle of a crisis and suspect you've stopped thinking, find a friend or a co-worker who is willing to brainstorm with you—not dither with you. You don't need any more of that right now.

Then force yourself to think of at least three courses of action that may save the day. Not sure-fire solutions—just possibilities worth exploring.

Try not to dismiss them before you give them a chance. You're likely to be negative anyway, right now. You'll be tempted to say, "No, that won't work," rather than, "It can't hurt to try."

Meanwhile, don't scare yourself even more. Thoughts such as, "This was my one big chance!" and "I'll never get another one!" do you no good right now. They keep you scared, and may keep you paralyzed.

Finally, even if you can't avoid a catastrophe this time, don't beat yourself up. There are enough other people around who will do that. Learn from your mistakes, then forgive yourself completely.

All successful people experience failure from time to time. We know that the courage to take risks is more important to one's success than a perfect record.

QUESTIONS ON CONTENT AND TECHNIQUE

1. How can you combine the suggestions in the article into one sentence?
2. What repetition occurs in the piece? How does the writer reinforce it? Is it effective?
3. Why does Niki Scott use just one woman executive as an example? What effect would several examples of different businesswomen have?
4. Normally, a writer avoids shifting point of view from first person (I, we) to second person (you) to third person (she, he, or it). Find where the author shifts her point of view and explain why she made that choice.

WRITING ASSIGNMENTS

Process

1. Write of a time when you panicked. Give a step-by-step account of the situation.
2. Attempt a spoof on how to drive your (boss, co-workers, relatives, spouse) to panic and madness.

Work and Play

1. The author advises you to force yourself to think of courses of action that may "save the day." Describe one incident at work or play where your actions "saved the day."
2. "We know that the courage to take risks is more important to one's success than a perfect record." Do you agree or disagree? Illustrate your argument with specific examples.

Chapter
6

Comparison and Contrast

In everyday speech and writing we are constantly comparing different things. To do this we may use clichés: "Your room looks like a pigsty"; "She's a fox" or, on a more literary note, "My love is like a red, red rose."

We also contrast things in a similar fashion. "I'm so neat and you're such a slob." "Men tend to hide their feelings, but women need to express theirs."

Individually, these descriptions are called similes, metaphors, hyperboles—figures of speech. But when the same process is used in a lengthy essay or article, we call this writing mode exposition by comparison and contrast.

Writers use comparison and contrast because it is an easy way to communicate clearly with the reader, who is able to understand the unfamiliar when it is described in terms of the familiar. Consider the image used in Winston Churchill's speech defining the Cold War: "An iron curtain has descended across the Continent."

In the articles in this chapter, we see how writers use comparison and contrast to make the strange seem familiar. Ellen Goodman describes the double standards that parents, because of fear, impose on their daughters. Charles Krauthammer's piece about Type A and Type B personalities delineates these two groups of people by comparing each group.

On a simpler level, George H. Gurley, Jr., contrasts the quiet era of the 1950s with the 1980s by describing the minor issues a high-school journalist faced 30 years ago and then contrasting them with the issue of school newspaper censorship that went all the way to the Supreme Court.

In almost every article, the unfamiliar is clarified for the reader by comparing it with or contrasting it to the familiar. Through these two methods the writers communicate clearly, achieving the primary goal of all writing.

WHEN YOU WRITE COMPARISON AND CONTRAST

- Draft a thesis statement that lets your readers know that a comparison and/or contrast will follow.
- Realize that your purpose is to make your audience aware of differences or similarities by comparing the familiar with the unfamiliar, old with new, artificial with natural, or one viewpoint with another.
- Choose points of comparison or contrast that are parallel and drop any details that do not serve this function.
- Plan the order of your comparison or contrast. Two common arrangements are **block**—to discuss one type including all points and then to move to another type to discuss the same points, or **alternating**—to move back and forth between the two types being compared. Help your readers by summarizing the major points in your conclusion.

Male and Female English

Anne de Courcy

Although Anne de Courcy is with the *London Evening Standard,* this article appeared in the *Chicago Tribune* on January 3, 1988.

WORDS TO KNOW

contradict to deny or say no

entitlement having a right to

erodes wears away

propitiate gain the favor of

reciprocal mutual

Do men and women understand the same things from the spoken word? Judging by the misinterpretation, misunderstanding and general mystification that can arise from a single simple sentence, there are grave reasons for doubt.

In fact, I would put it even stronger: Do we even speak the same language?

First—and contrary to the general impression—men use it more. From the classroom, where study after study has shown that boys talk roughly three times as much as girls (with the result that they receive most of the teacher's attention—and thus often a better education) to adult life, men consistently outtalk women. Nor does it take an expert to realize that this constant acceptance of second place erodes self-esteem.

"Like everyone else, I used to believe that women were the talkative sex," says Dale Spender, a specialist in sociolinguistics who has taken her tape recorder to more dinner parties than you and I have had.

"But when I analyzed the results of over 240 recorded conversations between men and women, the result was quite the opposite," Spender says.

"Whether we're talking about social gatherings or business meetings, one element is unvarying: In any conversation with a man, a woman who talks more than a third of the time is seen as talking too much. The point I'm making is that both men and women have very set notions about how much women are allowed to talk. And if women go over this entitlement, then they are seen as rude and aggressive by both men and women," she says.

Nowhere is Spender's Law more obvious than on radio or TV talk shows.

As one popular talk-show host was heard saying, "It's difficult to find the right kind of woman to participate in this program. Most of them find they can't stand up to the men and so stay silent. They also find interrupting a bit—er, tricky."

The reason for this may be that most men see talk as a form of rivalry: Talk is the easiest way for a man to draw attention to himself—women have other methods—so in any competitive situation they pick up that instrument and get down to work.

In a group, this can have a paralyzing effect on the female larynx. Part of the reason, points out Spender, is that many women see their role in any conversation as encouraging men to talk.

Man's belief in his prior claim to the airwaves is underlined by a major female conversation characteristic: the conviction that conversation should be a reciprocal exchange rather than an attempt to hold the floor.

"For women, talk is co-operative rather than essentially competitive," says sociologist Jennifer Coates, author of "Men, Women and Language."

"When a woman in a group of women raises a topic, the others will encourage, sympathize or elaborate. The next female speaker may enlarge on some point, add a personal anecdote, or simply make sympathetic interjections. But one thing she won't do is flatly contradict the previous speaker and abruptly change the subject. But men in a group with women often get bored with what they see as the slow build-up of a topic," she says.

Their method of avoiding this hazard is by doing what most women hate: interrupting.

Two California sociologists, Candace West and Donald Zimmerman, found that men interrupt women far more often than they interrupt other men—and more frequently than women interrupt anybody.

When psychologist Pamela Fishman recorded many hours of male-female conversation, she found that topics introduced by men succeeded (that is, developed further) 96 percent of the time, whereas those brought up by women were only 36 percent successful.

The effect constant interruption has on women is that they become silent, says Coates. It isn't solely that the male view of conversation is that it is a contest ("which means that, once men have made a point, they expect to be attacked—and do the same") but also as a clash of styles.

"We all think we know what a question is. But with men and women, it triggers different reactions. Men think questions are requests for information, whereas women think they are part of the way in which a co-operative conversation works—in other words, I feed you a question so that you can have a turn. Women don't like it if one member of a group isn't speaking; they always try to draw him or her in.

"Thus, if a woman asks a man a question, she's trying to keep the conversation going, while the man thinks this is a request for information so he gives her a lecture," she explains.

In social situations, Coates says, this cross-purpose view of the polite inquiry often can cause a certain amount of bad feelings. "The woman thinks, 'What's his problem? I don't want a run-down on company accountancy,' and the man thinks, 'Why is she looking so upset? If she didn't want to know, why did she ask?'"

Though her upbringing, past, and general social conditioning often give the average woman a greater sensitivity than her husband or brother to what the other person is feeling, it is equally true that, in situations where power is concerned, the male cut-and-thrust style is the norm.

Female language, as most women know, is altogether more tentative. "Would you like to eat now?" we sometimes ask when what we mean is "Dinner's ready." As harmless as this might be at home, carrying the same technique into the office can mean death to a career.

"Male language allows them to have clear goals, stick to decisions, answer directly without fudging and assert themselves," says Natasha Josefowitz, author of "Paths to Power." "Women say, 'I think

I can,' where men say, 'I can.' And though, theoretically, the woman may be right—who knows if she can carry out a particular task until she is doing it?—what employers go for is confidence."

Even when it comes to asking for a raise, a man is much more likely to ask for it as something that is his due—and get it—while a woman feels she has to justify herself.

One school of thought suggests these soft words and patball questions hinge entirely on power. Women always have felt the need to propitiate; and, interestingly, similar female speech patterns are found among people in subordinate or lower positions. Conversely, many women executives subconsciously have cultivated a male style; when they take this home, confusion and conflict can occur.

Jennifer Coates believes female politeness involves other factors as well. "Partly, it is a recognition that other people may not want to be imposed upon. What it's doing is giving the other person a chance to get out of an obligation without losing face."

Partly, too, it is a question of giving what Coates calls "positive face," which means reassuring others about their own value.

"If you meet someone, you say 'hello' and try to smile, even if you're in a bad mood—ignoring them casts doubt on their social worth," Coates explains.

And women are far better at both these aspects of communication than men—as well as more sensitive to the nuances involved. Which is why, say Coates, a woman will feel personally slighted if a man walks past her wearing a frown, whereas another man simply will assume he was preoccupied.

The reason for such discrepancy in interpretation is something that frequently makes male English a completely different tongue from the female version. Most men use language to conceal their feelings and women see it as an arena for self-disclosure.

Thus, when women are in conversation with women, talk tends to be about their own feelings, worries, problems. Men in a group almost never discuss their emotions or anxieties. This lack of skill and practice, in talking of their own feelings, is, believes Coates, a weakness in male language. "At work it can make negotiation far more difficult: at home or in personal life, all sorts of misunderstandings can involuntarily occur," she says.

Recent research suggests that the female need to confide and be confided in arises because a woman's identity is largely confirmed by the way she relates to other people (whereas a man's depends more on what he does).

Whatever the reason, women undoubtedly find refusing, rejecting, criticizing or dismissing particularly difficult to do. Yet, as

Natasha Josefowitz points out, an ability to say "no" clearly is a basic need for anyone on a career pathway as well as an invaluable asset in private life.

For men, learning to show weaknesses as well as strengths, and listening in a receptive way that allows awareness of the other person's mood, as well as comprehension of the words involved, can only be beneficial—though possibly a little more difficult.

But, then, learning to speak someone else's language never is easy.

QUESTIONS ON CONTENT AND TECHNIQUE

1. What multiple sources does de Courcy use to build her comparison?
2. "Most men use language to conceal their feelings and women see it as an arena for self-disclosure." Convert this general statement into specific examples.
3. How does de Courcy smoothly enter quotations into her article? Jot several sentences down to illustrate her technique and remember to do the same when you write.
4. What myths does the author explode?
5. How does de Courcy's tone affect the reader?

WRITING ASSIGNMENTS

Comparison and Contrast

1. Give two different points of view on a current political, social, or ethical problem.
2. To show how a writer can evoke feelings in his reader, take any animal, object, person, or scene and write a positive and negative description. Use as your theme: Beauty is in the eye of the beholder.

Social and Political Issues

1. De Courcy writes, ". . . many women executives subconsciously have cultivated a male style; when they take this home, confusion and conflict can occur." React to this statement and explain your position.
2. Using the model of de Courcy, construct an imaginary conversation between a man and a woman in which you reveal the differences in approach and content of male-female English.

Type A and Type B

Charles Krauthammer

Charles Krauthammer is a syndicated columnist in Washington.

WORDS TO KNOW

coronary relating to the heart

insatiable incapable of being satisfied

ostentatious seeking attention

validation fact or truth

zeitgeist general spirit of an era

In "Sleeper," Woody Allen wakes up 200 years from now and learns that, in the interim, science has discovered that cigarettes are good for you. Well, life plays better jokes than art. Remember the Type A personality: ambitious, aggressive, competitive, hostile and driven? It was long supposed to cause heart attacks. Surprise. It prevents them.

In the current issue of the "New England Journal of Medicine," a 22-year study shows that Type B men, laid-back and mellow, had about twice the chance of dying from heart disease as Type A's. The Type A personality, it seems, has an "apparently protective effect" in preventing coronary death.

The authors modestly note that theirs is "an unexpected result." Unexpected, and devastating to an entire industry that has grown up around the myth of mellow. Goodby, TM, yoga, mantras and all the groups and schools for venting aggression and finding your center. Time to get out of touch with your feelings. Heart problems? Try commodity futures.

Of course, the whole idea of a relaxation industry—mellowness training—is so cockeyed that belief in it requires a partially bent mind to begin with. But that is part of its charm. Less charming is the accompanying ideology. Ideologies are always looking for "objective" validation in biology. Anti-A ideology—as practiced by, say, the anti-macho, new-age militants bent on getting all the popguns out of toy stores—was buttressed by the argument that competition is not just ill-mannered, it kills.

Buttressed no more. On Wall Street, traders have just been given, literally, a new lease on life. Main Street, too, rejoices. The price of health today for the average guy is already too high: bran flakes in the morning, a 5-mile jog at noon, more roughage at night, no cigar, no booze, no eggs, no butter, no pastrami. And then they order him to get a personality change! Now, at last, the tide is turning; still no pastrami, but he can keep his personality.

Type A personality was first postulated to cause heart disease in the 1950s. The idea reached its peak of pop popularity during the '70s when the contemplated navel and transcendental relaxation were in vogue. Shortly thereafter, in 1981, the link was officially consecrated as scientific fact by an independent review panel that declared Type A behavior to be a risk factor for (that is polite medical talk for "cause of") heart disease. The panel, in fact, called Type A "coronary-prone behavior."

The debunking of that idea could just be what the flagging '80s need for a revival. After all, Type A is the '80s type: all greed and drive and excess. Science's rehabilitation of Type A should give pause to the Zeitgeist sniffers who have declared the '80s dead.

We can now view another anti-'80s tract, Oliver Stone's "Wall Street," in an entirely new light. The movie is a parable about Type A's. They are all villains: greedy, shifty, ostentatious, insatiable, and casually cruel. The movie's one cartoon good guy, the working stiff, is laid-back. He doesn't pace when he talks. No phone in his car or bathroom. He is content with his job, his family, his bar. He is not out to make a buck or a splash. He's a double B.

And then, wouldn't you know, by God, he gets the heart attack. Stone makes it happen right after the A's betray him, ruin him and turn his only son against him. Stone wants you to blame the heart attack on the A's, those rascals. But now we know better: The B's do it to themselves. You can look it up.

So arise all you hard-driving, bone-crushing, swashbuckling, nerve-racking, flame-throwing A's. You who have endured the gentle scorn of your Type B friends, saddened, they aver, that you insist on killing yourself. And all that time you were applying layers of Type A protection to your coronary arteries.

There is a new self-confidence descending upon the Type A's of this world as they enjoy the vindication of retroactive justice. If they can just resist the smugness—which can be dangerous to your health since it is a gateway to B-hood—they can, with scientific certainty, turn to their tormentors and pronounce on them that most awful of curses: We will bury you.

"Wall Street's" Gordon Gekko will live to be a 100. (In jail, it is true, but you can't have everything.) It's Alan Alda who'd better be stocking up on nitroglycerin.

QUESTIONS ON CONTENT AND TECHNIQUE

1. How does Krauthammer correct a common misconception?
2. Choose some words and phrases of Krauthammer which show that he is targeting a specific audience.
3. What is his attitude toward Type A? Type B?
4. Find his sentence fragments and see if it is possible to attach them to a preceding or succeeding sentence. Rewrite them by combining or developing.
5. How does the author maintain the reader's interest?

WRITING ASSIGNMENTS

Comparison and Contrast

1. Compare different types of personalities within your family.
2. Show your reaction to some event, as Type A and then Type B. Be specific.

Science and Technology

1. "The price of health today for the average guy is already too high." Agree or disagree with this statement, giving pertinent details.
2. Think of a commonly held belief or practice that no longer is held true. Show how facts dispel beliefs or that new data and experiments can change so-called facts.

Freedom of Speech

George H. Gurley, Jr.

George H. Gurley, Jr., writes a column "Behind the Lines" in the *Kansas City Times.*

WORDS TO KNOW

allegory symbolic representation

gothic type of ornate lettering

halcyon most pleasant

ruminate think

sardonic disdainful

virulent extremely severe

The Supreme Court's decision to permit censorship of student newspapers caused me to ruminate about my high school days.

What was the status of freedom of speech in the halcyon '50s? What were the issues that troubled our young, impressionable minds?

Luckily I was able to retrieve a copy of my school newspaper, The Hilltop, from a scrapbook my mother kept for me. It's more than a memento. It's a valuable document of cultural history. Let's take a look at student journalism as represented on the distant day of April 1, 1959.

 [The title is ours.]

The first thing we notice is that the name of the paper has been altered to suit the occasion. It's become The Hillflop. The lead story on the front page, in gothic print, bears the headline "A Sort of Allegory." Close reading reveals that it's a scathing, sardonic attack on the school itself.

Under a thin veil various teachers and administrators are referred to as "tyrannical wretch," "toady," "fat," "terrible," "doting," "timid," "meek," and "bumbling."

The gist of the allegory was that the people who were entrusted with our education were a stupid and incompetent lot.

How were we permitted to say such things back then? Were the rights of students more respected in the '50s than they are today? Not necessarily. That same year a student made fun of a teacher in his student council campaign speech. The next day, he was gone.

I can only conclude that our teachers were in fact a little dense and that the barbs of our newspaper were too subtle for them. . . .

Another disturbing revelation: The students from Hazelwood, Mo., who lost the Supreme Court decision, had written about pregnancy and divorce, subjects their overseers felt were too sensitive.

Nowhere in this issue of the Hillflop can I find a discussion of pregnancy, divorce, AIDS, drug addiction, alcoholism or any of the other issues which today's youth must wrestle with.

"Bahstow Dorm Scene of Raid," reads one headline. "Police are holding 21 Pembroke Country Day School students who were apprehended in last night's so-called panty raid at the swank Bahstow School Dormitory."

There's a full page parody of Kansas City's weekly journal of society, The Independent. A photo of an English teacher illustrates an ad for "Jeritol."

Alas, it appears that students in the halcyon '50s didn't have important issues on their minds. Consequently, perhaps, their elders didn't pay enough attention to them to bother with censorship. . . .

I have come to think of myself as a champion of free speech. But to my astonishment I found in the same scrapbook a virulent advocacy of censorship titled "Comic Books: Blue Prints for Delinquency," which I'd written for an eighth-grade debate.

"Many of these so-called comic books are chronicles of sex and violence," I ranted. "One of them depicted an evil-looking bandit overpowering a scantily clad girl and 19 murders, including disintegration in a vat of acid."

What do you make of it? A prig at age 13, a freethinker at 46. . . .

"Men are never so likely to settle a question rightly as when they discuss it freely," says Macaulay. The danger is not "by what breaks out of the public mind, but by what stays in it."

Censorship is a power that's almost certain to be abused, I say. Yet, if we give our kids freedom of speech, how can we be sure that what they say will be in good taste? It's enough to make you wring your hands.

What solace can we give to the disappointed students across the land who feel that there's one rule for their parents, another for them? In the words of a KU journalism prof, "This too will pass. Kind of like a kidney stone."

QUESTIONS ON CONTENT AND TECHNIQUE

1. Is the purpose of this article to (a) entertain, (b) explain, (c) persuade? Explain your choice.
2. Why does Gurley spend 85 percent of his article on one side of the comparison?
3. Words such as "prig," "barbs," "toady," "champion" carry emotional charge. Take any sentence from the article and slant it toward an opposite point of view.
4. The author argues his case from primarily one source. What is it? Is it effective? Why? Why not?
5. What changes have occurred in Gurley's point of view toward freedom since his high-school newspaper days?

WRITING ASSIGNMENTS

Comparison and Contrast

1. The author implies attitudes have changed. Compare your attitude toward any social issue now and in the past, for example, women in the military, single parenthood, racial segregation.
2. Find any issue that is debated, whether on TV, in a newspaper, or magazine. Give both points of view.

Social and Political Issues

1. Take any belief that you held as a teenager and compare it with your changed attitude today, showing the factors that led to reversal.
2. You are a reporter on your college newspaper. Write an editorial on an issue that needs to be addressed.

The Double Safety Standard

Ellen Goodman

Ellen Goodman, a nationally known syndicated columnist, compares daughters and sons.

WORDS TO KNOW

congenitally existing from birth

exponentially how many times a number is factored; greatly

foolhardy reckless

Boston—The two girls are inside. It is ten o'clock and dark. They are thirteen. The mother is not being unreasonable when she tells them that visiting hours are over. She doesn't want them on the street late at night. They know that.

Instead, their friends will walk over here for ice cream and cookies and conversation. That's different. The friends are boys, and boys are allowed out on the street at night.

The mother, scooping the ice cream out of the container for all of them, thinks to herself: It has begun—the slow separation between what boys can do and girls cannot.

Not long ago, the freedom of all four was curtailed by the joint fact of their childhood. They were equally small, young, weak, protected. Now they are growing out of the vulnerability of their youth. But the girls acquire a new vulnerability: their sex.

She has known these boys most of their lives. Their independence, mobility, physical freedom are growing exponentially. The freedom of the girls is growing, too, but carefully, within certain fences and fears, prearranged routes and routines.

Are the parents of daughters overprotective? the mother asks herself. Do we stunt their growth with our caution? What else can we do in the face of the reality of their greater risk?

There is one statistical fact that slams down like an iron door against their freedom of movement. The fact of assault.

Just recently, a woman was raped in the neighborhood. At that time, there was hardly a neighborhood in which a woman was not raped. That is the painful truth that divides the lives of growing boys and girls.

If parents are congenitally concerned with safety for all their children, we still worry differently about daughters. We don't want to, but we have to.

Years ago, during a wave of crimes against women in Israel, a council of men asked Golda Meir to put a nighttime curfew on females. Meir said no. If men were the problem, she answered, let the council enforce a curfew against men.

Now, a mother who had cheered Meir puts a curfew on her daughter. Like generations of parents before her, she chooses safety over growth for her child, protection over risk. It's what parents usually do, and she is, for better and worse, no exception.

The son of a friend has just returned from California. At twenty, he traveled back and forth by thumb. His father worried, but he also accepted this as a rite of passage, an adventure of adulthood. The risk was worth the returns of self-confidence, experience, independence.

But if the young man had been a young woman, the balance of payments for this adventure could have been quite different: the real risks greater, the anxiety greater.

In Simone de Beauvoir's book, "The Prime of Life," she describes a year during her life when she took leaps, deliberate physical challenges. Among other things, the writer hitchhiked regularly and alone.

As a woman, the mother understands de Beauvoir's deliberate rebellion, her need to act as if she were completely free. De Beauvoir forced herself to unlearn fear, to learn independence.

But as a mother, she thinks such behavior is foolhardy. As a mother she teaches her daughter the lessons that she may someday have to unlearn. She watches other parents teach these same lessons. She sees older girls not allowed to walk home from movies alone, older girls who learn that they need a man to be safe from men.

It is eleven o'clock now and the thirteen-year-old boys have to be home. Today, only an hour separates their freedoms. But that gap will grow.

The mother will do what she can. She will, at some point, buy lessons in self-defense. She will encourage other, safer kinds of growth and risk. She will struggle against her maternal anxiety.

And she will also rage. Rage in sorrow against the violence that forces parents, of all people, to become the agents of their daughters' suppression.

QUESTIONS ON CONTENT AND TECHNIQUE

1. What basically creates the double safety standard in American society, according to Goodman?
2. How does Goodman use time as a symbol?
3. "He traveled back and forth by thumb." Why would this be considered a rite of passage?
4. At what age does the author suggest the double safety standard begins?

WRITING ASSIGNMENTS

Comparison and Contrast

1. Select an event or situation in your childhood and compare the double standard of safety (male/female) being applied.
2. Compare a "rite of passage" in a family, a community, or a culture that has changed in the last decade or two.

Social and Political Issues

1. Write about a risk you took as a child and its outcome.
2. What conditions in your city have put men and women, young and old, at risk? Discuss possible solutions.

Coastal Cousins Are Two of a Kind

Joel Stashenko and Doug Willis

Joel Stashenko and Doug Willis of the Associated Press had their article printed in the *San Francisco Examiner.*

WORDS TO KNOW

brash impulsive

dynamo electrical generator; an energetic individual

huckster peddler

IF CALIFORNIA AND NEW YORK WERE NATIONS, THEY'D BE AMONG THE WORLD'S 10 RICHEST. THEY'RE FIRST AND SECOND IN POPULATION AMONG THE 50 STATES. FROM WALL STREET AND HOLLYWOOD, MADISON AVENUE AND SILICON VALLEY, THEY OFTEN SET AN AGENDA FOLLOWED BY THE REST OF THE COUNTRY, SOMETIMES GRUDGINGLY. HERE, WRITERS IN ALBANY, N.Y. AND SACRAMENTO RESPECTIVELY, LOOK AT THE WAYS AND MEANS AND MYTHS OF THE EMPIRE STATE AND THE GOLDEN STATE.

California and New York, coastal dynamos that generate much of the nation's intellectual, financial and social energy, are far apart in tradition, outlook and image.

New and old. Los Angeles cool and Manhattan brash. Hollywood hipster and Madison Avenue huckster.

New York and California have long been targets of the nation's wisecracks. Yet the profound influence they exert over the nation's way of life, finances and collective consciousness is no joke.

Nearly one-half of those who made Forbes magazine's list of 400 richest Americans live in the two states.

Those who make it big in either place—from President Reagan and tax rebel Howard Jarvis to Gov. Mario Cuomo and real estate mogul Donald Trump—usually end up as familiar figures in the rest of the nation.

In economic terms, California is riding the crest of a boom as the nation's gateway to the thriving Pacific Rim. New York, which grew to dominance as the chief U.S. port-of-entry from Europe, is enjoying an upswing itself.

However, the Empire State also is struggling to replace its decaying industries with the kind of high-technology and defense-oriented firms that have become a mainstay of California's economy.

While New York's metropolitan area still is the nation's largest with 18 million inhabitants (including many in New Jersey and Connecticut suburbs), metropolitan Los Angeles' estimated population in 1986 was 13.1 million and growing so fast it could have more people than New York early in the next century.

The ports of Los Angeles and San Diego already have surpassed the port of New York and New Jersey in cargo volume.

"We're No. 1 in everything from peaches to Ph.d.s," said Gov. Deukmejian. "California is home to more engineers, more scientists and more Nobel laureates than any state in America."

Cuomo reacts defensively, noting that Deukmejian is a native New Yorker.

"If you compare us to California, we do better everywhere," Cuomo said. "They say they have more computer chip companies. Who cares? I mean, so what? You took one category, computer chips. . . . We have more bowling ball manufacturers."

Rivalries aside, if they were independent countries, California would have the sixth richest economy in the world and New York would be about two places back.

New York's Wall Street continues to be the world's financial nerve center.

California's TV and movie industries have long showed Americans how to walk and talk, what to wear and even how to hold their cigarettes.

New York's Madison Avenue advertising firms have told Americans what to buy, and where, and sometimes why.

New York and California project styles so distinct that many Americans are repelled without ever visiting either place.

Are the stereotypes of laid-back Californians and gruff New Yorkers really true?

On a recent sunny day in West Hollywood, a friend of Jane Thorne told the transplanted New Yorker he was going whale-watching. "I said, 'What?'" Thorne recalled, finding it hard to believe that someone would go to sea simply to eyeball a whale.

And Janet Lowry still thinks about her first visit to a pizza parlor after moving to New York from Los Angeles a few years ago.

"Whaddya want?" a counterman snarled.

"I'm thinking," Lowry said.

"Next!" the counterman yelled.

Political consultant David Garth has handled campaigns on both coasts and saw a clear difference in approach—but keep in mind he's from New York.

"In New York when they stab you, they stab you in the stomach," he said. "In California when they stab you, they stab you in the back. They rub your back first and then they put a knife in it. They're all nice."

California's political system produced Reagan and before him Richard Nixon; New York's produced Theodore and Franklin Roosevelt, among other presidents.

And yet the two states' political systems could hardly be more different.

In California, voters have directly enacted laws creating new regulatory agencies and have used the state's unusual voter confirmation process to oust their chief justice and change the direction of their highest court.

California's Proposition 13, pushed by Howard Jarvis in 1978, cut local property taxes in half, chopped $7 billion a year out of the local government tax base, and set off a national tax revolt movement.

In New York, where there is no initiative process, only the 211 state legislators vote on such issues.

Misconceptions about the two states abound.

Electronics and tourism, not entertainment, are California's biggest industries. Farming remains a key component of the economy.

Despite being the nation's most populous state with more than 28 million people, California still has stretches that remain sparsely settled.

When fires swept over nearly 1,200 square miles of California's mountains last year, an area larger than Rhode Island, only 31 homes were destroyed.

And for all of New York's urban image, the state is home to the 6 million-acre Adirondack Park, the largest wilderness area east of the Mississippi.

Three million of the state's nearly 18 million inhabitants live in rural areas.

New York's Department of Economic Development classifies agriculture as the state's No. 1 industry.

"They have strengths we don't have," Cuomo said of Californians. "They have a defense industry we don't have. We have the financial industry."

"We're both very strong states."

QUESTIONS ON CONTENT AND TECHNIQUE

1. Besides style, what other comparisons do the authors make?
2. Why do Stashenko and Willis weave back and forth from New York to California rather than simply discussing one and then the other?
3. "California and New York are far apart in tradition, outlook, and image." What other trait(s) would you choose for comparison or contrast?
4. How do the authors keep the reader interested?

WRITING ASSIGNMENTS

Comparison and Contrast

1. Compare two rivals: politicians, teams, companies, colleges, products, or cities.
2. Compare or contrast two areas of your town, community, or state.

Memories and Reflections

1. One often hears the cliché "two of a kind." Write of two persons you know who appear different but have underlying similarities.
2. Narrate an experience where you competed against someone else and became number 1.

How Prison Differs for Men and Women

Jim Bencivenga

Jim Bencivenga compares the inequalities of prison conditions between women and men in this article from the *Christian Science Monitor*.

WORDS TO KNOW

contraband illegal goods

endemic native

incarceration imprisonment

Bedford Hills, N.Y.—An inmate at New York's Bedford Hills prison, a maximum-security facility for women, laughs when she thinks of how little people really know about women in prison. B. J. Close recalls a phone call from a couple who are friends of hers.

"He's a university professor," she said, "and he and his wife wanted to come and visit, take me out for dinner. They wanted me to just tell them where a nearby restaurant was and they'd be sure to get me back in on time." The visit took place inside the prison in the visitors' room.

The steel-bar doors in women's prisons clang just as loud as in men's. Concertina wire (a ribbon of looped, razor-blade steel) scrapes the tops of walls and fences and snakes along the ground at the outer perimeter of the facility. Electronic searches of visitors for weapons and contraband are just as thorough, just as impersonal. All movement is confined and controlled.

But differences are quickly apparent. Some are grounds for sex discrimination lawsuits, criminal-justice experts said. Others offer possibilities for change in the premises for which people are imprisoned.

Overcrowding is not the problem for women that it is for men. Fewer than 28,000 women are doing hard time in state or federal prisons, contrasted with 542,500 men in similar institutions.

But fewer women behind bars means the cost of rehabilitation per inmate is greater for women than men. "You just don't have the economy of scale for women that you do for men," said Kay Monaco, a lawyer in Santa Fe, N.M., who is a former state deputy secretary for corrections. The result is fewer education programs and pre-release work opportunities for women, she said.

"Women get the short end of the stick when it comes to prison industries," Monaco said. "Lots of resources go into men's programs. There's an inequality for women."

The qualities that should be rewarded with more opportunities result in fewer, because in the competition for scarce resources men win out each time, she said.

"They didn't come in with high job skills," said Christine J. Herlinger, executive director of the Guilford County Women's Residential/Day Center, an alternative setting for incarceration of women. If they spend 10 years in prison, where education programs are limited, where being a hairdresser is the model offered, what can they do when they leave? she asks.

The rate of increase in incarceration for women last year was 12.3%, more than double that for men. If that rate continues, a crisis in overcrowding will occur very quickly for women, and it will be difficult to manage, because state systems have far fewer options for shifting female populations among prisons.

Incarceration plays itself out differently for women in terms of self-respect, said Michael A. Millemann, a professor of law at the University of Maryland. Men inmates preserve an element of dignity that does not exist in women's prisons. The guards know how potentially violent men are, and there are sections (especially in the residential cellblocks) where "treaties" are reached between inmate and guard. Not so in women's facilities, he said.

"The biggest problem by far," Millemann said, "is that our perception of women inmates is distorted in that we do not, and cannot, relate to the idea of a woman as inmate."

Women's records suggest that more women offenders could be given alternative sentences or paroled, he said. But because society confuses them with male inmates, it is not willing to take what it considers risks in releasing them, he said.

This problem is endemic to modern corrections, said Anthony Travisono, executive director of the American Correctional Assn. "We equate punishment with putting someone someplace," he said.

This mentality limits alternative forms of sentencing better suited to the offense and the offender. Few women in prison ever dreamed they would be incarcerated. Many men, especially the 60% who are repeat offenders, knew they faced such a possibility. And although the majority of women commit their crime with a man, they do their time without one. Rarely, if ever, are there any men in the visiting room. Sisters, mothers, daughters, aunts—but seldom men.

In most cases, locking up a woman means locking up a family. "When a woman does time, her entire family does time," said Bedford Hills inmate Karen Ely. Child custody reverts to the state except in the rare instance when a father is present.

This increases the potential ripple effect for children entering the criminal-justice cycle as offenders themselves, said Jo Ann Potter, an advocate for women's correctional issues at the Edna McConnell Clark Foundation in New York City.

It would take five to 10 years to verify, Monaco said, but she is convinced fewer kids would turn up in the juvenile justice system if fewer mothers were locked up.

Violence is less likely in women's prisons.

Although there's always a hard-core element intimidating other women, the smaller number of women prisoners allows prison officials to isolate the predators and maintain a physically violence-free facility, he said.

"Idle men often lead to trouble in prisons. Women bring less attention to themselves, in that they do not deal with idleness in a violent way," said John DiIuilio of Princeton University's Wilson School of Government.

"Women are not going to riot," said Susan Hallett, an inmate at Bedford Hills. "We'll just nest."

It is common to see curtains in a cell, or find one inmate surprising another with a hot meal or a handcrafted gift.

In a perverse way their gentleness works against the best interests of women inmates, Potter said. Riots and court intervention have resulted in better rehabilitation programs for men. In contrast, the absence of violence in facilities for women has let state corrections departments be more responsive to male than to female inmates, she said.

Ironically, a little-known fact in the history of corrections is that many humanizing innovations originated in women's prisons at the turn of the century: Those include education classes, libraries, art and music programs, work release, recreation, vocational training, and placement by age, offense, and length of sentence.

The high price tag on corrections (average annual cost of keeping an inmate in a state medium- or maximum-security prison is $17,500; in some industrialized states, costs reach $30,000) is forcing many states to consider alternative modes of punishment and incarceration, Travisono said, adding they are much more likely to be adopted for women than for men, because women present less of a threat to others.

"One of the current catches of the criminal-justice system is that murderers of a spouse or lover are not a risk to you or me," Monaco said. "We are talking about a serious crime, certainly, but how many years is enough? Ten, 15, 25?"

If the risk is near zero that a 45- to 55-year-old inmate would injure anyone else or commit another crime, punishment becomes the only reason, not safety at all, she said.

QUESTIONS ON CONTENT AND TECHNIQUE

1. Give several ways women are different from men prisoners.
2. With what techniques does the writer help the reader visualize prison?
3. How do each of Bencivenga's sources strengthen and support his thesis? What is the impact on you?
4. Is the purpose of the article (a) informative, (b) argumentative, (c) both? Defend your choice.

WRITING ASSIGNMENTS

Comparison and Contrast

1. Write of a place (church, college, place of employment) where you feel women have been treated differently from men.
2. Compare any situation that you might have experienced with "being behind bars."

Crime and Society

1. "In a perverse way their gentleness works against the best interests of women inmates." Relate an event in which you felt this to be true.
2. Assume that you are a judge and the jury has declared Jennifer X guilty of murdering her abusive spouse. Discuss her background, give your sentence or alternative correction program, and explain your action.

Columbus and the Moon

Tom Wolfe

Tom Wolfe, one of the first to report in the "new journalism," wrote this comparison of the expeditions of Columbus to the New World and NASA to the moon.

WORDS TO KNOW

lured attracted

ignominy humiliation

testy irritable

traumatized cause physical or mental anxiety

The National Aeronautics and Space Administration's moon landing 10 years ago today was a Government project, but then so was Columbus's voyage to America in 1492. The Government, in Columbus's case, was the Spanish Court of Ferdinand and Isabella. Spain was engaged in a sea race with Portugal in much the same way that the United States would be caught up in a space race with the Soviet Union four and a half centuries later.

The race in 1492 was to create the first shipping lane to Asia. The Portuguese expeditions had always sailed east, around the southern tip of Africa. Columbus decided to head due west, across open ocean, a scheme that was feasible only thanks to a recent invention—the magnetic ship's compass. Until then ships had stayed close to the great land masses even for the longest voyages. Likewise, it was only thanks to an invention of the 1940's and early 1950's, the high speed electronic computer, that NASA would even consider propelling astronauts out of the Earth's orbit and toward the moon.

Both NASA and Columbus made not one but a series of voyages. NASA landed men on six different parts of the moon. Columbus made four voyages to different parts of what he remained convinced was the east coast of Asia. As a result both NASA and Columbus had to keep coming back to the Government with their hands out, pleading for refinancing. In each case the reply of the Government became, after a few years: "This is all very impressive, but what earthly good is it to anyone back home?"

Columbus was reduced to making the most desperate claims. When he first reached land in 1492 at San Salvador, off Cuba, he expected to find gold, or at least spices. The Arawak Indians were awed by the strangers and their ships, which they believed had descended from the sky, and they presented them with their most prized possessions, live parrots and balls of cotton. Columbus soon set them digging for gold, which didn't exist. So he brought back reports of fabulous riches in the form of manpower; which is to say, slaves. He was not speaking of the Arawaks, however. With the exception of criminals and prisoners of war, he was supposed to civilize all natives and convert them to Christianity. He was talking about the Carib Indians, who were cannibals and therefore qualified as criminals. The Caribs would fight down to the last unbroken bone rather than endure captivity, and few ever survived the voyages back to Spain. By the end of Columbus's second voyage, in 1496, the Government was becoming testy. A great deal of wealth was going into voyages to Asia, and very little was coming back. Columbus made his men swear to return to Spain saying that they had not only reached the Asian mainland, they had heard Japanese spoken.

Likewise by the early 1970s, it was clear that the moon was in economic terms pretty much what it looked like from Earth, a gray rock. NASA, in the quest for appropriations, was reduced to publicizing the "spinoffs" of the space program. These included Teflon-coated frying pans, a ballpoint pen that would write in a weightless environment, and a computerized biosensor system that would enable doctors to treat heart patients without making house calls. On the whole, not a giant step for mankind.

In 1493, after his first voyage, Columbus had ridden through Barcelona at the side of King Ferdinand in the position once occupied by Ferdinand's late son, Juan. By 1500, the bad-mouthing of

Columbus had reached the point where he was put in chains at the conclusion of his third voyage and returned to Spain in disgrace. NASA suffered no such ignominy, of course, but by July 20, 1974, the fifth anniversary of the landing of Apollo 11, things were grim enough. The public had become gloriously bored by space exploration. The fifth anniversary celebration consisted mainly of about 200 souls, mostly NASA people, sitting on folding chairs underneath a camp meeting canopy on the marble prairie outside the old Smithsonian Air Museum in Washington listening to speeches by Neil Armstrong, Michael Collins, and Buzz Aldrin and watching the caloric waves ripple.

Extraordinary rumors had begun to circulate about the astronauts. The most lurid said that trips to the moon, and even into earth orbit, had so traumatized the men, they had fallen victim to religious and spiritualist manias or plain madness. (Of the total 73 astronauts chosen, one, Aldrin, is known to have suffered from depression, rooted, as his own memoir makes clear, in matters that had nothing to do with space flight. Two teamed up in an evangelical organization, and one set up a foundation for the scientific study of psychic phenomena—interests the three of them had developed long before they flew in space.) The NASA budget, meanwhile, had been reduced to the light-bill level.

Columbus died in 1509, nearly broke and stripped of most of his honors as Spain's Admiral of the Ocean, a title he preferred. It was only later that history began to look upon him not as an adventurer who had tried and failed to bring home gold—but as a man with a supernatural sense of destiny, whose true glory was his willingness to plunge into the unknown, including the remotest parts of the universe he could hope to reach.

NASA still lives, albeit in reduced circumstances, and whether or not history will treat NASA like the admiral is hard to say.

The idea that the exploration of the rest of the universe is its own reward is not very popular, and NASA is forced to keep talking about things such as bigger communications satellites that will enable live television transmission of European soccer games at a fraction of the current cost. Such notions as "building a bridge to the stars for mankind" do not light up the sky today—but may yet.

QUESTIONS ON CONTENT AND TECHNIQUE

1. How many major points does Wolfe use for comparison and contrast?
2. What is a "spinoff"? Give other examples.

3. How does Wolfe develop and maintain your interest?
4. For what audience do you believe he intended his article? How well does he succeed?

WRITING ASSIGNMENTS

Comparison and Contrast

1. Compare and contrast two historical events, for example, the assassinations of Kennedy and Lincoln.
2. Choose two persons you know about who accomplished a "first" and contrast their achievements.

Science and Technology

1. You may have been influenced by some explorer or pioneer in a different field. Explain his or her effect on you.
2. You have accomplished something that no other human being has done. Describe your achievement and its impact on humankind.

Chapter 7

Definition

SHOE
Reprinted by permission: Tribune Media Services.

Sometimes a term or word is vital to one's well-being. A court case which centers on the interpretation of a legal term or a patient who misunderstands the medical terminology of her physician and suffers undue trauma are common examples. And often politicians redefine words to suit their platforms.

Most dictionaries state that to "define" means to give the exact meaning of a word. In practice, we shall see that this can range from a single sentence description, such as "ordeal, any difficult or painful experience," to a lengthy newspaper column, such as Jack Smith's amusing dissertation on the word "duologue."

Definitions can be as short or as long as the writer thinks necessary. Some are nothing more than a couple of synonyms while others become lengthy articles that include word origin and derivation, forms of usage, and background explanations. Examples using all of the latter are in Thomas H. Middleton's discussion of "Auld Lang Syne" and "Williewaught," and in William Safire's essay on love.

If you read further in your dictionary, you will gather that "define" has another meaning: "To determine the limits of, to describe exactly." From that explanation, a paper on "U.S. Foreign Policy in the Mideast" would be called a definition paper.

Simply put, a definition means giving a clear, distinct, and thorough explanation of a simple word or a complex situation. As writers you may use any method described in this anthology, from comparison, to cause and effect, to definition.

WHEN YOU WRITE DEFINITION

- Remember that usually your readers need a word defined only if it is new, unusual, unfamiliar, controversial, or abstract.
- Realize that a definition may involve an explanation of a single word or phrase, or a discussion of a complicated circumstance or happening.
- Be sure your readers fully understand the general group or class to which the term belongs as well as the subgroup that characterizes it; for example, Gothic is a style of architecture.
- Plan your essay answering the unheard questions of your readers: Why is this word important to know? To what is it similar? Of what value or significance is it? What examples could make it clearer?
- Check that after reading your definition the reader knows what was defined.

Duologue

Jack Smith

Jack Smith writes a daily column for the *Los Angeles Times*. This definition, newly coined, appeared in his column.

WORDS TO KNOW

circumvented to go around by trickery

dysfunctional not working

imperturbably calmly

lout a stupid, awkward person

monologue one person speaking

non sequitur a faulty inference that does not follow logically from a statement

oblique indirect, not straightforward

Tom Gilsenan's invention of the word duologue for a conversation in which neither party is responsive to the other has been well received by others who have always wondered what to call this common phenomenon.

In a duologue, each person answers the other with a non sequitur, so that the conversation takes up time and seems to be fulfilling a purpose, but in fact gets nowhere.

Perhaps the most common example of a duologue is one that may be heard in almost any home when the husband comes home from work to find his wife in a state of frenzied frustration and exhaustion.

She says, "What a day! You can't believe the things that have happened to me!"

He says, "What's for dinner?"

That is a duologue in its briefest form. It may go on from there:

SHE: "Don't you ever hear anything I say?"
HE: "Monday Night Football tonight."

But it sometimes ends with the first exchange, and with her realization that she is married to an insensitive lout and ought to divorce him.

Ronald Dethlefson, professor of communications at Bakersfield College, notes that the duologue was defined some time ago in the *Quarterly Journal of Speech* as a "communication denial."

"If a person is regularly a victim of communication denial," he points out, "then he or she will likely develop a low self-esteem." So we are not talking here about something inconsequential.

Prof. Dethlefson observes that teen-agers are often victims of the duologue, or communications denial, as in this conversation:

SON: "Dad, may I use the car tonight?"
FATHER: "Go help mother with the dishes."

Of course that may be reversed, and we get:

"Son, go help mother with the dishes."

"Dad, I need the car tonight."

I am delighted to hear from Rachel Pearson of Pasadena that Sir Arthur Conan Doyle sometimes used the duologue in the adventures of Sherlock Holmes. She recalls that the device was employed by Sir Arthur "to give Holmes a verbal advantage over the villain, Dr. Grimesby Roylott, in 'The Speckled Band'" as follows:

"'My stepdaughter has been here. . . . What has she been saying to you?'

"'It is a little cold for the time of the year,' said Holmes.

"'What has she been saying to you?' screamed the old man furiously.

"'But I have heard that the crocuses promise well,' continued my companion imperturbably.'"

"It would seem then," concludes Pearson, "that the key to managing a proper 'duologue' is to do it, as Holmes did, imperturbably."

John Trayne points out that the duologue is a device commonly employed by playwrights to depict monologues spoken at the same time. "It is customary to designate this mode by dividing the speeches with a horizontal line from beginning to end."

Trayne suggests that if the speakers' lines are simultaneous but on different subjects, it should be called an antilogue.

I'm sure we are all familiar with plays or movies in which two or more characters are talking simultaneously at cross purposes. The phenomenon Gilsenan describes, though, is a dialogue in which two people talk alternately, as in a true conversation, but their separate lines are not related.

Sara Bell Drescher suggests that, from her own marital experience, the duologue might possibly serve a therapeutic purpose in marriage.

"My former husband and I," she says, "spent a couple of years in 'conjoint' therapy and discovered that our communication was dysfunctional. Well, anything dysfunctional must be repaired or discarded, right? We couldn't repair it.

"Now I find that we could have continued this duologue forever and saved ourselves a lot of money and misery."

Drescher seems to be suggesting that a prolonged duologue between her and her husband might have circumvented their conjoint dysfunction and saved their marriage.

Perhaps she is right. Perhaps continuous duologues do not end as often in divorce as in a kind of disconnected harmony. Perhaps there is something safe in an oblique conversation, instead of the usual blunt confrontation:

"What's for dinner?"

"Get your own dinner."

That could lead to incompatibility and unhappiness.

We had a duologue at our house only this morning.

My wife said, "Did you get the paper?"

And I said, "Have you made the coffee?"

Of course I said it imperturbably.

QUESTIONS ON CONTENT AND TECHNIQUE

1. How did "duologue" originate?
2. What tone does Smith choose? See the glossary if necessary.
3. Notice how Jack Smith uses dialogue. What paragraph structure changes are there?
4. Are there possible advantages to using duologue?

WRITING ASSIGNMENTS

Definition

1. Coin a word of your own that explains a situation. Give its origin, modeling your paper after the article that you have just read.
2. Select one of the following nonsense words and create meaning through your own definition: singblat, funlo, banpo.

Language and the Arts

1. Illustrate a recent duologue in your family.
2. Discuss an event in your life where communication or lack of it caused a problem.

More Than One Way to Spell "Love"

William Safire

William Safire writes a column "On Language" for *The New York Times.*

WORDS TO KNOW

colloquialism an expression more appropriate to conversation than to formal writing

cordiality warm welcome

filial relating to son or daughter

hypocorism pet names

philologist one who studies human speech

unsullied unspotted

On Valentine's Day, philologists will be wondering: What's happening to love?

"O, my Luve's like a red, red rose—That's newly sprung in June . . ." wrote the Scottish poet Robert Burns in a 1794 song, deliberately using a variant spelling, luve. He was not the first or last to fiddle with the spelling or pronunciation of this fairly important noun and verb.

Love's root is not Latin: amor is what some Romans felt for each other, leading to our amorous. For the origin of love, we turn to the Saxons, whose Old English word was lufu, and the Gothic tribes of Central Europe, whose L-words led to our love, lust, and even libido. The English pronunciation began with LOO-voo, changed to LOW-vuh in Middle English, and now—as every lyricist knows—rhymes with dove, above, of, and shove.

The spelling variant that has gained in usage so much that it has lost its kinkiness is luv. This hypocorism started about a century ago, as friendly British barmaids clipped the word's pronunciation slightly to use it as a term of endearment: "What'll yer 'ave, Luv?" (You like hypocorism? It comes from the Greek and means "the use of pet names"; when a person calls everybody "Dahling," that word is hypocoristic. Glad to help, Guv.)

Today, luv is used to show affection, care or cordiality without getting serious. If you get a note signed with the dialectal form, the sender is saying, "Look, I'm being cheerfully affectionate, but this verbal embrace is no protestation of undying love; don't get any ideas." Much luv is to real love as ta-ta is to a serious farewell. A smiling "luvya!" is usually a friendly or filial equivalent to "see you soon," although it can conceal a genuine expression of love under a sassy colloquialism.

Love, spelled the traditional way, covers both spiritual and personal commitments. The powerful word is unsullied by the trend toward using make love to mean fornication rather than courtship: In 1897, the Century Dictionary defined to make love to as "to profess affection for (one of the opposite sex); strive to win the affection of"; but in 1976, the Oxford English Dictionary Supplement said the verb phrase's meaning has changed: "Now more usually, to copulate" (from the Latin copulare, "to join, couple"). Love's spelling, however, is firm and likely to last another thousand years.

Luv may also be here to stay.

QUESTIONS ON CONTENT AND TECHNIQUE

1. How many ways has love been spelled? Give examples.
2. What else does Safire suggest about love other than its spelling?
3. In what way does the writer make the word hypocoristic clear?
4. What other common words show "verbal embrace"?

WRITING ASSIGNMENTS

Definition

1. By specific example, explain what love means to you.
2. Select a word from the *Oxford English Dictionary.* Trace its history. Some examples might be sincere, curfew, companion.

Language and the Arts

1. Safire writes of the multiple meanings of love. Describe how possible misunderstandings can occur from this situation.
2. Discuss a film, book, or TV program that shows different types of love.

Hanukkah

A staff member of the Associated Press wrote this feature.

WORDS TO KNOW

Judah Maccabee Jewish patriot

secular not sacred

It was in the year 165 B.C. that Judah Maccabee and his followers defeated three Syrian generals and recaptured and rededicated the temple at Jerusalem.

Jews around the world still celebrate the event, Hanukkah, an eight-day holiday that this year begins the night of Dec. 3.

Hanukkah, the festival of lights, is one of the few holidays that unites Israeli Jews, divided at other times along religious and secular lines.

Secular Jews observe it as a celebration of the victory by the small band of Jewish rebels over their mighty Syrian rulers as a symbol for modern-day Zionism.

Religious Jews emphasize an ancient miracle said to have occurred at the temple after it was liberated, when an eternal flame burned for eight days on oil that should have lasted one day.

Whatever their level of observance, almost all Israeli Jews at some time light the menorah, the holy lamp that recalls the story of Judah and his followers.

Jewish tradition holds that when the rebels were purifying the temple of pagan rituals performed by the Syrians, they found enough oil for only one day to relight an eternal flame. But miraculously, the flame burned eight days until more oil arrived.

While the traditional menorah is described in the Bible as having seven candlesticks, a special candelabrum with nine candlesticks—the hanukkiyah—is used only to celebrate Hanukkah.

For the eight days of Hanukkah, Jews celebrate by lighting an additional candle each night on the candelabrum. A ninth candle in the middle, known as the "shamash" or servant in Hebrew, is used to light the other eight.

In Israel, menorahs adorn public buildings and flicker in the windows of homes. At Jerusalem's Western Wall, commonly known as the Wailing Wall and the last remnant of the rebuilt temple destroyed in 70 A.D., a large oil-burning lamp is lighted each night by leading rabbis and biblical scholars.

In the United States, Hanukkah is often marked by giving lavish gifts. But Hanukkah presents are rarely exchanged in Israel. Children receive small sums of money, known as Hanukkah "gelt" in Yiddish, or the traditional four-sided spinning top called a "dreidel."

Many believe that Hanukkah gift giving became popular in the United States because of the holiday's proximity to Christmas.

QUESTIONS ON CONTENT AND TECHNIQUE

1. What was the unusual event that led to the tradition of lighting the candles?
2. The writer often supports the definition with example, comparison, process, and description. Identify these as they appear in the article.
3. What differences are there in the way Hanukkah is celebrated in the United States and Israel?
4. What are some terms associated with Hanukkah?
5. How would you write a concluding paragraph that summarizes the article?

WRITING ASSIGNMENTS

Definition

1. Choose a religious or cultural term that your readers may not know and define it.
2. Define a national or cultural holiday including its historical origins.

Philosophical Values

1. Hanukkah in the United States is often marked by giving lavish gifts. Write an essay about a meaningful gift that you have received. Describe the situation, the gift, and its significance.
2. Do you or anyone in your family belong to any historical, national, or religious society that has influenced history? Relate its history to show its role in our country's development. Some examples are: Veterans of Foreign Wars, the Masons, National Organization of Women, American Civil Liberties Union.

Pouring a Guid-Willie Waught

Thomas H. Middleton

Thomas H. Middleton wrote this essay on definition for the *Los Angeles Times*.

WORDS TO KNOW

bibulously drinking readily

claymore a two-edged sword

convivial cheerful, festive

intuit quick insight

lees and dross dregs, settling in liquor

lexicographer dictionary maker

nostalgic yearning for something past

Almost every New Year's Eve for at least 45 years, I've joined hands with my fellow boys and girls, men and women, sometimes close friends, sometimes very nearly total strangers, and sung "Auld Lang Syne."

This year, Jeannie and I spent New Year's Eve at a pub in Santa Monica called the Darwin, where Rosie McHargue and a group of his always-fine jazzmen played our kind of jazz, which means most of the songs were written between about 1910 and 1955. At midnight, the jazzmen struck up “Auld Lang Syne,” and we joined hands or arms with convivial strangers and vocalized somewhat bibulously. It was great fun. The next morning, as I was clearing my head of last year’s lees and dross, I started thinking about the strange paradox that is “Auld Lang Syne.”

Here we have a Scottish song, about 200 years old, and I’ll bet that fewer than one “Auld Lang Syne” singer in 10 knows what *auld lang syne* means. We all sort of intuit the meaning, because we’re standing around holding hands, feeling nostalgic—for what, we don’t know. Seldom for the passing of the old year, I think. The common sentiment, in my experience, is more often than not, “Thank God that year’s over and done with!”

In fact, *auld lang syne* is fairly meaningless: literally, “old long since”; figuratively, “long ago,” and, still more figuratively, “the good old times.”

The song seems to have lost some of its popularity during the past 10 or 15 years. It used to be standard for every New Year’s Eve gathering, and everyone, of whatever national origin, would suddenly become as Scottish as Robbie Burns himself. People whose backgrounds were Swedish, Armenian, Italian, Chinese, Russian—you name it—would join together, tr-r-illing away: “. . . an’ never-r-r br-r-rought to min’ . . .”

The second verse is where I’ve always started spreading on the tr-r-r-ill with a 30 pound claymore: “Sae he-e-r-r-r-re’s a han’, ma tr-r-roosty fren’ / an’ gi’e’s a hand o’ thine, / An’ we’ll tak’ a r-r-right guid williewaught for-r-r Auld Lang Syne!” One of the friends I called was Henry Gibson. I asked him if he knew what a *right guid williewaught* is. If you know anything at all about Scotch or whiskey or the Scots of Burns or wee doch-an-dorises, you surely have a solid hunch that a right guid williewaught is a good stiff slug of highland dew. Henry knew all about that, so he said he thought some smart caterer to the *wee doch-an-dorises* crowd could make a bundle with a Williewaught Cooler, or a Williewaught Lite.

It wasn’t until 1988 that I took the time to find out why we sing about a right guid williewaught. This New Year’s Day, I looked it up in my Chambers Twentieth Century Dictionary. I chose that dictionary because it’s published in Edinburgh, and I figured that if anyone should know about williewaughts, it would be the lexicographers of Edinburgh.

Here’s what Chambers says: “williewaught . . . (Scot.) n. a deep draught. From misunderstanding of Burns, *Auld Lang Syne*, . . . ‘a right guid willie (or guid-willie) waught' (where 'guid willie' means 'good will'), a generous and friendly draught."

So a guid-willie waught is a goodwill drink. It figures that Burns, who wrote "We, sleekit, cow'rin', tim'rous beastie, / O, what a panic's in thy breastie!" would change "good will" to "guid-willie," thus confusing a lot of song publishers who thought he was talking about a good williewaught, instead of a good-willie waught. Most of my dictionaries explain "williewaught" as an illegitimate child, the bastard offspring of "guid-willie" and "aught."

The best way to make a Williewaught Cooler is to pour Scotch over rocks. For a Williewaught Lite, add water. Now, what did I do with that highland dew?

QUESTIONS ON CONTENT AND TECHNIQUE

1. How does Thomas Middleton take the very common phrase "auld lang syne" and make it so uncommonly interesting to the reader?
2. Where and how does the writer suggest sound in his article?
3. How does Middleton avoid repetition of the word beverage?
4. What feeling does the last paragraph create in you? Explain briefly.

WRITING ASSIGNMENTS

Definition

1. Select a word from an immigrant group that has entered and enriched our language. Trace its origin, history, and evolution of meaning; for example, moccasin, tortilla, zero, bouquet.
2. Find a historical term to define that has an interesting origin. For instance, Cinco de Mayo, Bastille Day, Shaker, gerrymander.

Language and the Arts

1. Write about a song or poem that is associated with some significant occasion in your life.
2. "The common sentiment in my experience is more often than not, 'Thank God that year's over and done with!'" Recount an experience where you could say, "Thank God that ___________ is over and done with!"

Origami: Art of Folding

Donna Kato

Donna Kato is a writer for the *Los Angeles Daily News*.

WORDS TO KNOW

discernable recognizable

diversion amusement

whimsical subject to unpredictable behavior

Fold a thousand origami cranes, and a seriously ill loved one is said to recover.

Teach a young child to make a fish or box or rabbit out of an ordinary square of paper, and that child will develop confidence and coordination in his hands and mind.

Peer into a Shinto shrine, and you're likely to find a few origami figurines on the altar. They have been a part of the religion's rituals for centuries.

Such is the significance of origami in Japan, a folk art that transforms sheets of paper into three-dimensional objects. Translated, origami simply means "folded paper." In its purest form, there is no cutting or gluing, just creasing, bending and folding until the paper takes on a discernable shape.

A calming diversion to some, and a mathematical challenge to others, origami shapes can range from menageries of animals to toys, flowers, musical instruments, furniture and more.

It may be an art form primarily passed on from mothers to daughters in Japan, but in this country, its calculative aspects are especially fascinating to computer whizzes, engineers and scientists—such as research physicist Robert J. Lang.

A recognized expert on origami, Lang's masterpieces currently are displayed at the Hall of Administration on the California Institute of Technology campus.

Among the thousands of origami designs he has created, there have been a few favorites: There's the impossibly intricate cuckoo clock complete with a pendulum and bird; a whimsical, buck-toothed beaver, mascot of Lang's alma mater, Caltech; and the musicians—one playing a violin, one playing a string bass and one playing a grand piano.

"It's a very fun hobby," said the Altadena resident whose career work involves such things as lasers and high-speed transistors at the Jet Propulsion Laboratory. "On days when I'm a bad physicist, it's a real stress reliever."

Lang, 27, said a first-grade teacher introduced him to the craft.

"Something about creating all these shapes from a flat piece of paper held my interest then as a 6-year-old," he explained.

While some youngsters might have quit out of frustration after attempting some of the involved directions in origami books, Lang persevered, mastering most of the common shapes with scrap tablets his dad would bring home from work. Like other small boys, Lang played army with toy soldiers. However, his soldiers were origami dogs and giraffes.

"Just from folding other people's designs, I learned the techniques for making other things," he said. "If I wanted an animal that wasn't in the book, I would experiment until I could make that animal." Deer became canines, and sometimes, canines were transformed into eagles.

"It stayed a pretty low-level hobby until my college days," said Lang, who did origami during his study breaks. "It was then that I started to really develop my own designs."

His book "The Complete Book of Origami" (Dover; $6.95) recently hit the bookstores, and another book, "Origami Zoo," co-written with Stephen Weiss, will be available later this year.

His personal origami collection is minimal, he said, because the paper pieces don't pack well and tend to come apart or discolor. He is working on mastering a technique that prevents the origami from splaying and unfolding, and would like to find a method of ironing out the creases that are inevitable after multiple foldings.

"I've done this for 20 years," Lang said. "But I still find new things about it to keep me challenged."

QUESTIONS ON CONTENT AND TECHNIQUE

1. What is the purpose of origami?
2. The original article had several photos of origami figurines. How might this affect the way the reporter wrote the piece?
3. Observe how the author uses the colon in paragraph 8 and explain its effectiveness.
4. The writer uses the terms "intricate," "time-consuming," and "meticulous" in describing paper folding. What do these adjectives suggest about the art?

WRITING ASSIGNMENTS

Definition

1. Define an art form through description, example, steps used in creating it, and its value to society.
2. Origami figurines are part of the Shinto ritual. Define a term used in a custom, ritual, or ceremony that may be of interest to someone not in that cultural group.

Language and the Arts

1. Origami is an art primarily passed on from mothers to daughters. Many parents teach a craft or a hobby to their children. Select one from your own experience and explain it to a person who is unfamiliar with it.
2. Several persons interviewed in the article create origami figures to relieve stress. Develop an essay describing the cause of stress in your life and how you deal with it.

The Kiwi

Hollace Weiner

Hollace Weiner of the *Fort Worth Star-Telegram* wrote of this exotic fruit.

WORDS TO KNOW

doughboy soldier

Down Under Australia, New Zealand

blokes guys

Multiple choice:

A kiwi is

(**A**) a nocturnal, needle-nosed bird.
(**B**) a hairy berry.
(**C**) a boot polish brand.
(**D**) a doughboy from Down Under.

Answer: All of the above.

The bird came first, and it's the namesake for all the rest.

But what does a bird have in common with the fuzzy green fruit decorating so many tarts and tables nowadays?

Nothing but the name.

Name recognition was exactly what the fruit needed back in the 60s because kiwifruit was first marketed as the Chinese gooseberry.

The fruit originated in the Orient, growing on a wild vine Chinese poets dubbed "mihoutau," or "monkey peach." When New

Reprint courtesy of the *Fort Worth Star-Telegram*. [The title is ours.]

Zealanders imported the vine as an ornamental plant in 1904, they rechristened it the Chinese gooseberry.

Over the next three decades farmers cultivated the fruit from a grape-sized lump into a 4-ounce berry containing less fat than a banana and more Vitamin C than a Florida orange.

But with a name like Chinese gooseberry, who could be tempted to look beneath its hairy skin? Not the American consumer. After all, the gooseberries common to North America are wild, lip-puckering little balls best doused with sugar and baked till infinity.

What's more, who would want to chomp anything Chinese in the '50s (Remember the Red Scare?) or in the '60s before Nixon opened the doors to China?

Try to convince consumers that a Chinese gooseberry—from some island Down Under—is actually a tangy fruit with emerald flesh and a flavor akin to melons and mango.

So these hairy berries were rotting on shelves, dying on the vine, being raised more for their showy white blossoms than their tropical fruit—which has as much vitamin E as an avocado.

In the mid-'60s, one California importer was brave enough to order them. Frieda Caplan, of Frieda's Finest, liked what she tasted and pushed for an ear-catching name.

The fruit's New Zealand exporter, Turners and Growers Ltd., responded. The firm considered "monkey peach" and tossed around "melonette," because when kiwifruit is cut in half, it resembles a Japanese musk melon.

But the growers knew better than to identify with a foreign country. The fruit needed a positive, national identity of its own.

It was John Turner, chairman of the board, who hit on "kiwi." He pointed out that kiwi birds are cute and peculiar to New Zealand. Their likeness appears on tins of Kiwi boot polish, used with spit throughout the English-speaking world.

Moreover, during World War I, New Zealand soldiers were such good blokes, the allies affectionately called them "kiwis."

Rechristened kiwifruit, the produce took off.

QUESTIONS ON CONTENT AND TECHNIQUE

1. Which is more exciting: Weiner's opening or closing? Why?
2. What various names has the kiwi had?
3. How does the writer cleverly insert the characteristics of the kiwi without distracting the reader from his main idea?
4. How did public attitude play a role in the marketing of the kiwi?

WRITING ASSIGNMENTS

Definition

1. Assume you are a horticulturist like Luther Burbank or a botanist like George Washington Carver. You have just created a hybrid fruit or vegetable. Name and define your new product through its characteristics, its use, its history, its process of growth, and its comparison with another product.
2. You can often influence the feeling of your readers toward your subject through your choice of words. Define any object or place first negatively and then positively, that is, a secondhand, beat-up rocker stuck in a corner; a cherished antique rocker nestled in a corner.

Natural Environment

1. Create a commercial for a new food product that has not hit the market yet.
2. Packaging a food product often encourages the consumer to buy it. Tell of a product that you bought because of its innovative packaging or marketing.

The Tamarack

Ben Groff

Ben Groff, a free-lance writer, wrote this article for the Sunday supplement of the *Seattle Times/Seattle Post Intelligencer.*

WORDS TO KNOW

arboreal living in trees

conifer cone-bearing tree

igneous relating to volcanic activity

marmot burrowing rodent

talus slope formed by rock debris

tarn steep-banked mountain, lake, or pool

From the pass we angle downward into shadow. Heather bells shake fitfully, with a small, dry noise, in the chill wind up from Granite Creek. A long slope of talus tumbles through the gray twilight under cliffs of the Cascade Crest to the outlet of Lewis Lake, whose soap-green water shimmers in a wedge of late-afternoon sun.

We zip our jackets and push on. Stunted islands of noble and alpine fir taper up a shoulder into meadowland, then disappear. Beyond this, only one tree shares the rocky world with the grasses and ground-hugging flowers. Here, at the base of Black Peak, on the rim of a tarn cold as a slab of steel ringed with stone, it perches on the

Reprinted with permission of the author. [The title is ours.]

low bluff that keep Wing Lake from falling 3,000 feet and holds its fantastic yellow arms against a blazoned sky.

It is October. It is the tamarack.

And it is well worth a trip. Experienced hikers of the high Cascades have long planned their late-season forays with an eye to one of the true botanical glories of the region—the autumn foliage of Larix lyallii, the alpine larch, commonly known as tamarack.

Autumn foliage? You thought you left all that behind in New England? Hillsides mosaicked with oak and maple, strolls down dappled lanes of birch, fallen leaves as brilliant in the wheel ruts as fresh-minted coins, scattered with so wild and free a hand that you counted them with your feet . . . but the Northwest mountains are made of sterner stuff, are they not? Rocky clambers, tearing fogs, snouts of snow, and here and there an evergreen uprightly shouldering the first white dust of winter, white on black?

Yes, and no. The tamarack is a tree-line conifer of the North Cascades which has the delightful habit of shedding its needles for the winter—and going a fiery yellow-orange before it does so, as if it thought it were a hickory in Pennsylvania. The contrast between these pastoral associations and the stark landscape it calls home light a fire in the mind brighter than the one you'll almost think this tree stands in the middle of.

Seasons are a fluid thing in this high country, changing several times in a day, let alone a month or trio of months, as we are wont to think of them here below. It may be spring in the sun and fall in the shade, summer on the south and winter on the north side of a pass. You may climb from July to November between lunch and dinner, get bee-stung in the morning and frost-nipped the very same night. More than anything else, the seasons here are a sequence of four colors.

Snow is white, mud is brown, grass is green, and tamaracks—tamaracks are golden. By late September, the lilies are only a memory, the sedge and grasses have once again become effective camouflage for marmots, and the firs have mysteriously assumed their stiff and stoical look of winter darkness. If you go then to the places where the forest trickles out and the peaks trickle down in piles of stone, it won't be hard to pick out the tamaracks. They're the ones that shine.

They've a lot to be happy about, as the noblest species of a noble order. There are some 10 different kinds of larches inhabiting the temperate forests of the northern hemisphere—all deciduous conifers —and tamarack is a name applied to many of them without discrimination. Though it originally belonged to the eastern larch

(Larix larcina) beloved of lumbermen, it has long since stuck, despite the chagrin of botanists, to other more exotic cousins as well.

One of them is the western larch (Larix occidentalis), itself a beautiful tree, tall and tapering, quite common at moderate elevations on the slopes of Northwest mountains. But the tree of poetry, the living sculpture, the Giacometti with roots, is the alpine larch, the "tamarack" of which I sing.

It grows in a limited swatch of the North Cascades, and only above 5,000 feet. At the lower range of its habitat, as in protected sites higher up, the alpine larch is not necessarily a small tree, occasionally reaching 60 to 70 feet in height, in open, parklike groves with spreading crowns. But the typical tamarack, more lovely still, stands about as high as a human being and prefers, like many human beings, especially the mountaineering kind, to be alone.

Unlike alpine fir or whitebar pine, with whom it often shares the summit of arboreal adaptation, the tamarack is rarely deformed into krummholz—German for "crooked wood," meaning the densely matted, prostrate form that time wreaks on trees in the land of wind and snowpack. Instead, it just shrinks into a small human being, slightly corkscrewed in the trunk but still upright, at 8,000 feet a very old tree only three feet tall, an ancient child.

To be alone with him, go to tree line from mid-September to mid-October just about anywhere north of Wenatchee and east of the Cascade Crest. Take a sweater, a warm hat, and a camera loaded for color. In the Enchantment Lakes he will enchant you, between Ingalls Pass and Mount Stuart he will take your breath away, around Heather Pass of Park Creek Pass or in the Chiwaukum or Okanogan or Entiat Mountains he will welcome you home with open arms. You can even see him from your car along Route 20 near Washington Pass.

Gone is the deep forest smelling like a hope chest. The trees grow sparser; hemlock, heather, and the humming of bees. Beneath the surface of a tarn shivering in its igneous bowl, an igneous wind tumbles upside-down clouds through an upside-down sky. Climb higher among purple heather into the purest landscape, place reduced to its essentials: at the head of a small cirque, a lake held under heaven in a granite circle.

Next, as the guidebooks like to say, go above that iron-black lake, follow the line of a ridge up smooth slabs to a snowfield to a rocky step, and up the step to the summit. It will be lonely here, falling off in the manner of loneliness many thousands of feet into another basin. A sudden fog should nervously erase and reveal again the cliffs of a neighboring peak. Having arrived, you will not care to remain. You stumble back down the mountain.

Over the tarn, the blue of the sky has deepened and gentled, brimming with distant light. Through its emptiness sail great clouds of snow-white and lavender, and the almost-unnoticed, icy shard of the moon. Near at hand a cricket sings. The dry bells of the heather shake in a silent wind.

Across the water, on the rocky bank, three orange trees twist upward, spark-needled in the late light, like flames.

QUESTIONS ON CONTENT AND TECHNIQUE

1. Define the tamarack in one sentence.
2. How does the writer avoid repeating tamarack?
3. Where does Groff personalize the tamarack, giving it human qualities?
4. How many senses does Groff use in developing his description?

WRITING ASSIGNMENTS

Definition

1. Choose a season and give its meaning for you.
2. Define a term associated with ecology or the natural environment; that is, greenhouse effect, smog, cyclone.

Natural Environment

1. Relate an incident where you felt nature was abused either by greed or ignorance or both.
2. "You stumble back down the mountain." The writer describes the possible danger of natural elements. Tell of a moment when you feared nature.

Going with Hapkido's Flow

David Barry

David Barry is a staff writer for the *Los Angeles Herald-Examiner.*

WORDS TO KNOW

aesthetic relating to beauty

choreography arranging dances

martial relating to war

relentless mercilessly severe

versatile having many abilities or uses

The strike comes without warning, the kicker's right leg flashing upward, his foot snapping up far above head height. Then, in a movement too quick for the eye to follow, his heavily calloused foot springs back to the mat.

The kicker, a slender, earnest-faced man with dark brown hair, stands ready for his next move.

This is hapkido karate, a devastating but obscure Korean self-defense system with a devoted cult following in Los Angeles. Fluid in form and abstract in philosophy compared to the more orthodox tae kwon do karate demonstrated at the 1988 Olympics, hapkido is shaping up as the intellectual's martial art for the '80s.

"Yes, hapkido is a form of self-defense," says hapkido master Bong Soo Han in his Santa Monica dojang, the Korean word for teaching studio. "But it is also an art of gracefulness and harmony," continues Han, a slender, broad-shouldered man with thick silver hair. "The concept is to flow with nature, instead of against it."

Han began his martial arts study as a teen-ager in Korea in the early 1950's, when karate was just emerging from decades of being forbidden.

Developed as defense against warrior swordsmen in the feudal periods in Japan, Korea and China, karate had evolved into a highly sophisticated fighting art by the late 19th century.

During the Japanese occupation of Korea, which stretched from 1910 until 1945, Korean martial arts were banned. Martial artists, driven underground, kept the teachings alive by secretly practicing in Buddhist monasteries.

Like most martial arts masters, Han emphasizes mental and spiritual development, but focuses even more on the aesthetic of the techniques that make hapkido unique.

"Hapkido is versatile," he says. "The beautiful thing about it is the philosophy of cooperating with your opponent. It is self-defense, but also an art."

With decades of the rigid discipline of practicing and teaching hapkido behind him, the hawk-faced Han has a commanding presence. An eighth-degree black belt, he has a stern, critical manner that drives students to relentless pursuit of perfection in technique.

Even after 15 years of advanced study, senior instructor Eric Friske, a third-degree black belt, constantly looks for flaws in his form as he demonstrates a roundhouse kick for the camera.

"Master Han's going to see this photograph and find something wrong with my roundhouse technique," says Friske, 38, a building contractor, after executing a series of lightning-fast kicks.

"A kick may look perfect to you and me," says Friske, "but not to Master Han."

During a typical hourlong class, two new students wearing beginner's white belts practice the primary hapkido forms. One of them, a middle-aged entertainment attorney, has been studying at Bong Soo Han's for three weeks.

"Zen is the root of the martial arts. The martial arts are the shape of Zen." These words are Bong Soo Han's, who is given to quoting Chinese Taoist philosopher Chuang-Tzu. Serious hapkido students, which means anyone who lasts as a student for more than a year, take the Zen philosophy that is central to hapkido seriously. They believe that the spiritual heart of karate is balance, and accept the yin and yang of harmony and wholeness and its contribution to a discipline of fully formed consciousness in which violence is avoided.

But ironically, the means to mastery of harmony in hapkido is perfecting a repertoire of violent choreography in which all parts of the body become potential deadly weapons: Feet, elbows, fists, palms, and knees all become lethal weapons.

QUESTIONS ON CONTENT AND TECHNIQUE

1. According to the author, students of hapkido take Zen philosophy quite seriously. What are some Zen beliefs?
2. Give several examples of the discipline needed in hapkido.
3. How has hapkido evolved?
4. In what ways are the opening and closing paragraphs similar? How do they create satisfaction in the reader?

WRITING ASSIGNMENTS

Definition

1. From music, ballet, voice, art, dance, or martial arts, select a term not commonly known and explain it to a general audience.
2. From a lecture or discussion in philosophy, geography, religious studies, biology, or any other college course, choose a word or term that you didn't know before and define it.

Philosophical Values

1. Bong Soo Han stresses harmony and balance. Show how mind and body must harmonize to obtain maximum efficiency in one of the following areas: sports, job skills, or leisure activities.
2. Tell of any athlete whose activity on or off the field you admire.

Once Yuppies, Now "Moss"

Ron Katz

Ron Katz, a San Francisco lawyer at work on a book about the "moss" phenomenon, wrote this article for *The New York Times*.

WORDS TO KNOW

affluent wealthy

bestow give

bisque light grayish brown

ostentatious showy

parlance manner of speaking

yuppie young, upwardly mobile, materialistic professional

About a year ago, yuppies suddenly faded from view and nothing seems to have replaced them. I, however, have an idea what the next new and catchy pop signature for our times will be: "moss"—middle-aged, over-stressed, semi-affluent suburbanites.

Moss (like moose, the singular and plural are the same) will soon be common parlance. Not only did most yuppies become moss (or mossy if you prefer the adjective), but the term moss is more encompassing, because it includes nonprofessionals.

Don't reject the term moss out of hand. "Yuppie" didn't sound that good at first either, nor did most Beatles songs on first hearing.

The average moss:

- Is 41 years old; more over-stressed than overworked; affluent (but doesn't feel that way).
- Has been married twice to virtually the same person; has 2.5 children (2 biological and .5 step); hires three child care persons per year.
- Stays home at least 50 percent of all Saturday nights; takes comfort from the fact that Tom Hayden seems to have matured somewhat; has been known to disappear for hours on Saturday afternoons and return home faintly reeking of frozen yogurt.
- Takes most vacations with at least two family members to places previously visited; owns at least one publication about cholesterol; understands why not everyone gets to the top; sees the benefits that skin moisturizers bestow upon society.
- Is faithful, more as a result of the Centers for Disease Control than as a result of wedding vows; has less sex but enjoys it more; approves of new sex roles but cannot tell you what they are; is beginning to comprehend the difficulty of aging gracefully; claims to be a Democrat.
- Is beginning to understand why the world hasn't changed more over the past 25 years; hopes that the world changes somewhat less over the next 30 years.
- Appreciates the ease of parking at shopping malls.

A principal focus of moss is children, many of whom are named Jason and Jennifer. These youngsters, born when their parents were in their 30's, tend to be like yuppies without the benefit of having gone through the 60's.

They know more about condoms than any other pre-adolescent generation in history. Jason's or Jennifer's first trip abroad is likely to be to the country where their parents were Peace Corps volunteers.

The children, unwittingly crueler than the proverbial serpent's tooth, are starting to indicate that their parents are not "rad" meaning radical (their word for "cool"). This is despite the fact Mom and Dad were on the cutting edge of rock-and-roll and attended numerous teach-ins at some of the very best schools.

As yesterday's baby boomers, today's moss have been cradled from infancy in the arms of the mass market, which lovingly anticipates their every whim and need. There soon will be all-natural bisque Pepto Bismol, college tuition junk bonds and environmentally conscious second homes. Although not quite there yet, moss are beginning to think that it might not be too ostentatious to drive a Jaguar—with a subdued color.

In general, moss are less interesting than yuppies and are proud of it. The flower children are now receiving the Smith & Hawken catalogue. They are moss: no longer rolling stones, but not yet the grateful dead.

QUESTIONS ON CONTENT AND TECHNIQUE

1. What is "moss"?
2. Katz mentions "crueler than the serpent's tooth." What is the source and meaning of this quotation?
3. By what means does Katz expand his definition?
4. How do the terms moss, yuppie, and flower children affect you?

WRITING ASSIGNMENTS

Definition

1. Make up a label for a group and describe its characteristics.
2. Select a slang term with which you are familiar and define it.

Philosophical Values

1. Have you ever experienced someone stereotyping you? Describe the situation and its impact on you.
2. Choose a group to which you belong and explore your reasons for joining, its influence on you, and the activities its members share in common.

Chapter
8

Classification and Division

"What category was that?"

One of the best ways to present an all-encompassing subject is to break it down into subgroups or divisions and then describe each of them separately. This technique, classification and division, is also used in politics, government, business, and science.

For example, consider the task of an election campaign manager who has to canvass thousands of potential voters. One way to reach those voters is to study the demographics that show which population subgroups should be contacted. If the candidate is a Democrat, the campaign manager knows from the statistics that voters who usually favor that party are younger, less affluent, hold more liberal social views, and are likely to favor changes in the status quo. By classifying these characteristics, the experienced manager determines how to find these voters and then targets them with mailings to their homes, with speeches before specific groups, or with advertising in appropriate periodicals.

In a similar way, businesspeople target the most receptive groups for their products, government agencies determine which segments of the population need public assistance, and scientists investigate medical concerns such as the effect of excessive smog on older people.

In "Kinds of Fatigue," Jane Brody employs classification and division to uncover the reasons why complaints of fatigue are so common. Russell Baker applies the same approach to the humorous problem of why and how inanimate objects bewilder humankind. While being serious, Stuart Silverstein still maintains a humorous tone in his classification of bad bosses. Edmund Andrews classifies types of mousetraps, and Garry Abrams explores the background and psychological makeup of mass murderers.

By using the mode of classification and division, each of these writers is able to break down a mass of information into manageable segments for their readers. And so can you.

WHEN YOU WRITE CLASSIFICATION AND DIVISION

- Divide a general group into subgroups (kinds, types, classes) to help your readers understand better the subject matter. For example, there are several forms of literature: the novel, the short story, drama, poetry, and the essay.
- Introduce the reader to the general group early in your paper and indicate for what purpose you intend to separate the different elements for study.
- Plan an effective order of presenting the groups, using effective transitions and keeping your readers aware of the principle(s) being discussed. Your categories should cover all possibilities and not overlap.
- Select the best details and examples that illustrate each of the components and reflect differences or similarities.
- Be certain that your readers clearly understand the principle(s) discussed and their relations to the subgroup as well as to the whole.

The Plot Against People

Russell Baker

Russell Baker, author of *Growing Up* and other books of collected personal essays, wrote this article originally for *The New York Times*.

WORDS TO KNOW

baffled puzzled

inanimate not alive

invariably always

plausible reasonable

Inanimate objects are classified scientifically into three major categories—those that break down, those that get lost, and those that don't work.

The goal of all inanimate objects is to resist man and ultimately to defeat him, and the three major classifications are based on the method each object uses to achieve its purpose. As a general rule, any object capable of breaking down at the moment when it is most needed will do so. The automobile is typical of the category.

With the cunning peculiar to its breed, the automobile never breaks down while entering a filling station which has a large staff of idle mechanics. It waits until it reaches a downtown intersection in the middle of the rush hour, or until it is fully loaded with family and luggage on the Ohio Turnpike. Thus it creates maximum inconvenience, frustration, and irritability, thereby reducing its owner's lifespan.

Washing machines, garbage disposals, lawn mowers, furnaces, TV sets, tape recorders, slide projectors—all are in league with the automobile to take their turn at breaking down whenever life threatens to flow smoothly for their enemies.

Many inanimate objects, of course, find it extremely difficult to break down. Pliers, for example, and gloves and keys are almost totally incapable of breaking down. Therefore, they have had to evolve a different technique for resisting man.

They get lost. Science has still not solved the mystery of how they do it, and no man has ever caught one of them in the act. The most plausible theory is that they have developed a secret method of locomotion which they are able to conceal from human eyes.

It is not uncommon for a pair of pliers to climb all the way from the cellar to the attic in its single-minded determination to raise its owner's blood pressure. Keys have been known to burrow three feet under mattresses. Women's purses, despite their great weight, frequently travel through six or seven rooms to find hiding space under a couch.

Scientists have been struck by the fact that things that break down virtually never get lost, while things that get lost hardly ever break down. A furnace, for example, will invariably break down at the depth of the first winter cold wave, but it will never get lost. A woman's purse hardly ever breaks down; it almost invariably chooses to get lost.

Some persons believe this constitutes evidence that inanimate objects are not entirely hostile to man. After all, they point out, a furnace could infuriate a man even more thoroughly by getting lost than by breaking down, just as a glove could upset him far more by breaking down than by getting lost.

Not everyone agrees, however, that this indicates a conciliatory attitude. Many say it merely proves that furnaces, gloves and pliers are incredibly stupid.

The third class of objects—those that don't work—is the most curious of all. These include such objects as barometers, car clocks, cigarette lighters, flashlights and toy train locomotives. It is inaccurate, of course, to say that they never work. They work once, usually for the first few hours after being brought home, and then quit. Thereafter, they never work again.

In fact, it is widely assumed that they are built for the purpose of not working. Some people have reached advanced ages without ever seeing some of these objects—barometers, for example—in working order.

Science is utterly baffled by the entire category. There are many theories about it. The most interesting holds that the things that don't work have attained the highest state possible for an inanimate object, the state to which things that break down and things that get lost can still only aspire.

They have truly defeated man by conditioning him never to expect anything of them. When his cigarette lighter won't light or his flashlight fails to illuminate, it does not raise his blood pressure. Objects that don't work have given man the only peace he receives from inanimate society.

QUESTIONS ON CONTENT AND TECHNIQUE

1. Summarize the categories of inanimate objects that Russell Baker uses.
2. How does Baker use words to imply personal malice of the object against its owner?
3. Why do you think the author wrote this article?
4. How does he prove his thesis? See the glossary if necessary.

WRITING ASSIGNMENTS

Classification

1. Select an object that has plotted against you and show three ways that you would retaliate against it.
2. Classify three different methods of completing a household task.

Science and Technology

1. Computers and robots are the Darth Vaders of the twenty-first century. Agree or disagree, stating your reasons.
2. Can you think of any plot against people—any technological development that limits human values? Explain its causes, its effects, and a means of combating it.

Kinds of Mass Killers

Garry Abrams

Garry Abrams is a staff writer for the *Los Angeles Times.*

WORDS TO KNOW

annihilate destroy

enigma puzzle

narcissistic self-loving

paranoia a tendency toward excessive suspiciousness

He led a life of frustration and failure.

He apparently felt threatened by a breakup of his family, a "precipitating event" similar to unemployment or divorce.

He was a loner—living in a state of "social isolation."

He was familiar with and had access to firearms.

* * *

R. Gene Simmons, Sr., the 47-year-old former Air Force sergeant who allegedly killed 14 family members and two others in Arkansas over the holidays and then said, "I've gotten everybody who wanted to hurt me," would appear to fit the profile, which matches other rampage murderers.

Simmons apparently had moved around a lot and is older than

 [The title is ours.]

the typical single-victim murderer, who generally is a male in his late teens or early 20s.

A majority of mass murderers have been white, mobile males in their late 20s to 40s, according to Jack Levin, one of the sociologists at Northeastern and co-author with colleague James Fox of a 1985 book, "Mass Murder: America's Growing Menace."

"It takes a long-standing, cumulative set of frustrations (to make a mass killer)," Levin said.

Levin, Fox and others who study the phenomenon—and have, in one instance, even categorized the types of mass killers—have had ample opportunity in the past few months, especially as 1987 waned. . . .

Levin estimated that currently there are 30 to 40 cases a year of mass murder in this country, or an average of about three per month.

Park Elliott Dietz, an associate professor of law at the University of Virginia and a forensic psychiatrist and criminologist who works with the FBI on unusual crimes, is skeptical that mass murders are on the rise.

"There's no evidence of an increase," Dietz said. But the frequency with which he gets calls on new instances of mass killing is "hard to ignore anymore," he said.

Dietz himself has developed a list of three types of mass killers.

The most common kind of mass murderers are "the family annihilators" who "often are not newsworthy" beyond their local area, Dietz said. These killers often kill pets as well as their family and themselves.

Family annihilators "almost uniformly have some sort of mental illness—depression and paranoia—which leads them to believe this (murder) is a solution to a dilemma," Dietz said. He added, "They always have trouble seeing the options."

Family killers, especially those who do not commit suicide, may be narcissistic, Dietz said. Such killers may choose death for their loved ones because they believe "it would hurt the family too much if I died," he explained.

Dietz has tagged the second most frequent kind of mass killer "the pseudo-commando." These killers—such as out-of-work security guard James Oliver Huberty, 41, who killed 20 people at a McDonald's restaurant in San Ysidro, Calif., in July 1984—usually own "multiple firearms and have a fascination with arms," he said. Huberty was killed by a police sharpshooter.

When pseudo-commandos go on their killing sprees they are wearing "some element of military clothing" and they probably have "fantasized about the glory of mass murder," Dietz said.

These killers generally are discontent with society at large rather than specific individuals, Dietz and others said.

"If they're not angry at any particular person, they go after people in general," said Northeastern's Fox.

His colleague Levin added, "I think that the more random the massacre, the more likely the killer is to be psychiatrically insane."

Sometimes the distinction between targets appears to be hazy, said Dr. Alfred Coodley, professor emeritus of psychiatry at USC. In the case of last month's Pacific Southwest Airlines crash, David Burke, 35, a fired airline employee who apparently caused the crash, probably shot his boss and then caused the death of himself and 41 others because everyone on the airliner was "joined together in his mind as the major heavies in the piece," Coodley said.

Dietz's third—and rarest—category of mass murderers are "set and run killers" who use some lethal method—arson, bombing, product tampering—that allows them to escape. Unlike the previous two groups, these killers—such as the Tylenol poisoner who killed seven in Chicago in 1982—may have no serious mental disorder and are motivated by revenge and anger, Dietz said. In another such case, 45 people, including 38 elementary school students were killed in a series of dynamite explosions at the Bath, Mich. Consolidated School. However, the bomber, school board member Andrew Kehoe, then blew himself up, along with the school superintendent.

While the mental processes of mass killers largely remain an enigma and while their actions probably never will be predictable, several experts said that today's availability of military-style weapons and firearms in general may be important in some massacres. . . .

QUESTIONS ON CONTENT AND TECHNIQUE

1. What is the effect of the four opening sentences on the reader?
2. Name the types of mass killers.
3. How do Abrams's sources enhance his article?
4. Where do these mass killers appear?

WRITING ASSIGNMENTS

Classification and Division

1. Classify some groups that are special targets for violence.
2. Classify some industrial hazards in your community.

Social and Political Issues

1. React to the statement, "The time has come for gun control." Develop your position logically.
2. How many times have you heard "There ought to be a law"? Select a social or political problem and explain in what way a law would be beneficial or not.

Kinds of Fatigue

Jane Brody

Jane Brody, a health expert, wrote this article for *The New York Times.*

WORDS TO KNOW

induced caused

metabolic relating to processes in maintaining life

pathological related to disease

tedium boredom

Fatigue is one of the most common complaints brought to doctors, friends, and relatives. You'd think in this era of labor-saving devices and convenient transportation that few people would have reason to be so tired. But probably more people complain of fatigue today than in the days when hay was baled by hand and laundry scrubbed on a washboard. Witness these typical complaints:

"It doesn't seem to matter how long I sleep—I'm more tired when I wake up than when I went to bed."

"Some of my friends come home from work and jog for several miles or swim laps. I don't know how they do it. I'm completely exhausted at the end of a day at the office."

"I thought I was weary because of the holidays, but now that they're over, I'm even worse. I can barely get through this week, and on the weekend I don't even have the strength to get dressed. I wonder if I'm anemic or something."

"I don't know what's wrong with me lately, but I've been so collapsed that I haven't made a proper meal for the family in weeks. We've been living on TV dinners and packaged mixes. I was finally forced to do laundry because the kids ran out of underwear."

The causes of modern-day fatigue are diverse and only rarely related to excessive physical exertion. The relatively few people who do heavy labor all day long almost never complain about being tired, perhaps because they expect to be. Today, physicians report, tiredness is more likely a consequence of underexertion than of wearing yourself down with overactivity. In fact, increased physical activity is often prescribed as a cure for sagging energy.

There are three main categories of fatigue. These are physical fatigue, pathological fatigue, and psychological fatigue.

Physical This is the well-known result of overworking your muscles to the point where metabolic waste products—carbon dioxide and lactic acid—accumulate in your blood and sap your strength. Your muscles can't continue to work efficiently in a bath of these chemicals. Physical fatigue is usually a pleasant tiredness, such as that which you might experience after playing a hard set of tennis, chopping wood, or climbing a mountain. The cure is simple and fast. You rest, giving your body a chance to get rid of accumulated wastes and restore muscle fuel.

Pathological Here fatigue is a warning sign or consequence of some underlying physical disorder, perhaps the common cold or flu or something more serious like diabetes or cancer. Usually other symptoms besides fatigue are present that suggest the true cause.

Even after an illness has passed, you're likely to feel dragged out for a week or more. Take your fatigue as a signal to go slow while your body has a chance to recover fully even if all you had was a cold. Pushing yourself to resume full activity too soon could precipitate a relapse and almost certainly will prolong your period of fatigue.

Even though illness is not a frequent cause of prolonged fatigue, it's very important that it not be overlooked. Therefore, anyone who feels drained of energy for weeks on end should have a thorough physical checkup. But even if nothing shows up as a result of the various medical tests, that doesn't mean there's nothing wrong with you.

Unfortunately too often a medical work-up ends with a battery of negative test results, the patient is dismissed, and the true cause of serious fatigue goes undetected. As Dr. John Bulette, a psychiatrist at the Medical College of Pennsylvania Hospital in Philadelphia, tells it, this is what happened to a Pennsylvania woman who had lost nearly fifty pounds and was "almost dead—so tired she could hardly lift her head up." The doctors who first examined the woman were sure she had cancer. But no matter how hard they looked, they could find no sign of malignancy or of any other disease that could account for her wasting away. Finally, she was brought to the college hospital, where doctors noted that she was severely depressed.

They questioned her about her life and discovered that her troubles had begun two years earlier, after her husband died. Once treated for depression, the woman quickly perked up, gained ten pounds in just a few weeks, then returned home to continue her recovery with the aid of psychotherapy.

Psychological Emotional problems and conflicts, especially depression and anxiety, are by far the most common causes of prolonged fatigue. Fatigue may represent a defense mechanism that prevents you having to face the true cause of your depression, such as the fact that you hate your job. It is also your body's safety valve for expressing repressed emotional conflicts, such as feeling trapped in an ungratifying role or an unhappy marriage. When such feelings are not expressed openly, they often come out as physical symptoms, with fatigue as one of the most common manifestations. "Many people who are extremely fatigued don't even know they're depressed," Dr. Bulette says. "They're so busy distracting themselves or just worrying about being tired that they don't recognize their depression."

One of these situations is so common it's been given a name—tired housewife syndrome. The victims are commonly young mothers who day in and day out face the predictable tedium of caring for a home and small children, fixing meals, dealing with repairmen, and generally having no one interesting to talk to and nothing enjoyable to look forward to at the end of their boring and unrewarding day. The tired housewife may be inwardly resentful, envious of her husband's job, and guilty about her feelings. But rather than face them head-on, she becomes extremely fatigued.

Today, with nearly half the mothers of young children working outside the home, the tired housewife syndrome has taken on a new twist, that of conflicting roles and responsibilities and guilt over leaving the children, often with an overlay of genuine physical exhaustion from trying to be all things to all people.

Emotionally induced fatigue may be compounded by sleep disturbance that results from the underlying psychological conflict. A person may develop insomnia or may sleep the requisite number of hours but fitfully, tossing and turning all night, having disturbing dreams, and awakening, as one woman put it, feeling as if she "had been run over by a truck."

Understanding the underlying emotional problem is the crucial first step toward curing psychological fatigue and by itself often results in considerable lessening of the tiredness. Professional psychological help or career or marriage counseling may be needed.

QUESTIONS ON CONTENT AND TECHNIQUE

1. What are the three kinds of common fatigue? Give an example of each.
2. How does Jane Brody convince her reader that fatigue can be overcome by exercise?
3. What technique does Brody use to define "the housewife syndrome"?
4. Why do you think the author uses dialogue?

WRITING ASSIGNMENTS

Classification and Division

1. Classify three types of complaints common among your peers.
2. In an essay, use three different techniques to tell how you deal with one of the following: the common cold, backaches, headaches.

Science and Technology

1. Narrate an incident where your fatigue brought unforeseen consequences.
2. Describe what bores you and give a means of escape.

Dealing with Bad Bosses

Stuart Silverstein

Stuart Silverstein is a staff member of the *Los Angeles Times.*

WORDS TO KNOW

demeaning degrading

vindictive revengeful

If your boss ignores, bullies or otherwise abuses you, it's good to:

(a) Mutter under your breath, exchange gripes with co-workers and, in general, develop an attitude.
(b) Take the problems in stride at work and then go home and scream at your family.
(c) Tell the boss' wife what really happened at the last office party.
(d) Find a tactful way to suggest to your boss how your working relationship could be improved.

Congratulations if you picked (d). Although it's a simple idea, management consultants say most people with difficult bosses neglect to take a straightforward, constructive approach to improve matters. "Doing nothing is by far the most common employee strategy," says Mardy Grothe, a Boston psychologist.

Doing nothing, that is, besides suffering, bellyaching and perhaps trying to make the boss look bad. "They hold symposiums at the Pizza Hut about what a lousy guy their boss is," says Patricia

King, a New York management training consultant and author of "Never Work for a Jerk."

Fortunately, experts say there usually are much more effective techniques for dealing with a bad boss. In fact, a growing legion of consultants are lecturing and writing about the topic, often at the request of companies that want their personnel to work together more efficiently.

Employees first ought to size up how bad their situation is. At their worst, bad bosses can degrade you, violate your civil rights and encourage illegal or unethical activities. Said Christopher J. Hegarty, an executive training consultant and author of "How to Manage Your Boss," "Unemployment is a more intelligent risk than working under someone who is truly demeaning."

Here are some types of bad bosses frequently cited by consultants, along with suggestions on what to do:

Nice-Guy Bosses When disputes among employees arise, nice-guy bosses are reluctant to act and afraid to criticize. "The thought of sitting down with an employee and discussing a touchy subject makes them nervous," says Grothe, co-author of "Problem Bosses: Who They Are and How to Deal with Them."

Nice-guy bosses, considered by Grothe to be the most common type of bad boss, let down subordinates who count on their supervisors to crack down on lazy or incompetent colleagues. And they frustrate workers who want honest appraisals and constructive criticism.

When trying to draw a comment from a nice-guy boss, listen carefully and probe for more details, Grothe says. If that fails, he recommends the "sting and listen approach." If the boss doesn't offer any criticism, Grothe suggests you say: "I'm surprised, because I can think of a bunch of ways you could improve as a boss."

Judith Segal, a Westwood management consultant, suggests a more delicate approach. She explains that these bosses (she calls them "feelers") are very concerned with interpersonal relations. Consequently, she says, appeal to their concern for other people's feelings by indicating that Joe's 90-minute coffee breaks are a source of frustration to you and perhaps some of your co-workers.

Overreactors The perfect example is Mr. Dithers, who barks at Dagwood in the "Blondie" cartoon. Overreactors, known for their volcanic tempers, often are people who simply can't handle their anxieties.

They also frequently are the owners of small, privately held businesses. "Once you become the top person," Grothe explains, "there's a little bit of a feeling that you can do anything you want."

Sometimes, Grothe says, overreactors aren't aware of how their outbursts demoralize employees. If they appear to be basically reasonable, fair-minded people (despite their constant screaming), they might benefit from being told that their behavior is hurtful.

But, Grothe says, if an overreactor has a vindictive streak, an employee's smartest move might be to get a transfer or a new job.

Pushers These bosses are more concerned with results than anything else, and they like to act decisively and take responsibility. The trouble is, they have a tendency to trample other people and make big demands without fully explaining what they want.

Segal says when dealing with pushers—or almost any boss, for that matter—get them to spell out what they want. "It lets them know you're interested in doing what they want," Segal says.

Further, she advises, indicate how much time it will take and what the job entails. That also will help avoid misunderstandings.

Credit Takers Remember Dabney Coleman in the movie "Nine to Five"? Credit takers tend to need lots of ego stroking and hog the credit for successful projects.

To get your share of the recognition, make it a point in the early going to have your name appear on the project. Tell the boss: "It would really make me proud for people to know I'm part of your team," Segal advised.

And what if you work for a slave-driving, credit-taking, overreacting nice guy? Or if none of these scenarios apply perfectly to your situation? Don't consider it a good excuse to do nothing. "We see tons of examples of people who are miserable working for turkeys," Grothe explains. "They pay a great cost in self-respect and feelings of self-esteem."

QUESTIONS ON CONTENT AND TECHNIQUE

1. What is the most common employee strategy in dealing with a bad boss?
2. Where and why does Silverstein use slang?
3. If the labels for bosses were removed, how would you lead the reader from one category to another?
4. How does Silverstein gain your confidence that he can solve the problem?

WRITING ASSIGNMENTS

Classification and Division

1. Give and illustrate three kinds of problems that you meet at your college or workplace.
2. Explain three defense mechanisms that you have used in an unpleasant situation.

Work and Play

1. Discuss a situation where your self-respect or self-esteem was compromised.
2. Write a paper showing your technique of dealing with a wife or husband, teacher, sales clerk, or any other authority figure.

Better Mousetraps

Edmund Andrews

Edmund Andrews wrote this column for *The New York Times.*

WORDS TO KNOW

squeamish easily nauseated or disgusted

The world is still seeking a better mousetrap.

Even with thousands of mousetrap designs, ranging from spring-loaded jaws to glue snares to poisoned cheese, a new mousetrap patent appears every few weeks.

The new inventions come in roughly two types: traps that kill more effectively and traps that kill more tastefully. To be sure, mousetrap inventors say, the pathways to their doors have not been trampled with customers.

But they also think that the current state of the art bears improvement.

Here are the highlights of four mouse-catching devices recently patented:

QUICK DEATH BY ELECTROCUTION

First, consider the Electric Mouse Exterminator, invented by Claude G. Coots, a textile worker in Mentone, Ala.

Coots said he got the idea after chasing a rat without success; it escaped through a hole it had chewed in one of his walls.

The inventor stripped a 120-volt electric cord and stretched the bare wires across the hole. When the rat emerged, the wires touched its nose and neatly electrocuted it.

The inventor's new mousetrap is a small rectangular box, with an entrance at one end and bait at the other.

To reach the bait, mice have to poke their snouts between two horizontal wires. When they do, they close an electric circuit and die instantly. The device plugs into a standard wall outlet, and is configured to protect humans from accidental shocks.

Coots, who has yet to market his invention, said the device should cost less than $10.

He received patent 4,780,985.

NOT BETTER, JUST NEATER

Clifford R. Feldman, a student at Chicago Medical School, decided that the world did not need a new mousetrap as much as it needed to make the original spring-loaded trap more tidy.

"With all the jillions of mousetraps, the best one is still the simplest," Feldman said.

But, he said, such traps can produce an unpleasant sight because they typically crush the rodent's neck. Feldman added a small plastic bag, attached to an extension of the trap's bar, that envelops the animal when the device is triggered. Users can simply flip the trap over and remove the bag without looking at their quarry.

The inventor added that people who feel squeamish about killing mice can modify his device so that it only bags the animal for later removal.

Feldman said he hopes to market his invention after he completes medical school.

He received patent 4,779,374.

FEW WHO ENTER EVER RETURN

Neatness also preoccupied Richard W. Copenhaver, a former state patrolman living in Kansas, Okla., who recently patented a preset, prebaited, disposable trap.

"I thought, there's got to be a better mousetrap," said

Copenhaver, who has devoted himself full time to marketing his invention.

The trap consists of a long spring-loaded box with an opening at one end and bait at the other end.

In order for a mouse to get to the bait, it must chew through an adhesive strip blocking the way midway through the box.

When the strip breaks, springs pull the two ends of the box together and block the opening. The inventor said the plastic trap suffocates the animal within a few hours.

Copenhaver acknowledged that buyers were not yet beating a path to his door, either. "It's easy to come up with ideas, but you've really got to hustle on the marketing," he said.

Copenhaver, who said his invention should sell for $2.50, received patent 4,769,942.

TRAP LETS THEM DIE IN THEIR SLEEP

A similar trap, invented by Cornelius Chow of La Jolla, Calif., uses gravity to trap mice without actually killing them outright.

The trap consists of a curved tube, weighted so that the front end rests flat on the ground and the rear end curves up.

When a mouse enters in search of bait at the rear end, the tube rocks backward and a door slams shut. Chow received patent 4,744,170.

But some inventors think such approaches are cruel, because they often leave the mouse to die a slow death by starvation, thirst, or suffocation.

With that in mind, James Smith of Ontario, Canada, won patent approval for a mousetrap that knocks out its targets with an anesthetic, allowing them to suffocate peacefully.

Smith's invention consists of a slender tube, with bait mounted on a hook inside at the far end.

The hook is connected to a rod that holds open a door over the entrance. When the mouse plucks the cheese, the rod slips loose and the door swings shut.

When that happens, the door breaks a small vial containing the anesthetic, which puts the mouse out of its misery.

Smith received patent 4,763,439.

QUESTIONS ON CONTENT AND TECHNIQUE

1. What two types of mousetraps do the latest inventions fall under?
2. How does Edmund Andrews lift a rather grisly subject with light touches of humor?
3. At the end of each subdivision, the writer gives the patent number. What effect does it have on you?
4. What other occupations do some of the inventors hold?

WRITING ASSIGNMENTS

Classification and Division

1. Humorously write about three kinds of pests around your home.
2. Classify some psychological traps that people use.

Science and Technology

1. Write about a time that you attempted to change, improve, or repair a device that was not working for you. Describe the situation, the process you used, and the result.
2. Animals from the city pound should not be used for medical experimentation. Agree or disagree.

Four Kinds of Reading

Donald Hall

Donald Hall—a poet, editor, playwright, and teacher—wrote this classification essay for *The New York Times.*

WORDS TO KNOW

advent arrival

continuum scale

narcissism excessive love of self

narcosis state of unconsciousness or stupor

piety devotion to religion

tangible able to be touched, real

Everywhere one meets the idea that reading is an activity desirable in itself. It is understandable that publishers and librarians—and even writers—should promote this assumption, but it is strange that the idea should have general currency. People surround the idea of reading with piety, and do not take into account the purpose of reading or the value of what is being read. Teachers and parents praise the child who reads, and praise themselves, whether the text be *The Reader's Digest* or *Moby Dick.* The advent of TV has increased the false values ascribed to reading, since TV provides a vulgar alternative. But this piety is silly; and most reading is no more cultural nor intellectual nor imaginative than shooting pool or watching *What's My Line.*

It is worth asking how the act of reading became something to value in itself, as opposed for instance to the act of conversation or the act of taking a walk. Mass literacy is a recent phenomenon, and I suggest that the aura which decorates reading is a relic of the importance of reading to our great-great-grandparents. Literacy used to be a mark of social distinction, separating a small portion of humanity from the rest. The farm laborer who was ambitious for his children did not daydream that they would become schoolteachers or doctors; he daydreamed that they would learn to read, and that a world would therefore open up to them in which they did not have to labor in the fields fourteen hours a day for six days a week in order to buy salt and cotton. On the next rank of society, ample time for reading meant that the reader was free from the necessity to spend most of his waking hours making a living of any kind. This sort of attitude shades into the contemporary man's boast of his wife's cultural activities. When he says that his wife is interested in books and music and pictures, he is not only enclosing the arts in a delicate female world; he is saying that he is rich enough to provide her with the leisure to do nothing. Reading is an inactivity, and therefore a badge of social class. Of course, these reasons for the piety attached to reading are never acknowledged. They show themselves in the shape of our attitudes toward books; reading gives off an air of gentility.

It seems to me possible to name four kinds of reading, each with a characteristic manner and purpose. The first is reading for information—reading to learn about a trade, or politics, or how to accomplish something. We read a newspaper this way, or most textbooks, or directions on how to assemble a bicycle. With most of this sort of material, the reader can learn to scan the page quickly, coming up with what he needs and ignoring what is irrelevant to him, like the rhythm of the sentence, or the play of metaphor. Courses in speed reading can help us read for this purpose, training the eye to jump quickly across the page. If we read *The New York Times* with the attention we should give a novel or a poem, we will have time for nothing else, and our mind will be cluttered with cliches and dead metaphors. Quick eye-reading is a necessity to anyone who wants to keep up with what's happening, or learn much of what has happened in the past. The amount of reflection, which interrupts and slows down the reading, depends on the material.

But it is not the same activity as reading literature. There ought to be another word. If we read a work of literature properly, we read slowly, and we hear all the words. If our lips do not actually move, it's only laziness. The muscles in our throats move, and come together when we see the word "squeeze." We hear the sounds so accurately that if a syllable is missing in a line of poetry we hear the lack, though we may not know what we are lacking. In prose we accept the rhythms, and hear the adjacent sounds. We also register a track of feeling through the metaphors and associations of words. Careless writing prevents this sort of attention, and becomes offensive. But the great writers reward this attention. Only by the full exercise of our powers to receive language can we absorb their intelligence and their imagination. This kind of reading goes through the ear—though the eye takes in the print, and decodes it into sound—to the throat and the understanding, and it can never be quick. It is slow and sensual, a deep pleasure that begins with touch and ends with the sort of comprehension that we associate with dreams.

Too many intellectuals read in order to reduce images to abstractions. With a philosopher one reads slowly, as if it were literature, but much time must be spent with the eyes turned away from the pages, reflecting on the text. To read literature this way is to turn it into something it is not—to concepts clothed in character, or philosophy sugar-coated. I think that most literary intellectuals read this way, including the brighter professors of English, with the result that they miss literature completely, and concern themselves with a minor discipline called the history of ideas. I remember a course in Chaucer at my university in which the final exam largely required the identification of a hundred or more fragments of Chaucer, none as long as a line. If you liked poetry, and read Chaucer through a couple of times slowly, you found yourself knowing them all. If you were a literary intellectual, well-informed about the great chain of being, chances are you had a difficult time. To read literature is to be intimately involved with the words on the page, and never to think of them as the embodiments of ideas which can be expressed in other terms. On the other hand, intellectual writing—closer to mathematics on a continuum that has at its opposite pole lyric poetry—requires intellectual reading, which is slow because it is reflective and because the reader must pause to evaluate concepts.

But most of the reading which is praised for itself is neither literary nor intellectual. It is narcotic. Novels, stories and biographies—historical sagas, monthly regurgitations of book clubs, four and five-thousand word daydreams of magazines—these are the opium of the suburbs. The drug is not harmful except to the addict himself, and is no more injurious to him than Johnny Carson or a bridge club, but it is nothing to be proud of. This reading is the automated daydream, the mild trip of the housewife and the tired businessman, interested not in experience and feeling but in turning off the possibilities of experience and feeling. Great literature, if we read it well, opens us up to the world, and makes us more sensitive to it, as if we acquired eyes that could see through things and ears that could hear smaller sounds. But by narcotic reading, one can reduce great literature to the level of *The Valley of the Dolls.* One can read *Anna Karenina* passively and inattentively, and float down the river of lethargy as if one were reading a confession magazine: "I Spurned My Husband for a Count."

I think that everyone reads for narcosis occasionally, and perhaps most consistently in late adolescence, when great readers are born. I remember reading to shut the world out, away at a school where I did not want to be; I invented a word to name my disease: "bibliolepsy," on the analogy of narcolepsy. But after a while the books became a window on the world, and not a screen against it. This change doesn't always happen. I think that late adolescent narcotic reading accounts for some of the badness of English departments. As a college student, the boy loves reading and majors in English because he would be reading anyway. Deciding on a career, he takes up English teaching for the same reason. Then in graduate school he is trained to be a scholar, which is painful and irrelevant, and finds he must write papers and publish them to be a professor—and at about this time he no longer requires reading for narcosis, and he is left with nothing but a Ph.D. and the prospect of fifty years of teaching literature; and he does not even like literature.

Narcotic reading survives the impact of television, because this type of reading has even less reality than melodrama; that is, the reader is in control: once the characters reach into the reader's feelings, he is able to stop reading, or glance away, or superimpose his own daydreams. The trouble with television is that it writes its own script. Literature is often valued precisely because of its distance from the tangible. Some readers prefer looking into the text of a play to seeing it performed. Reading a play, it is possible to stage it oneself by an imaginative act; but it is also possible to remove it from real people. Here is Virginia Woolf, who was lavish in her praise of the act of reading; talking about reading a play rather than seeing it: "Certainly there is a good deal to be said for reading *Twelfth Night* in the book if the book can be read in a garden, with no sound but the thud of an apple falling to the earth, or of the wind ruffling the branches of the trees." She sets her own stage; the play is called *Virginia Woolf Reads Twelfth Night in a Garden.* Piety moves into narcissism, and the high metaphors of Shakespeare's lines dwindle into the flowers of an English garden; actors in ruffles wither, while the wind ruffles branches.

QUESTIONS ON CONTENT AND TECHNIQUE

1. Can you think of any kind of reading that Hall omitted? If so, label and illustrate it.
2. What is Hall's attitude toward each of the four types of reading?
3. In the context of the article, what does the coined word "bibliolepsy" mean?
4. What metaphors and similes does Hall use? Are they effective for this piece? Explain. Use your glossary if necessary.

WRITING ASSIGNMENTS

Classification and Division

1. Select one type of fiction (mystery, western, comedy, adventure) and write a paper on classification of types that fall within that division.
2. Write a classification essay on three or four kinds of TV viewing.

Education

1. Do you agree with the author's feelings on "narcotic" reading? Defend or attack with several examples of your own.
2. If your livelihood did not depend on certain courses in college but only on the completion of a certain number of units, how would this fact affect your life and choices?

Chapter
9

Cause And Effect

DENNIS THE MENACE

"MY KITE WOULDN'T FLY. I THINK THE SKY HAD THE WIND KNOCKED OUT OF IT."

From our earliest years we are conditioned to cause and effect: "It's raining so you can't go out to play." "Your calling the right signals on that last play gave us the winning touchdown."

People are fascinated by cause and effect because they constantly seek causes or explanations for whatever they observe. "The ceiling downstairs is leaking because the drain in the bathtub is clogged." "I caught the flu because I didn't take my Vitamin C."

Although the relationship appears simple, cause and effect can often become a trap when it is based on fallacy. For example, in Mark Twain's *A Connecticut Yankee in King Arthur's Court,* the time-traveler Hank Morgan knows when a solar eclipse will take place and uses this knowledge to convince the credulous folk of the sixth century that he caused the sun to go dark. Two things happening concurrently does not always mean one caused the other. Did the stock market crash of 1929 cause the Great Depression or was it merely a symptom of economic distress?

In David Streitfeld's article on names, he proposes that bizarre first names are blamed for a tendency to criminal behavior. Possibly that's true, or could it be that the parents who give their children odd names also provide an environment that is conducive to crime? An in-depth study of each family involved would be needed before deciding which premise is correct.

Gwen Yount Carden's story about executive women claims that tallness is a trait of women who succeed, but one of the successful women cited is only five-feet-two-inches tall. Explains the writer, rather lamely, the woman "thinks of herself as tall."

Since cause and effect can be ambiguous, it is necessary to use this method correctly. If you watch out for false analogies in what you read, you will avoid making them when you write.

WHEN YOU WRITE CAUSE AND EFFECT

- Choose a sequence of events that you wish your readers to examine carefully because a meaningful relationship exists that they may not have noticed.
- Realize that there may be single or multiple causes and single or multiple effects, and that your responsibility is to examine apparent as well as less apparent factors.
- Select specific examples, facts, statistics, comparisons, and details to illustrate this relationship.
- Gain the confidence of your readers by your unbiased and careful reporting of opinions, inferences, assumptions, and facts.
- Remember the possibility of new data changing the interpretation of your cause and effect relationship.

What's In a Name? Danger!

David Streitfeld

David Streitfeld of *The Washington Post* suggests in this article that one's given name can affect one's life.

WORDS TO KNOW

consensus collective opinion

coronaries heart attacks

fraught filled

neurosis nervous disorder

Would you name your son Barrett rather than Michael? Would you name your daughter Norma or Jennifer? If you had a choice between two job applicants of equal merit, whom would you call in first: Elroy or Douglas? Would you go on a blind date with a woman named Gertrude or a man named Elmer?

Fairly or unfairly, images have always attached themselves to names. Certain ones call forth stereotypes at their mention. Naming a child is an activity fraught with pitfalls. That's why many parents—who often place too much emphasis on pleasing relatives, honoring their favorite TV show or making a harmonious combination with the family name—might want to put some extra effort into it.

Consider the "Dynasty" boom, which has caused otherwise normal folk to select Alexis, Krystle (or Krystal or Crystal) and even Fallon for their offspring. In 20 years, they might be regretting it. "Trendy names eventually work against you because they let people know when you were born," says Christopher Andersen, author of "The Baby Boomer's Name Game." "Most Tammys were born in the late '50s, when Debbie Reynolds' "Tammy and the Bachelor" was a hit. To be pegged so perfectly is something you want to avoid."

Andersen cites a recent study by Edwin Lawson, a researcher at New York State University at Fredonia who asked 225 men and 225 women to rank 453 male names on six dimensions: Good-Bad, Strong-Weak, Active-Passive, Sincere-Insincere, Intelligent-Dumb and Calm-Emotional. The results tend to confirm any suspicions you might have about the relative value of names.

Gary received the best rating from men, with an overall score of 85.7. He was closely followed by John, Daniel, David, Kurt and Erik. Women gave the highest score to Moses, at 91.9. He was followed by Gregory, Mike, Jon, Brad and Luke. The sexes didn't agree on the best names. Only four in the top 20 were chosen by both men and women: John, David, Mike and Steve.

When it came to the lowest overall scores, there was more consensus. Oswald was the most unpopular name with both sexes, with an approval rating of only 29.8 for men and 26.7 for women. Other names that got poor marks from both men and women were Angus, Boris, Delbert, Elmer, Melvin, Horace and Myron.

"Parents," Andersen said, "need to pay attention to what a name is going to do. Psychologists will say that if parents give their child a name that's going to make him an object of ridicule by his peers, then obviously those parents are either terribly ignorant of the damage that name can do, or on some subconscious level they want to make their child's life miserable. If you name your kid Lethal, it says something about your intentions."

"Lethal" comes up because of another study, a five-year examination of 10,000 delinquents at Cook County Psychiatric Institute in Illinois. Criminals misdeeds among those with such bizarre names as Lethal, Oder and Vere were four times more frequent.

Said one of the researchers, Robert C. Nicolary: "When a child is given a name that is an object of ridicule (such as Precious) or connotes snobbery (such as Throckmorton) or provokes embarrassment (Looney) or confusion as to sex (Marion), he is placed on the defensive and may have to fight for it."

This works in milder ways, too. The best names, Andersen said, are not too trendy (86 babies were given the name Tiffany in Washington in 1985), not too popular (national and local leaders were

Jennifer and Michael), and not too androgynous (such as Ivory and Jade, which were given to both girls and boys in '85).

He also suggests avoiding nicknames. "I tell parents not to let their kids be given nicknames they don't approve of. If they want their child to be known as Michael and not Mikey, make sure that's what he's called. Childhood nicknames often last into adulthood, and sometimes they have a profound impact on what someone thinks of you before meeting you. Lenny conveys a different impression from Leonard."

By the way, even if your first name is irrelevant to your chances for happiness, there's evidence that your last name can cause serious problems. According to Dr. Trevor Weston, a London doctor and hospital consultant who checked into a decade's worth of British mortality statistics, people whose last names begin with the letters S through Z died a dozen years earlier than the national average.

Furthermore, Weston's survey at a London hospital reportedly determined that end-of-the-alphabeters were twice as likely to get ulcers and three times as likely to have coronaries.

The schools are blamed for this unhappy state of affairs, which is labeled Alphabetical Neurosis. "The strain of all this waiting for our names to be reached—or always being last—renders us much more liable to become morose and introspective," Weston said.

QUESTIONS ON CONTENT AND TECHNIQUE

1. What is the main idea? Is it stated or implied?
2. Can you relate to the alphabetical neurosis mentioned in the last paragraph? Explain.
3. This article discusses stereotypical names. Give several other societal stereotypes.
4. What technique does Streitfeld use in the introduction to catch your attention?
5. What concrete forms of evidence does the article include? Is it convincing? Why or why not?

WRITING ASSIGNMENTS

Cause and Effect

1. Show how your name has affected you either positively or negatively.
2. Recall a comment that affected you. Write a cause and effect essay showing its impact.

Social and Political Issues

1. Describe several persons whom you have known who did not match their names. Explain why.
2. Select any name in the article and create a character sketch of the individual.

When Life Intrudes

Jerry Rockwood

Jerry Rockwood, who teaches theater at Montclair State College in New Jersey, reflects on the ideal versus the real in advising his son on aggression.

WORDS TO KNOW

audible capable of being heard

confrontation act of facing or opposing

accomplished competent

I never spoke back. I was quiet and obedient. And so I grew up without aggression, at least the kind of aggression that can be seen on the surface.

It has cost me dearly. I think one reason I became an actor was to be able to vent my squelched aggression and hostility through the characters I played on the stage. But one needs loads of personal aggression to make it in the theater, and, as a result, I never had the success I wanted. Eventually, I turned to teaching acting in college.

Now I have been watching my son, Matthew, a year out of college, display a similar lack of aggression. He reminds me of myself—the way I used to find myself shrinking back or turning away from unpleasantness. Matthew uses "I choose not to" as an excuse for avoiding things he ought to face. It troubles me. It makes me wonder about the values we impose in raising our children.

Education, to a Cherokee father, meant teaching his son to hunt with a bow and arrow, to tread noiselessly through the woods. To an Eskimo father, it meant showing his boy how to tap ice for strength and thickness, how to gauge the depth of the water. Education for these boys meant learning to deal with the environment.

Was it so with Matthew when he was a boy? I think not. His was a good school. Private. Expensive. With all the right and beautiful philosophies intended to help kids grow up to be interested and sincere and sensitive and cooperative and creative and aware—to shun violence and war and vice and double-dealings. Disputes in Matthew's school were mediated by sympathetic and understanding teachers. Feelings were aired, points of view pointed out, alternatives proposed. The right stuff.

But I cannot forget an episode that occurred when Matthew was 9 years old. A boy named Kevin, the leader of a small gang of bullies, had it in for him. I remember saying something like, "Look, Matt, if Kevin calls you filthy names and teases you, then he's not a very nice kid, and the best thing to do is to ignore him. Laugh it off and walk away."

"But he follows me. And then he starts shoving me. And today he knocked over a bike on me. I don't know what to do!"

Well, what do you do? Tell me, educators and psychologists, what should I have told my son to do? He had discovered that the world inside his fabulously equipped, psychologist-staffed and superior-teacher-laden school was not like the real world outside.

What I did do is this: when I learned that Matthew was determined to fight with Kevin, I first tried to talk him out of it. I asked him if he could beat Kevin. He said yes. I saw that he was determined, and so I agreed and even accompanied him. "My father is coming," Matthew had explained to the other boys, "just to make sure that two of you guys don't jump me at once."

We all walked along the beach looking for a secluded place. "Whatever happens, Dad," Matthew said on the way, "don't break it up." I said I wouldn't break it up.

I stood against a telephone pole, gripping with one hand the lowest of the metal spikes used for climbing it. A dozen or more kids stood nearby. Matthew was sturdier than the wiry Kevin; they were the same height. Each waited for the other to move first. Kevin sprang and, in an instant, had Matthew down and in a headlock. His fist smashed again and again into Matthew's face. There was no contest. Kevin was an accomplished street fighter; Matthew simply didn't know how to fight. At last, "Do you give up?" "Yes."

Matthew rose to his feet, his nose bleeding, his lips bloody and swollen. He tried to hold back the tears, but the anger and humiliation were too much. He made a lunge, and Kevin reached all the way back with his right fist and threw all his weight into a solid punch in the neck. There was an audible intake of breath from the spectators at the sound of the punch. Matthew was stunned and gave a strangulated cry. "Do you give up?" A nod of the head. I put my arm around my son's shoulder and took him home to bathe his wounds.

Later, I tucked him in bed and kissed him goodnight. I knew that his bruises would heal, but I wasn't sure about the humiliation. Even now, all I'm sure of is that Matthew remembers the incident as vividly as I.

I have since taught in New York City public schools, and the preparation in some of them is something else again. The kids in certain of my classes knew how to get what they wanted simply by taking it—or stealing it. They knew how to hassle a teacher so badly that the hours went by without an arithmetic or reading book's ever being opened. They knew how to discipline a teacher by slashing his tires.

I am puzzled. I reluctantly allowed my son to have his confrontation, and he did not shrink from it. But was that enough? Should I have taught Matthew to be a street fighter, as well? Should he have been trained to co-exist in this other world? The idea is monstrous to me. But so is the idea of his being beaten up by any punk who comes along. Are we wrong in presenting only half the picture? Do you train a sailor by showing him the ropes and neglect to tell him about wind direction and tides?

"Life intrudes," was one of the pet expressions of Stella Adler, a wonderful acting teacher with whom I worked for years. Life intrudes. No matter how solidly we build our dream cabin, we can't ever completely seal up all the cracks. Life will sneak in, force itself upon us. It is there no matter how often we mutter our yeses and noes and ifs and buts and maybes. It is there, and it may be unwise to pretend it is not.

I don't have an answer, just the uncertainty of how to wish the best for Matthew and all of us. If we can't train the street fighters to be gentlemen, must we train the gentlemen to be street fighters? Should we all be Boy Scouts? Be Prepared? Or is that akin to the craziness of putting a hair trigger on the gun?

QUESTIONS ON CONTENT AND TECHNIQUE

1. What is the dilemma that Rockwood faced?
2. Find examples of the author's skillful use of questions. What is the effect on the reader?
3. What is the purpose of Rockwood's narrative?
4. Does Rockwood feel that lack of aggression has limited his and his son's choices? Explain.
5. Discuss possible answers to the questions Rockwood raises in his conclusion.

WRITING ASSIGNMENTS

Cause and Effect

1. Select an unsolved dilemma that you have had or observed in a friend, child, or spouse. Follow the model of Rockwood in your personal essay, not solving but presenting the factors involved.
2. Describe a time when you walked away from a problem and its impact on you.

Philosophical Values

1. Find an incident from childhood that has remained with you because you were unable to solve it at the time. Assume that you have a child. How would you advise him to handle the situation?
2. "Matthew uses 'I choose not to' as an excuse for avoiding things he ought to face." Relate one time when you gave a false excuse. Why? What was the outcome? Would you do it again?

Kids and TV

Barbara Vobejda

Barbara Vobejda wrote this article for *The Washington Post.*

WORDS TO KNOW

correlated show a connection between

debunks exposes as false

inferences reasoned conclusions

mesmerized hypnotized

Contrary to popular belief, children do not passively stare at the screen when watching television but are as mentally active as when they read, according to an extensive review of research on the impact of TV sponsored by the Department of Education.

The study found that many other common beliefs about television, including that it has a powerful, negative effect on school achievement, are unsupported by scientific evidence. While the study does not assert that television is harmless, it draws some surprising conclusions:

—The clearest evidence indicates that television viewing, rather than displacing valuable thinking activity, most often takes the place of movies, radio, comic books and sports.

—There is no evidence that homework done in front of the TV is of poorer quality than homework done in silence, though the authors of the study warn that little research has been conducted on this question.

—While there is some evidence that TV viewing may reduce reading achievement, the impact seems to occur in the early years of elementary school and is probably temporary.

—There is no evidence that children become mesmerized by TV, and even preschool children show they make inferences about the programs they are watching. Children's conversations indicate that they speculate about how the plot may be resolved, for example, and what is motivating characters to act in certain ways.

At the same time, the study authors, Daniel R. Anderson and Patricia A. Collins, as well as other academics who reviewed the paper, said parents should not conclude that they need not monitor the amount or content of TV programs their children watch.

In fact, the researchers emphasize, children are learning actively from what they see on TV and "they may learn things parents do not want them to know," Collins said.

Anderson is a professor of psychology at the University of Massachusetts and a leading specialist in the field. Collins is a graduate student at the university.

"I can't believe how much television is blamed for in this society as far as children are concerned," Collins said. "Because television is such a popular medium and everybody's kids are being educated, people make these connections between TV and achievement scores. In fact, there's no scientific evidence to back it up."

Ron Pedone, an Education Department official, called the paper a "showcase piece" that opens the door for a new approach in research, shifting from a mind set that TV viewing is necessarily harmful to one looking at how the medium might be used constructively.

The paper, which does not contain original research, is a compilation of virtually all research done on TV's effect on cognitive development. The paper covered research in various fields, including education, psychology and medicine.

Some of that research compared thinking skills of children in towns with and without TV. In other cases, children were exposed to TV and their behavior was observed immediately after. Sometimes researchers correlated the amount of TV viewed with a child's performance on reading or other tests.

"I was really excited about this because it flies right in the face of the conventional wisdom about television," Pedone said. Much of the discussion of TV viewing and its effects has been "emotionally charged," he said. "What we may be arguing over is what we value rather than what the concrete evidence indicates."

Anderson said his review found no evidence that children's mental activity while watching TV is different from their mental activity while reading. Children are more mentally active when the material on TV is demanding or when it is assigned for them as a learning activity.

But the same is true for reading—when children are reading comic books or other entertainment material, they are less mentally active than when reading educational material.

Most of what the TV children watch is entertainment rather than educational but it does not appear to be replacing educational reading, the authors said.

"Kids weren't reading much before TV and they are not doing much now," Collins said. "It doesn't mean that more reading wouldn't be good. It's just that TV is not the culprit."

Other researchers in the field have not disputed the authors' conclusions but some feared it could be misinterpreted as evidence that TV viewing is harmless.

"To say parents should not be concerned about monitoring television would be a travesty," said Laurie Krasny Brown, a former researcher at Harvard University's graduate school of education, who reviewed the publication. "This was just one paper."

She said the most nagging questions, which have not been adequately addressed in research, are those concerned with what behavior and attitudes children pick up from television. "There is clear evidence that children are learning behavior from television even if they don't act on it at the time," she said.

She told of experimental studies in which children were shown a cartoon in which one character repeatedly punches another. After the program, children demonstrated increased aggressiveness by punching dolls or clowns, especially when the punching behavior in the cartoon had not been punished.

And Brown cautioned that, while the effects of TV on cognitive development may be small, "that doesn't mean they aren't there."

Without commenting directly on the Anderson-Collins paper, Tannis MacBeth Williams, an associate professor of psychology at the University of British Columbia, said that the relationship between TV and school achievement has been oversimplified.

In her research, Williams found that children living in a Canadian town without TV were better able to generate ideas—to think of alternative uses for an object, for example—than their counterparts in towns with TV.

Two years later, after TV was introduced to the town, the children's ability to generate ideas dropped to the same levels as those in the towns with TV.

Also, adults in the town without TV were able to solve creative thinking problems faster, and persisted longer in trying even when they failed to solve the problem, than adults in the towns with TV, she said.

Other researchers said they welcome the Anderson-Collins paper because it debunks many common myths.

"This is an extraordinary review of the literature, and I think the conclusions are correct," said Aletha Huston, a professor of human development at the University of Kansas and co-director of the Center for Research on the Influence of Television on Children.

While Huston cautioned that there is little research on some of the questions Anderson and Collins examined, she said there has been enough research to say "probably, in and of itself, television viewing does not have much effect on school achievement."

Several of the researchers cited other studies showing that up to about 10 hours of TV viewing a week correlated with improved school achievement, while more viewing correlated with lower achievement.

That does not indicate, however, that TV viewing causes the child to perform better or worse in school. The specialists agreed that other factors, including intelligence, socioeconomic status, family routines or parental attitudes about television, are just as likely to account for differences in achievement.

QUESTIONS ON CONTENT AND TECHNIQUE

1. What were several surprise findings in the article?
2. How many sources does Vobejda cite? What is the most common type that she uses?
3. In what ways does the author use comparison? How does each comparison expand the piece?
4. Upon what do the specialists agree about TV viewing?

WRITING ASSIGNMENTS

Cause and Effect

1. Select one TV program that you feel has provided a service to the public. Describe its production and explain its impact.
2. There need not be a conflict between TV viewing and reading. Write about favorable results from using both.

Education

1. Write on any conflict that television has created in your home.
2. "Television viewing does not have much effect on school achievement." Agree or disagree with this statement, giving examples and reasons for your position.

What Propelled Women to Executive Positions?

Gwen Yount Carden

Gwen Yount Carden wrote this article for the New Orleans *Times Picayune.*

WORDS TO KNOW

echelons levels of authority

nurturing taking care of

Women may travel different paths to the top echelons of the executive suite, but many of the road signs along the way are similar. That is the conclusion of British researcher Rosalind Miles, who interviewed 44 top women executives in the United States and Great Britain about their backgrounds and experiences and put them into a book called "Women and Power" (Salem House, 1985).

"Each woman received the same detailed questionnaire in which I asked them almost everything about themselves except their shoe size," says Miles. "There were tremendous similarities in terms of early experiences and the influence of family members."

To meet the criteria for Miles' survey, the women questioned had to have "made it on their own" with no financial support from any family source.

"The women I interviewed were also in a position of seniority and power and made decisions about large amounts of money," she explained.

Almost all the women said their most important influence was a grandmother who took an active role in the family.

"The grandmothers weren't necessarily kind," says Miles. "In fact, many of the women described them as 'old bats' or 'terrors,' but because they were strong, independent and powerful the women executives had seen themselves as coming from a line of strong women."

The mothers were influential not because they were nurturing, but because they shunned domesticity. It was their mothers' attitudes that had the greatest impact.

"As a rule, the mothers disliked domestic duties and taught the girls to despise them also," she says. "They encouraged their daughters not to spend their lives doing housework."

Ironically, when the daughters did well with their careers many of the mothers became jealous. Some of the women executives also reported having strained relatons with their mothers.

"These women all idolized their fathers," Miles says. "Almost all the women described their fathers in glowing terms." The fathers told their daughters they could do anything they set their minds to, and actively encouraged their daughters' pursuits and successes.

Many of the women's fathers had failed in business or had died while the girls were still dependent on them, says Miles.

"You can't learn to rely on a man as a significant breadwinner if your father has died or failed at business and left your family in financial difficulty," Miles says. This early experience with insecurity, she believes, made the girls self-reliant and determined to depend only on themselves for their well-being.

Most of the women were the eldest child in the family. Many had only one sibling, usually a younger brother.

A number of the women said they did not feel like "one of the gang" when they grew up, Miles says. Many had an experience such as a serious illness or an achievement that set them apart from others their age.

"One girl became a cheerleader for her hometown university at the age of 15," Miles pointed out.

"Not one of the women interviewed was born in the countryside," Miles says. "I think if you live in or near a city your eyes are open to the wide horizons of the world. Cities usually have better schools, libraries and a wide range of opportunities."

Most of the women have a background in dance or theater, or had been active in sports. "This prepared them," Miles contends, "to confidently appear in front of people without worrying that people were looking at them. These women liked being center stage."

More than three-fourths of the women in Miles' survey were taller than the average female; 30 percent of those were taller than the average man. "The taller the woman, the better her chances of being in a position of power because she is perceived by the power-holders as being more like them," Miles explains.

Two top-achieving women who were not part of Miles' study were interviewed to find out what their backgrounds had in common with those of the women in Miles' book.

Lois Becker, founder of the multimillion-dollar jewelry business Lois Becker Collection, Inc., in Shaker Heights, Ohio, was astounded to learn how similar her background and characteristics were. Her mother, a housewife, always spoke admiringly of career women as she plodded through life "bogged down" by family responsibilities. Becker, who was breast-fed for about one month, says her relationship with her mother was stormy.

Her relationship with her father, on the other hand, was just the opposite. "He told me that because I was young I could do anything I wanted. I believed him and admired him very much," she says, adding that he had failed several times in business during her childhood.

She admitted to feeling different from other children. "I felt alienated and didn't know why. I think a lot of it had to do with the fact that my brother was born when I was just 13 months old. I felt left out and set apart. There was a lot of rivalry between us that probably resulted in my becoming competitive."

At only 5-feet-2-inches tall Becker is shorter than the average successful woman, but thinks of herself as tall. "I know how to make my presence felt," she says.

Martha Gottfried opened a real-estate firm specializing in selling mansions in Palm Beach, Fla., about 11 years ago. Selling properties including John Lennon's oceanfront estate, her annual income is well into seven figures. She says her mother was a traditional housewife, but always encouraged her to have a career.

"She let me know she would rather have been doing something besides being a housewife," Gottfried says. "She just went through the motions of domesticity as did all women who lived in the Midwest at the time."

Gottfried does not know if she was breast-fed or not, and was unable to find out because her mother is deceased. She admitted feeling set apart from her peers as did the women in Miles' study and credits an inner drive to achieve at an early age.

"I didn't have time to do the things other kids did," she says. By the age of 7 she had started her first business, going door-to-door selling Christmas cards. She greatly admired her father, a successful salesman. "He was always very special," she says. "I think he always expected me to achieve."

Gottfried, the oldest of four children, was born in Evansville, Ind. She modeled after high school for her first employer, a drug manufacturing firm. At 5-feet-6-inches tall she was well-suited for it. She was on the volleyball and baseball teams in high school.

"I get no butterflies in my stomach walking into a room full of important and powerful men," she says. Neither of her grandmothers influenced her other than by being loving. But her paternal grandfather took her with him "to business" on weekends beginning in her early childhood and that had an impact on her, she says.

QUESTIONS ON CONTENT AND TECHNIQUE

1. Carden uses two different types of sources. What are they? Are these reliable enough to make generalizations? Attack or defend.
2. How are mothers and grandmothers characterized in the survey? Fathers and grandfathers?
3. The author gives ten influences that encouraged women to become executives. Name and explain any eight.
4. What similarity among women in power positions seems least significant?

WRITING ASSIGNMENTS

Cause and Effect

1. Explain in an essay how a parent or grandparent influenced your life.
2. Think of a person whom you know or a person in the public eye who has "reached the top." Write about the pressures on the person's family.

Work and Play

1. Discuss how you and a friend, spouse, or relative have become alienated in work or play.
2. Carden writes, "Women may travel different paths to the top echelons of the executive suite." Discuss some routes to power that men and women choose.

Golden Gate Built to Bridge Depression

McClatchy News Service supplied this article to the *Los Angeles Daily News.*

WORDS TO KNOW

malign speak evil of

moribund dying

scrounge collect by foraging

viscera internal organs

San Francisco Take it from French Gales, it wasn't the genius of its planners and the daring of its builders that were responsible for the Golden Gate Bridge. . .

"What made that damned bridge was hard times," said outspoken Alfred P. Gales, a one-time bridge worker who for most of his 87 years has been called Frenchy because of parental derivation. "Pretty near everybody voted for it because pretty near everybody was out of work. They voted for the job, that's all they voted for."

In 1933, Frenchy was living precariously in Sausalito, just north of where the bridge now ends. Like so many others at the time, his was a hand-to-mouth, odd-jobs existence, digging ditches, cutting or hauling wood, whatever came along. He still grumbles about the last work he'd been able to scrounge before he began a four-year career on the bridge as a dollar-an-hour laborer.

"I put up a gas station for Standard Oil in Sausalito," said Gales, who lives in Stinson Beach northwest of the bridge. "Hung the folding doors and worked Friday and Saturday. Two days, two 10-hour days for seven . . . dollars! That's 35 cents an hour! See how it was? That's what I'm saying, everybody was red-hot for that bridge."

Those hard times were favored times for public works, giving governments a chance to try to pump life into the moribund U. S. economy. Works Progress Administration jobs, the too-much-maligned WPA, paid 50 cents an hour when a person could get aboard. The Tennessee Valley Authority, with its hydroelectric complex, and such monumental projects as Hoover (then Boulder) Dam on the Colorado were federal pump-primers.

But the Golden Gate Bridge wasn't founded by the feds, as were the great dams of that era; nor by the state, as was the neighboring San Francisco-Oakland Bay Bridge. It didn't seem to be a project worth gambling on.

The Golden Gate itself, for instance, is a mile-wide, three-miles-long-cleft in the Coast Range. Once it had been a gorge through which the outflow of inland rivers emptied into the Pacific. But now it was a stormy channel connecting ocean and a great harbor. . .

Then there was the missing population factor. Bridges always had been built to link masses of people. But north of the Golden Gate lay Marin country (1930 population: 41,000), Sonoma County (62,000), and beyond that little else but cows and forest until you got to Portland 600 miles away.

So the bill for the Golden Gate Bridge was picked up by taxpayers from a new district carved out of six counties expressly for that purpose. In bleak 1930 they approved a $35 million bond issue that nobody was certain ever could be repaid, and they voted it in by a 3–1 margin. It remains perhaps the most courageous—and eventually successful—example of bootstrap self-help to come out of the Great Depression.

"I didn't work steady at first," said French. "I'd go out there every day and stand around and maybe I'd get a couple of hours' work. There was a bunch of guys hanging around Fort Baker waiting for somebody to get killed, fall off, or waiting for somebody to get canned. If you got caught on the job standing around on one foot, that was the end of it. And you didn't have no coffee breaks. Even if you got up and went to the can more than once, you took a chance."

When the job was finished in May 1937 and the bridge district owned the longest suspension span in the world, it even found it had $1.3 million left from the original bond issue. The construction itself—bond interest, engineering and inspection fees and administrative costs aside—came in at $27,125,000, which was $40,000 under the contractors' bids. New York's George Washington Bridge, 700 feet shorter and completed six years earlier, cost almost twice as much.

Records are made to be broken, as they say. It shouldn't be a surprise, then, that the Golden Gate Bridge, which held the ranking of the world's longest suspended span for 27 years, is now in third place. And by next year, if everything goes according to schedule in Japan, it will be a distant fourth.

Funny thing is, though, its numbers ratings are superfluous. Most people heard about the Verrazano-Narrows when it replaced the Golden Gate at the top of the charts. But the fame wasn't lasting. After all, it was only 60 feet longer, and face it, a bridge between Brooklyn and Staten Island doesn't exactly stir the viscera. As for its successor, the one in England, where's Hull?

The Golden Gate remains the world's most famous bridge, the one that still springs to mind when bridges are mentioned, the one that captures the imagination, the one that unleases imagery as well as professional admiration.

But then the bridge tends to have that effect. For something 746 feet high and weighing a million tons—a regular Godzilla of utilitarian devices—it has always had a curiously lifting effect on people's spirits.

"In its structural beauty," sculptor Beniamino Bufano wrote as one of its designers in 1935, "its engineering and architectural simplicity, and of course its color—like red terra cotta—it moves and molds itself into the general beauty and contours of the hills. It is this structural simplicity that carries to you my message of admiration."

No wonder. If you walk out on the bridge, the effect is uncanny. It shakes under your foot. The screen that discourages people from tossing junk on old Fort Winfield Scott vibrates like a harp. The great suspender "ropes" of wound steel wire three inches in diameter visibly vibrate. The whole thing pulsates. It seems alive.

QUESTIONS ON CONTENT AND TECHNIQUE

1. In what ways does Golden Gate capture the imagination?
2. What purpose does the interview with Gales have aside from the facts that emerge?
3. Why does the journalist switch from third to second person in the closing paragraphs?
4. How do the various comparisons enrich the article?

WRITING ASSIGNMENTS

Cause and Effect

1. Built during the Depression, the bridge is a symbol of "making ends meet" and necessity calling forth inventiveness. Can you write of another time when money was tight and you "made ends meet"?
2. The taxpayers gambled on the successful completion of the bridge. Relate an incident where you took a chance and it worked out well for you.

Science and Technology

1. Observe a worker or craftsman on the job and through your interview create for your reader a feeling for the object or task.
2. Choose a landmark or manufactured structure in your community and give its origin, description, and significant details to create for it a feeling of respect or admiration.

Tea—Did It Cause British Colonialism?

Russ Parsons

Russ Parsons is the food editor for the *Los Angeles Herald-Examiner.*

WORDS TO KNOW

colonialism policy of ruling colonies for profit
defray pay
de facto in reality
infusion steeping in fluid without boiling
knell stroke of a bell
poultice warm, medicated dressing
raucous noisy
spate flood
tisanes dried leaves or flowers
waffled went back and forth

". . . The last time she saw them they were trying to put the Dormouse into the teapot."

Lewis Carroll might have been exaggerating just a tad, though to look at the spate of herbal and flavored teas on the market today you wouldn't really know it. Have you ever opened up one of those teabags? Flowers, leaves, twigs, branches, dried bits of peel—it's more like the Dormouse's nest.

But really, those aren't teas. Those are tisanes or infusions, one step away from a poultice, two steps away from a soda pop. Real tea, at least the kind of real tea we'll all be sipping and slurping through the UK/LA festival is a very specific, very special thing.

Like Jaguars, tweed and National Health, tea is definitively British. As the brothers Schapira point out in "The Book of Coffee and Tea" (St. Martin's Press, $8.95), "He starts with tea as an eye opener and goes on with tea for breakfast and for the morning break. He has tea for lunch and tea at four, then tea with dinner and tea for a late-night snack. The Briton, to be happy, must have his tea."

But while most of our food cravings are of fairly minor consequence in the grand scheme of things (it is hard to imagine how the rage for sun-dried tomatoes will affect world politics), tea has a most significant history. To begin with, it provided the motive that helped power the engine that was British colonialism. First China, then Japan and finally (and most completely) India were exploited for the tea they could provide.

Oddly enough, though, it was the Dutch who gave the British their first taste of tea (and tea-politics). In 1602, the Dutch East India Co. was chartered to bring some order to a raucous East Indies trade as well as acting as the de facto government in those areas. In those days, tea was supplied primarily by China and Japan and was an item of extreme luxury.

When prices for tea (and, coincidentally, black pepper) rose too high, the British East India Co. was formed with governmental powers that even exceeded those of their Dutch counterparts. Known as the John Company, it could annex territory, raise armies, declare war and mint currency. One of the company's first actions was erecting a string of armed trading camps in India to protect their troubled, violence-plagued trade routes to the tea-bearing areas of China. They failed to realize that India itself was prime ground for tea cultivation.

British tea consumption was given a great boost when Charles II married a Portuguese princess, Catherine of Braganza, who was a devoted slurper. It also had the backing of the British government, most of them John Co. stockholders, which regarded (quite rightly, it seems) coffeehouses as hotbeds of political dissent. By the start of the 18th century, when Queen Anne made something of a fashion statement by substituting tea for ale at breakfast, it was on its way to becoming popularly acceptable.

But the winds of change were blowing ill for the John Co. Simply put, too much money was being made by too few people at a time when the idea of free trade was gaining common currency.

We colonials struck the first blow with the revolution. Remember the Stamp Act? Parliament passed it in 1765, taxing tea, among other things, to help defray the costs they incurred defending us during the French and Indian Wars. We protested. They waffled. In 1773 we threw tea into Boston Harbor. So there. The death knell sounded not long after when Richard Twining (a surname familiar to tea-lovers), organized 30,000 London tea dealers in a protest against unfair trade practices. Parliament officially ended the monopoly in 1813. To make up for the loss of income, the company began the government-sanctioned exporting of Indian-grown opium to China. Not until recently have East-West relations begun to thaw.

What the demise of the John Co. did accomplish was the opening of new areas for tea cultivation. Once the market was opened, many companies rushed to meet the tremendous demand for more tea—more than the old sources could supply. The Dutch planted in Indonesia, especially Java, and the British tried Ceylon and India. After much experimentation, these non-traditional teas began to reach the markets in commercial quantities in the 1860s, at last making the drink really affordable to the general public.

And as such, it has become the very picture of a stolid British middle class.

As Rupert Brooke wrote:

> Say, is there Beauty yet to find?
> And Certainty? and Quiet kind?
> Deep meadows yet, for to forget
> The lies, and truths, and pain?. . .
> oh! yet
> Stands the Church clock at ten to three?
> And is there honey still for tea?

QUESTIONS ON CONTENT AND TECHNIQUE

1. From what novel does the opening quotation come?
2. Russ Parsons states that tea affected world politics. What other areas did it affect? Explain.

3. What present-day consumer products do you feel have such an impact on international relatons?
4. List some of the parenthetical elements used in the article. What other ways might the information be integrated into the sentence?
5. Why does the writer end his essay with a poem?

WRITING ASSIGNMENTS

Cause and Effect

1. Think of a historical event and its effect on you, for example, the death of Martin Luther King, Jr., the Vietnam War, the disaster of *Challenger* space shuttle.
2. Write an essay tracing the cause and effect of a present-day social problem, for instance, lack of day-care centers, homelessness.

Social and Political Issues

1. Describe a popular consumer product and show the cause of its popularity and its effect on you the consumer.
2. Parsons writes, "The Briton, to be happy, must have his tea." Write on the topic: The American, to be happy, must have ______.

Mood Swings

Verna Noel Jones

Verna Noel Jones wrote this article for the *Rocky Mountain News Sunday Magazine*.

WORDS TO KNOW

correlation act of seeing connection
euphoria elation
grandiose splendid
sedate quiet and dignified
sociopathic characterized by anti-social behavior

People often do wild and crazy things, but some people have little control over the impulses driving them to do so. An artist from Westminster recently fell into deep legal trouble after wild spending sprees, during which she wrote numerous bad checks.

A usually sedate Denver librarian suddenly put all her money into an investment scheme, got involved in some sexual indiscretions and made extended trips to Hawaii—all things out of character for her.

The condition driving these people to such erratic behavior is known as bipolar affective disorder. This manic-depressive illness affects more than 3 million Americans, according to Loveland psychiatrist John Nagel. Of those, he says, perhaps 20% are unaware that a treatment exists to control the drastic mood swings they experience.

During a manic state, someone with bipolar disorder can experience grandiosity, euphoria, and hyperactivity. They may invest wildly in the stock market or drive themselves to exhaustion working nonstop on projects.

On the flip side, such people have episodes of profound depression. They may lose interest in everything that was important to them, and feel there is little hope.

Bipolar disorder seems to have an unexplained correlation with creativity and achievement. One study found that 38% of Pulitzer Prize-winning poets showed signs of the disorder. Music composers such as Mahler, Schumman and Handel were manic-depressive, as were political greats Winston Churchill, Theodore Roosevelt and Abraham Lincoln.

In addition, says Nagel, "Doctors, lawyers and bank presidents sometime have bipolar disorder, yet are able to function well; they don't necessarily do bad things as a result."

Characteristically, these people have above-average intelligence and ability, yet suffer terrible mood extremes. "In the good times, they do very well, but during depressive episodes they get awfully disorganized and troubled," he says.

The manic state often is enjoyable because the person's creativity peaks, says Nagel. He recalls one patient who composed television and radio jingles for a living. On a manic high, he could turn out 10 to 12 a day. But when his mood was controlled with lithium, he could do only two or three a day.

However, some people experience spectacular failures because their judgment goes awry, says Robert Freedman, professor of psychiatry and pharmacology at the University of Colorado Health Sciences Center.

Others become manic to the point of rage. One of Nagel's patients became extremely violent with his wife, threatening her with knives and guns. In another case, a woman had a fight with her daughter, leading to a car chase at speeds exceeding 60 mph, during which she ran a police roadblock and smashed her car into police cars.

Diagnosis of bipolar affective disorder is based on three things. First, the patient's family history is checked for others in the family who show exaggerated mood swings, suicidal tendencies or antisocial, sociopathic behavior. An example of an antisocial act might be participation in grandiose schemes.

"I had one man who bought an eight-plex (condominium) when

he really didn't have the money to do that. He later got in trouble because of it," says Nagel.

The psychiatrist says alcoholism also can be a clue to manic-depressive disorders. "Many people will try such self-medication to help with mood swings."

The next thing Nagel looks for is a history of mood swings—low and high mental states lasting weeks or months that the person recognizes in himself. Finally, Nagel considers the person's current mental status, should he be in the midst of a manic or depressive state.

The patient is then put on a clinical trial with lithium, a drug treatment that corrects imbalances in the brain, to see whether it makes the person more stable. If so, this is taken as evidence that the person has a manic-depressive disorder, says Nagel.

Lithium is the treatment of choice for most bipolar patients. However, about 10% of patients have an adverse reaction to the drug. Such people often can be helped instead with an anticonvulsant called carbamazsepine.

In addition to the drug treatment, those with bipolar disorder undergo therapy to help them learn more about their illness and how it can affect them.

"Most people have specific trigger points and stressors that throw them into mania or depression," says Nagel, "and very often they get interpersonal clues that it's about to happen. Something like losing a job can throw them into emotional overload."

When a person is headed into a manic episode, the first sign often is irritability and out-of-control rage from relatively minor stimuli. Drugs also can be a precipitant A first experience with cocaine or reactions to prescribed drugs such as steriods or asthma medications can set off manic episodes in susceptible individuals.

Manic-depressive illness often doesn't appear until a person reaches his late 20s or early 30s, although children as young as 2 have been thought to have it, says Freedman.

"And of all the mental illnesses, manic-depressive illness seems to be the most heritable," he says.

Researchers outside Colorado have been working with Amish families in search of a gene responsible for manic-depressive illness, and "a location on the human chromosome has been identified," says Freedman.

In other equally large families, different locations have been identified, leading scientists to believe there may be several genetic types of the illness.

Locally, Freedman is researching the function of norepinephrine, one of the neurotransmitters in the brain thought to be involved in manic-depressive illness.

"We're looking at how excess norepinephrine disrupts brain function," he says. "One thing we've found is that it makes people more susceptible to perceptual abnormalities, such as grandiose schemes."

QUESTIONS ON CONTENT AND TECHNIQUE

1. Identify at least four strategies (comparison, classification, etc.) in the article.
2. Who are the Amish families mentioned in the article? What would be the value of studying their behavior?
3. Identify any appositives. See the glossary if necessary.

WRITING ASSIGNMENTS

Cause and Effect

1. "Most people have specific trigger points and stressors that throw them into mania or depression." Show how a "trigger point" in your life caused elation or depression.
2. Choose a human behavior (shyness, fear of failure, anger) and write about some of its effects on you and others.

Science and Technology

1. Describe a person you know who exhibits eccentric behavior and explain what may be the cause or causes.
2. Recall a situation where an unreasonable amount of work had to be done in a short time and show how you handled the situation.

World Turns Deaf Ear to Noise

Jean Marbella

Jean Marbella of *The Baltimore Sun* reports the dangers of overloading our hearing in the modern world.

WORDS TO KNOW

audiologist hearing specialist

brunt main impact

decibels measurement of sound

obliterated completely removed

The sound and the fury are becoming louder and more furious. And our ears, not to mention our nerves, are bearing the brunt of an increasingly noisy world.

Walkmen, computer printers, supersonic jets and answering-machine beeps are just a few of the newer ways we've devised to overload our hearing.

How much noise is too much? Not only does the answer vary from person to person, it varies from environment to environment.

In the workplace, for example, the Occupational Safety and Health Administration says if the noise averages 90 decibels over an eight-hour shift, workers must wear ear protection. And new homes generally can't be built in the area near an airport where the noise level exceeds 65 decibels.

But except for a relatively few areas for which the government has set noise standards, we're on our own.

"The federal government has laws for noise in the workplace, but no regulations for non-occupational noise," said William Clark, a St. Louis, Mo., specialist in physiological acoustics who has studied noise in baseball stadiums. "We tend to ignore the amount of noise we're exposed to during leisure-time activities."

One problem with noise is that it's something of an invisible hazard.

If only ears would bleed when hearing loss were occurring, people would be more wary about exposing themselves to deafening dangers, Stephen Seipp, a Lutherville, Md., audiologist said, partially in jest.

"A person isn't aware it's happening until it's pretty far along," Seipp said. "You have to have pretty significant damage before it will show up on an audiogram."

"People have different sensitivities to noise," he added. "Someone can work eight hours a day with 90 decibels (for years) and suffer no apparent problems; someone else can work there two months and suffer permanent hearing loss."

Decibel levels are a way of measuring the intensity of noise. Ten or 20 decibels is about the lowest level most people can hear, above 80 or 90 (traffic, loud music) starts getting uncomfortable for some, and 120 (a jackhammer) or so is usually painful and damaging to the ear.

Decibels don't work on a simple, progressive scale. An increase of 20 decibels, for example, will not sound just 10% louder but about twice as loud.

We hear sounds when sound waves vibrate the air and the outer ear directs those vibrations into the ear canal. The ear drum vibrates, and the vibrations travel through the bones of the middle ear into the fluid of the snail-shaped cochlea of the inner ear. There, the tiny hairs lining the cochlea pick up the vibrations and transform them into nerve impulses. The auditory nerve transmits the impulses to the brain.

Loud noise, however, damages the cells of those delicate hairs and can cause deafness.

"They get broken off or bent or completely obliterated," Seipp said. "When this happens, the transfer (of sound) doesn't take place."

Because hearing of the highest frequencies is lost first, people don't realize they're going deaf until they start losing the middle ranges, which is where human speech falls, hearing experts say.

Clark said that 30% to 50% of the hair cells can be damaged before you notice any loss of hearing. The damage to those cells is permanent.

Besides the obvious physical problems of going deaf, "there's the emotional, psychological impact of starting to get cut off" that individuals who suffer hearing loss face, Seipp said. "They gradually withdraw."

"Noise is probably the largest cause of hearing loss in this country," he said. "Estimates are that 10 to 15 million people have suffered hearing loss because of noise. And it's the one cause that's preventable."

The solution, he says, is simple: "Either eliminate the noise, get away from the noise or wear hearing protectors."

Getting away from noise can be a problem; it's all around. A random check of noise at various locations in Baltimore found some real noise-makers.

A downtown nightclub, for example, registered in the neighborhood of 106 decibels one recent evening. A concert by singer James Taylor ranged from 80 to 104 decibels. A helicopter overhead: 72 decibels. A telephone ringing in an office: 83 decibels. The whistle of an incoming subway car: 85 decibels. A police van with sirens blaring on a downtown street: 104.

Another suggested solution—wearing ear protection, especially on the job—is often seen as a nuisance by workers, some say.

"They'll wear glasses to protect their eyes," Seipp said. "They'll wear steel-toed boots. But they won't wear ear protection."

Leroy McClelland, Sr., a commiteeman for the Steelworkers of America Local 2609, a Baltimore union with more than 2,000 members, offered another reason for the resistance.

"Some of the guys are resisting wearing ear protection because they depend on sound for doing their job," he said. "The machine talks to the guy. We don't see everything we do; we hear some of it."

From the sound some machines make, McClelland said, a worker can tell if it's operating at the right speed, or if there's a defect, or any number of other factors the worker needs to know.

McClelland says that companies should try to muffle the sound of the machinery, rather than rely on hearing protection devices.

That generally is preferable, when possible, said Gail Brinkerhoff, an industrial hygienist with OSHA's enforcement division in Washington.

"It's a more absolute solution to the problem," he said. "The easy way out is to just put a protective device on a person."

Sometimes, though, either there is no technology available to make machinery more quiet, or it's too expensive.

QUESTIONS ON CONTENT AND TECHNIQUE

1. What purpose does Jean Marbella's article serve?
2. Find several one-sentence paragraphs and indicate how you would combine, develop, or delete them.
3. Why does she insert the process of hearing sound into her cause and effect article?
4. At what level does sound usually become unpleasant? Why is it easier for one not to recognize ear damage?
5. Give several reasons that workers avoid ear protection.

WRITING ASSIGNMENTS

Cause and Effect

1. Write an essay focusing on pleasant and distressing sounds and their effects on you.
2. Marbella mentions that with deafness people "gradually withdraw." Select an example of another situation where people might withdraw and show the cause and effect.

Science and Technology

1. Narrate an incident where you or someone else "turned a deaf ear" when medical or technical advice was given.
2. Defend or attack the use of background music for people waiting in restaurants, on the phone, in doctors' offices, shopping in stores, or riding elevators.

Illiterate Voters

Michelle Hiskey

Michelle Hiskey is a staff writer for *The Atlanta Journal.*

WORDS TO KNOW

illiteracy inability to read

irony use of words to express the opposite of literal meaning

precinct district of a city

rote repetition by memory

On Election Day in the past, Marlin Harper has set out for his precinct, but he's never quite made it.

The Super Tuesday primary won't be any different—Marlin Harper won't vote because he can't read.

"Plenty of times I've gone to the polls, but that's what chickened me out," said Harper, 33, a high school graduate from Atlanta. "I would have voted if I could read."

One of every four adults in Georgia is functionally illiterate. They might be able to sign their names and read basic words, but they may not be able to write a check or read directions—such as those inside a voting booth. They are much less likely to register and vote than someone more educated, according to Bill Crane, the spokesman for Secretary of State Max Cleland, and a recent study shows that they are much less likely to know how to vote.

Fear and pride often keep them from the polls. Usually, illiterate adults do not vote for the same reason they might not drive, or shop, or work: Other people could find out they can't read. Ironically, even though the law guarantees them the right to have someone help them vote, that's one reason they don't—assistance in public could be embarrassing.

If they do vote, their inability to read still handicaps them. Often they decide solely on a candidate's television image and must rely on rote memory when they enter the vote booth.

U. S. Sen. Wyche Fowler (D-Georgia) tells a story about being stopped on a street in downtown Atlanta by a woman just before an election.

"Please tell me what number you are on the ballot," she said, "I can't read, but I know I want to vote for you."

Nellie Whitehead, a great-grandmother from Atlanta who dropped out of school in the third grade, said she last voted in 1968, for Richard Nixon.

"I thought he was good for our country. When he was on talk shows, I picked it up from there," said Mrs. Whitehead, who is enrolled in a first-grade level reading course at Literacy Action in Atlanta.

But after Nixon "messed everything up," during the Watergate scandal, she gave up voting. She said that when she learns to read the newspaper, "maybe I'll vote, but that's way off."

For an illiterate adult, voting is part of a world where reading and writing are taken for granted, a world illiterates avoid because they don't feel equal.

"I dodge a lot of things, like voting," said Loretta Harris of Decatur, who also is in a first-grade level reading course at Literacy Action. Voting booths are intimidating, she said, because "they've got a lot of words in there. Maybe I'll vote when I learn to read better."

"I didn't think my vote would make a difference anyway," said Rosetta Battle, 29, of Atlanta, a classmate of Harper's in a third-grade level Literacy Action course.

In the 1985 mayoral election, Ms. Battle carefully memorized the name of the candidate she liked. She went to her precinct, entered a booth and pulled the right lever.

But as for the rest of the ballot, she "just pressed anything," because she could not read the names, referendums or directions.

Illiterate voters are much more likely to make a mistake while voting, according to a 1987 study.

"There is a tendency for people who haven't completed high

school to punch more than one button and waste their vote," said K. Farouk Brimah, director of research for the Voter Education Project in Atlanta, which conducted the study.

Election officials in Georgia and other Southern states once used literacy tests to disqualify black voters. The Voting Rights Act of 1965 outlawed such tests and guaranteed the right of illiterate voters to have someone help them vote.

In Georgia, an illiterate voter must verify—either by signature or mark—an oath swearing that he or she is disabled, with a check beside this reason: "Unable to read."

Once registered as disabled, a voter can step into the booth with anyone except his or her boss, an official of the voter's labor union or someone who has already aided 10 other disabled voters. Federal law requires that an elections superintendent be present at polls to help anyone who does not bring a qualified assistant.

Harper said that prospect intimidates him because he has no one he trusts to help him vote.

"People could tell me anything because I can't read the ballot," he said. "The person helping me might say he wants this guy to be president, so he might tell me George Bush and it might really be Jesse Jackson. When I go in to vote, I would like to read for myself."

QUESTIONS OF CONTENT AND TECHNIQUE

1. How is functional illiteracy defined in the article?
2. By what technique does Michelle Hiskey develop sympathy for the illiterate voter?
3. What sources does she use and how does she blend them into the piece?
4. Although the writer states the age of most of the people that she interviewed, one lady does not reveal her age. How does the writer let the reader know her general age anyway?

WRITING ASSIGNMENTS

Cause and Effect

1. Fear and pride often keep illiterate voters from the polls. Describe an incident where they kept you from a task. Examine the causes and effects.
2. Illiteracy is a major problem in the United States. Write an essay explaining what you believe are the causes and their effects upon the individual and society.

Education

1. Do you believe a literacy test should be given to voters? Write a persuasive argument.
2. Recount a situation where you were intimidated by your lack of knowledge.

Females in the Comics

Iris Krasnow

Iris Krasnow wrote this piece for United Press International.

WORDS TO KNOW

protagonist hero or heroine

pathetic pitiful

regression movement backward

syndicate an organization that sells comic strips and features to newspapers

voluptuous shapely

It may seem like women have come a long way in the comics, with thinking, achieving characters like Cathy now cresting at the top of the strips.

Yet there have been potent females starring in other eras of the industry that started in 1895 with "Yellow Kid."

By 1901, Jean Carr's Lady Bountiful appeared as an assertive and independent Gibson Girl. The first working woman came in 1906, "Sally Snooks Stenographer," by Dink Shannon. More than a half century ago, female cartoonists actually outnumbered males.

Brenda Starr, who hit the ground running in 1940 as a reporter, was created, written and drawn by a woman, Dale Messick. She changed her name from Dalia and mailed her work around after coming up against male editors who didn't take a woman seriously.

The striking Brenda, who was modeled after Rita Hayworth and named after debutante Brenda Frazier, was as able as any man on the staff of the Globe newspaper, later renamed the Flash.

"Comics have always reflected the popular culture of the day," says Catherine Yronwode, co-author of "Women in Comics" (Eclipse Books), which details the founding mothers of the cartoon industry. "During the late '20s, there was a tremendous amount of syndicated strips featuring female protagonists who were flappers, or showgirls," among them the legendary Nell Brinkley, a romantic cheesecake beauty created by a namesake artist "who was quite an eyeful herself," her obituary read.

"Those strips were considered the equivalent of today's 'Cathy.' I think people tend to forget history very fast," Yronwode says. "These flapper strips addressed issues like women getting the vote, women bobbing their hair, women in the work place as secretaries. Now Cathy is not a secretary, she works in an office, but that mirrors what has happened in society."

So when Winnie Winkle did stenography and Tillie the Toiler was a part-time office worker and model in the '20s, no one was thinking that women were portrayed in lowly jobs. Rather they personified the typical working women of the era, just like real-estate agent Lois of "Hi and Lois" is a character '80s womanhood can claim as their own.

"The evolution of women in comics has kept pace with the real evolution of life," says Bill Yates, a cartoonist who draws "Indian Chief" and "The Small Society." "Cartoons don't lead, they follow what's going on. If the big bomb blew us away and some Martians came in they could tell a lot about our culture and politics through the ages by reading our comics."

The evolved woman starring in the comics pages these days is generally very much her own person. LuAnn, who started in 1985, gives a sophistication to teen-age girlhood, getting involved with social issues such as coming out strongly against drugs. Both women in "The Middletons," created in 1982, have careers. Sally Forth juggles family and job. Adam, launched five years ago, is a house husband and his wife is the breadwinner.

"Doonesbury" is in a class all its own.

"Readers today assume the woman works in good jobs, no one is surprised," says Jay Kennedy, deputy comics editor for King Features, which syndicates all the above, except "Adam" and "Doonesbury" of Universal Press Syndicate.

Elly, the heroine of "For Better or for Worse," doesn't fit the picture of an '80s superwoman. She is predominantly a wife and mother, yet her character holds great appeal to modern couples because she is real.

She is not beautiful. A hair is permanently sprung out of place. Her kids are challenging, doing things like making an anatomically correct snow man as an aghast mother looks on. Her girlfriend gives birth to a baby that has six fingers on each hand. And Elly feels great conflict about falling short as a good mother.

"She is believable," says Lynn Johnston, who created "For Better or for Worse" in 1979. "She's not a super hero. What makes any character lovable is her vulnerability. Super heroes are unattainable. Even Lois Lane, you could never say 'That's me.' And so often I wear my heart on my sleeve and I tell it like I feel it.

"I don't mind being vulnerable on the pages because it's therapeutic," says Johnston, who lives in Ontario and has two children, 11 and 15. "She makes mistakes. She's sometimes a real heroine. And that's the way we all are."

Recently, Elly has entered the workplace part time at a local library where she performs duties like arranging window displays. But don't expect Elly to eventually become an executive. "I show her being capable at home, more than I show her being capable at work. The personal relationships between people are more interesting to me than being obsessed with your career. Primarily, Elly is a mother."

During the '30s, the tenor of the female strip began to turn toward more fluffy characters. Blondie, originally a showgirl, married Dagwood Bumstead, a millionaire's son who was disowned for taking a bride "beneath" him. By the onset of World War II, comic women became voluptuous pin-ups for the boys at war.

"Prior to World War II, you had flappers like 'Polly and her Pals,'" Kennedy says. "Polly wore short dresses, was very independent, she took charge of her own life. Then by the time you get to the war, over all, you saw a regression for women. You were seeing pin-up strips like the 'Glamour Girls,' and a bunch of others like that. I think it was for the lonely men in the trenches cut off from American women in a foreign land. You had an idealization of women as a sex image.

"And those pin-ups survived all the way into the '60s. Then they just dropped off like flies," Kennedy adds.

The big burst of women returning to the kitchen in the 1950s with strips like "The Farm Kitchen" by Ethel Hays Simms also began to wane.

Submissive bubbleheads are virtually nowhere on today's comic pages. Blondie, which along with "Peanuts" is the most widely distributed syndicated strip in the country, may appear to be a ditzy blonde, but a closer look shows just who is boss.

Blondie, age 58, is the one who gets Dagwood dressed. She gives him an allowance and gets him a raise. She is absolute monarch of the house. The continuing thread of humor in many of these vintage strips is that bumbling men are dominated by their women.

Look at old Jiggs, an immigrant construction worker turned millionaire, being ruled by his social climbing wife in the 75-year-old "Bringing Up Father." Maggie wants opera, Jiggs wants to low-life with the boys at the pub. When he comes home drunk, she beats him over the head with a rolling pin.

"The '70s brought another upsurge in strong female protagonists," author Yronwode says. "We've regained the subject matter we had in the '20s but of course the jobs being shown now are the better jobs women have in society."

Landmarks of the onset of the feminist age have been apparent across the comics in subtle and brash ways. When "The Phantom," that macho superhero who has fought off 52 years of pirates and assassins, finally became engaged to be married in 1977, his choice was no-stay-at-cave type.

He picked longtime companion Diana Palmer, who agreed to the proposal only if he would agree to marry a career woman. Rather than idle away her days in his Skull Cave in Bengali, she wanted to keep her job as a U.N. administrator in New York and commute between the two cities.

In 1975, a teen-ager became pregnant in the "Mary Worth" strip. Rich Marschall, the country's leading comics historian, remembers that scenario well. At the time, he was comics editor of the Field Newspaper Syndicate that has since merged with King Features.

"I said to Allen Saunders, creator of 'Mary Worth,' 'Have you ever considered doing something that isn't a safe theme with a predictable ending, like teen pregnancy?'" says Marschall.

"And he said—this bowled me over—he had wanted to do a story on that but was afraid the syndicate would veto it. So he did a high school girl who decided to keep the baby. Now we're talking about 1975, and it became grist for newspaper headlines—'Mary Worth Enters the Modern Age.'"

The following year Cathy Guisewite's "Cathy" strip was born, and in 1982, lawyer turned artist Greg Howard introduced professional everywoman "Sally Forth." By 1984, Blondie wore her first pair of pants, and the readers loved it.

Howard's heroine Sally made him a hero among feminists. Last September, he traveled from his Minneapolis home to receive a Good Guy Award from the National Women's Political Caucus in Washington.

"I don't make a conscious effort to take a feminist point of view in the strip. It's just my point of view," Howard says. "I am married to a woman who wouldn't permit me to be anything else but sensitive to women's issues. She first worked as a nurse, and now she is coordinator for the bone marrow transplant unit at the University of Minnesota hospital."

QUESTIONS ON CONTENT AND TECHNIQUE

1. How has the attitude toward women in the United States affected the heroines in comic strips?
2. Can you classify certain types of female comic strip heroes?
3. Do you feel that the reader has to be familiar with the comic strip to comprehend the hero? Explain your answer.
4. Give examples of Krasnow's powerful use of description and detail.
5. What were the sources of information for the article?

WRITING ASSIGNMENTS

Cause and Effect

1. Describe your favorite comic strip character, explain its philosophy of life, and what keeps you reading daily.
2. Clip a political cartoon from the newspaper and explain its significance.

Social and Political Issues

1. Compare yourself to some comic strip character.
2. Do you believe that comic strips have a positive or a negative influence on elementary school children? Explain.
3. Give three examples of the way cartoons portray one of the following: children, marriage, or social problems.

D'Artagnan on Ninth Street: A Brooklyn Boy at the Library

Pete Hamill

Pete Hamill, a novelist and screenwriter, wrote this essay for *The New York Times.*

WORDS TO KNOW

abstract not expressing something specific

epitome ideal example

sallow yellowish, sickly color

sheaves bundle

truncate cut short

The library was on Sixth Avenue and Ninth Street on the south slopes of the Brooklyn hills and for a long time in my young life it was the true center of the world.

The formal name, back then, was the Prospect Branch of the Brooklyn Public Library, but to me it was always just The Library and it remains that way in memory. I seem always to have gone there on Saturday mornings, following the same route each time, hurrying past the grocery stores, bakeries, drugstores and bars of Seventh Avenue. At the corner of Ninth Street, I turned left and the broad street dropped away into the distant jumble of the waterfront. On clear mornings, I could see past the elevated tracks of the IND subway and glimpse the Statue of Liberty in the harbor and the vertical smudge of the skyline of Manhattan. But usually I ignored the view. I was locked into a sensuous, almost religious ritual, with the holy sanctuary of the library drawing me like an iron filing to a magnet.

I can feel now the way my blood quickened as I crossed the trolley tracks, passed the stately brownstones and the small synagogue and saw ahead the wild gloomy garden behind the library. As a gesture of support, I would run a finger along the menacing iron pickets of the garden's fence. I wanted that fence to stand forever, holding back the jungle; each spring, the riot of weeds and nameless plants seemed to grow more menacing. I sometimes imagined it spilling into the streets, marching steadily forward to link with Prospect Park. Or it would turn to the nearest target: the library itself. The vengeful blind force of untamed nature would climb those granite walls, seep under the windows and assault the books, those sheaves of murdered trees, sucking them back to the dark earth.

But then I would glance through the immense windows, relieved: the books were still there. Turning at Sixth Avenue, I would look up, feel momentarily dwarfed by the majesty of the mock Corinthian columns that framed the entrance. Then I would take the wide granite steps two at a time. Into my second home. I was 10 the first time I took that journey alone; I kept taking it until I was 17 and went off to the Navy.

Inside, behind walls as thick as any true fortress, I always felt safe. The high-roofed building was warm in winter and cool in summer, and although it seemed built to last forever, and the sense of space was unlike anything I knew except the lobbies of movie houses, the attraction was not merely shelter. I was there on a more exciting mission: the discovery of the world.

In those years during and after the war, I was a citizen of a hamlet we all simply called "the neighborhood" (now cynically renamed the South Slope by real-estate developers). There were strict rules (Pay Your Debts, Don't Cross Picket Lines, Don't Squeal to the Cops, Honor the Old) and powerful institutions (the church, the police station and Rattigan's Bar and Grill). There was wisdom in the hamlet, of course, and honor, and the safety of the familiar. But within the boundaries of this working-class parish there were also men who gave it a dangerous edge: sallow-faced characters with gray fedoras and pinkie rings who carried guns under their coats;

youth gangs called the Tigers and the South Brooklyn Boys, who wore pegged pants and rolled through the streets with the swagger of victorious armies. There were homeless rummies too, and deranged vets still fighting Tarawa or the Hurtgen Forest, and cops on the take and brawling dock wallopers and apprentice wise guys. As a boy, I was afraid of them, a condition that went beyond the normal fears of childhood. But I knew one thing: none of them ever came to the library.

So, in one important way, the library was a fortified oasis. At the same time, it alarmed me. The books seemed to look down upon me with a wintry disdain. Most certainly they were adult, and I stood before them as an ignorant child. They knew what I did not know; they were, in some ways, the epitome of the unknowable, full of mystery and challenge and the most scary thing of all, doubt. The harder I worked at cracking their codes, the more certain I was that the task was impossible. I will carry that awe before the printed word to my grave.

At first, in my tentative probes of the Caliph's palace, I was condemned to the children's room. I liked the bound volumes of a magazine called St. Nicholas, full of intricate pen drawings and the cheery innocence of the 19th century. I read through most of Robert Louis Stevenson (enthralled by "Treasure Island" and "Kidnapped," disturbed by "Dr. Jekyll and Mr. Hyde," defeated by "The Weir of Hermiston"); Dumas *pere* thrilled me with "The Count of Monte Cristo" and "The Three Musketeers"; I consumed "Howard Pyle's Book of Pirates." But the rest of the books meant nothing to me; they all seemed to be about kids living in idyllic country glades, rabbits who talked and an elephant named Babar who had adventures in Africa. Outside the library, I was already traveling through the Africa of Burne Hogarth's comic-strip version of "Tarzan" and plunging into the South American forest of Bomba the Jungle Boy. When I read "The Count of Monte Cristo," I began to think of the children's room as another version of the Chateau d'If.

But even in that brightly lit cell, a peculiar process had begun. On the street, I consumed the artifacts of what is now called popular culture: comics, movie serials at the Minerva and the Globe, boys' books that were not in the library (Bomba, the Buddy series, Tom Swift, even G. A. Henty) and radio serials about Captain Midnight, the Green Hornet, Captain Silver and the Sea Hound. Out there, I was swept away by the primary colors of melodrama.

The library took that instinct for the lurid and refined it. The books that were talked about in schoolyards and on rooftops gave me a need for narrative, for removal from the dailiness of my life. But they stood in relation to the books in the library as the raw does to the cooked.

At first, I didn't know one writer from another. It didn't even occur to me that books were actually written by a lone man or woman sitting somewhere at a desk. They were there on the shelf and you took them down and opened them and began to read. To this day, I don't remember learning to read any more than I remember learning how to breathe. And in those years, I read books with a joyous innocence I've only rarely felt in all the years that followed. I had not begun to read, as I do now, as a writer; that is to say (in Stevenson's phrase), I was not reading as a predator.

Looking back, it's clear to me that I was reading as a creator, bringing myself (and comics, radio, movies, the street) to a collaboration with the writer in the invention of an alternative world. These books were not collections of abstract symbols called words, printed on paper; they were real events that had happened to me. So I was D'Artagnan. I hid from Blind Pew. I discovered the hidden grotto. I fought duels with the henchmen of the evil Milady. But alas, I also discovered early that telling these tales to my friends could sometimes provoke boredom or scorn; the stories then became part of my buried private history, another solitary vice.

When I escaped at last from the children's room, I felt like an explorer who had been handed a map written in invisible ink. As in life, one thing always led to another. At 14, I was trying to understand Latin at Regis High School. In the stacks at the library, this led me to Stevenson's "Virginibus Puerisque," which I still read for pleasure and reward; to Cyril Connolly's "Unquiet Grave" (the byline read "by Palinurus"), and though I surely understood virtually nothing it said, and skipped all the passages in French, I was consumed for a week by its mood of romantic loss. I pored over a translation of Cicero's accounts of murder trials. I took home a book called "Daily Life of the Romans" and copied most of the line drawings of free men and slaves. None of this helped me much with Latin, but the journey did take me to the meditations of Marcus Aurelius, and that splendid book was to help me through the brief anguish of losing all faith in religion.

Other books provoked similar journeys. The Bomba books led me to the geography section of the library, to volumes about South America, to a biography of Simon Bolivar and the fevered discovery of the existence of the great Chilean Bernardo O'Higgins, as Irish as I was, the liberator of his country. In that time, I often rode through the Andes of my imagination, a member of a revolutionary army, about to charge hard upon the hated viceroys in the capital; or I was an old man, seeing the revolution betrayed, saying (with Bolivar): "I have ploughed the seas." These were wars, conflicts, tragedies in the real world, but they were not taught in our schoolbooks, and so they became (I arrogantly thought) my own private discovery. If you lived in Brooklyn in those years, you said words like Caracas and Lima, Cartagena and Bogota, the Amazon and the Orinoco, as if they were digits on a secular rosary. Years later, I would travel this private tributary to school in Mexico City, to Diego Rivera, David Alfaro Siqueiros and Jose Clemente Orozco, to Carlos Fuentes and Octavio Paz, Luis Bunuel, and Jose Luis Cuevas, Jorge Luis Borges and Julio Cortazar, the granite of Neruda and the magical groves of Macondo.

The library taught me one other thing that has survived and expanded through the course of my life: the love of books themselves as objects. I came to love the feeling of a well-made book, the look of type on fine paper, the leathery worked splendor of certain bindings. I even loved the aroma of certain books, the smell of drying paper, the moldy fragrance of the past. This also has a context: I grew up as the oldest son of seven children of Irish immigrants; we were, I suppose, poor; there were always books in the house but none of them were very fancy. The library allowed me to borrow the first beautiful things I ever took home. When I was not reading them, I would place them on tables, on the mantelpiece, against a window, just to be able to see them, to turn from dinner and glance at them in the next room. I hated to bring them back, and often borrowed some books three or four times a year, just to have them around. As a result, I am today one of those people with a book jones. There are 10,000 books in my library, and it will keep growing until I die. This has exasperated my daughters, amused my friends and baffled my accountant. If I had not picked up this habit in the library long ago, I would have more money in the bank today; I would not be richer.

In short, the library was a place where most of the things I came to value as an adult had their beginnings. Art was there, poetry, history and words. Millions of words. Trillions. Politicians have come and gone since many of them were written, empires have risen to temporal glory and collapsed into decay. But those words remain as powerful as they were when I was a boy and will be there long after I'm gone. I went to the library in a different time, of course, during the last years before the arrival of the great obliterating force of television. I went to the library in search of entertainment and discovered the world.

Today, kids don't seem to embark on that exhilarating journey as often as they did when I was young. Politicians keep chiseling away at the branch libraries, truncating their hours, reducing their staffs. The dumb forces of darkness still riot in the garden. But there, through the windows, you can still see the shelves. The books stand in eternal wintry challenge, full of wonder, fear, certainty and doubt, just waiting to be opened. Hey, young man, hurrying by, a Walkman plugged into your skull: pause a moment, mount those steps and enter. The world awaits you.

QUESTIONS OF CONTENT AND TECHNIQUE

1. How did the library evoke four or five changes in the author?
2. List some of the images and comparisons that Hamill makes of the library and tell how they enhance the article.
3. Although the author primarily uses cause and effect writing strategy, what other types of writing does he blend with it and why?
4. Hamill has great versatility of sentence length. Write an example of an extremely short and extremely long sentence and see if you can explain the reasoning behind his choice.
5. There are a number of sentences using the colon. Examine several and see if you can determine when a colon is appropriate.

WRITING ASSIGNMENTS

Cause and Effect

1. Write an essay showing how a place or a certain environment created a change in you.
2. Select three or four books in your childhood or adolescent reading that were especially significant for you and explain their value in your development.

Education

1. "In that time, I often rode through the Andes of my imagination. . ." Can you recall a period or an incident in your life where daydreaming or reading a book provided a magic carpet for your imagination? Explain its positive and/or negative effects.
4. Using the model of Hamill, select one of the following to show change in youth due to their association with the media: radio, television, movies, or theater.

When Practice Never Makes Perfect

Mary Conroy

Mary Conroy wrote this special feature for the *Kansas City Star.*

WORDS TO KNOW

compulsive obsessive, driven

dawdling wasting time

procrastinate put off

stultified nullified

Tammy was bright and talented by anybody's measure. She was a passionate reader, craved creative writing and threw herself into her piano lessons.

But somehow all that turned sour. She'd practice piano three hours a day, never happy with her progress, and spend the rest of the time holed up with a book. Never satisfied with how much she learned in college, she drifted from school to school. Finally, at home alone between semesters, she let everyone know how miserable she'd been: She took her father's gun and shot herself.

Not all perfectionists take their perfectionism to such extremes; some limit it to one field, such as sports. And not all perfectionalists are outstanding performers, either.

All perfectionists share one trait, however: No matter how well they do, they're dissatisfied with themselves. Guilt is a constant companion as they punish themselves for not measuring up to their own impossible standards.

Perfectionists set their sights high, but their drive to achieve isn't prompted by ambition alone. They're also propelled by fear of rejection, psychologists say.

"As children, perfectionists are afraid they're not going to be loved if they don't do well," says psychologist Colette Davison of the Virginia Frank Child Development Center in Chicago.

They feel worthless unless everyone approves of them, adds Susan Forman, psychology professor at the University of South Carolina. As a result, they spend all their time straining to please parents, friends and teachers.

Unlike such childhood problems as fear of the dark, perfectionism isn't a stage that children outgrow. Without intervention, the problem may persist into adulthood.

By that time, "you're dealing with very anxious people who don't take much pleasure out of anything," Davison says. "It limits their capacity to enjoy life—and everyone's capacity around them."

Instead of competing with others, perfectionist adults compete with themselves. They may have forgotten early experiences but still live up to expectations their parents would have had. There's no let-up: "They strive like crazy all through their life," Davison says.

They also strive, sometimes without realizing it, to make their children perfect.

"You see parents pass on perfectionism to tiny children," Davison says. "Rather than just letting them play with blocks, the parent interferes to get them to make something that looks good. It's likely that they're caught up in a generational quality that's hard to get rid of."

In fact, many people think perfectionism isn't bad. "I wish just one of my children would be a perfectionist," a Chicago woman complains. Then she explains: she simply wants to see them put more effort into household chores.

The goal setting that is typical of perfectionists is a healthy motivator, Davison agrees. But some parents have unrealistic expectations for their child. They hang multiplication flash cards around the child's bed or insist the child practice football every day. These parents live through their child, experiencing the child's success as their own.

Memories of perfectionistic parents don't die easily. "I remember bringing home a Spanish exam," says Katharine Kersey, chairman of the child study department at Old Dominion University in Norfolk, Va. "I had a 99⅔ on it. My father asked, 'Why not a 100?'"

Other parents may pass on perfectionism unconsciously. Some are never pleased with their own work. Others can't take compliments because they don't think they deserve them. Still others refuse to let their children see them making mistakes.

Some teachers also pass on perfectionism unwittingly. By praising only achievement and focusing on the best papers in the class, they give students a strong message: The only way to get attention is by being perfect.

Of course, not all children exposed to a perfectionist parent or teacher become a perfectionist themselves. "Some children just seem predisposed toward perfectionism," Forman says. Other children have risk factors that increase their likelihood of becoming a perfectionist.

Oldest children are especially vulnerable, Kersey says. Because they have no older siblings for models, "they compare themselves to their parents." Those comparisons establish a standard the children just can't reach. In time, they may assume that unreachable goals are a routine part of life.

Children of alcoholics and workaholics also are at risk, Kersey says. For these children, perfectionism fulfills two needs: It allows them to please the parent and helps them escape the parent's wrath.

Although perfectionism varies from one person to the next, certain characteristics are typical, such as a low tolerance for mistakes. Some children tear up school papers that aren't perfect. Others may lose a card game and throw all the cards on the floor.

Many perfectionists also have a compulsion to succeed in unlikely fields. Someone who once found it difficult to express ideas may become a writer, Davison says. "They cannot accept that there's a side of themselves that's weaker and will spend their whole life trying to overcome it with impossibly high standards."

Extreme concern about appearance also is typical. Some children spend hours making sure they have just the right clothes. They may become irate if a single hair is out of place.

Perfectionists also are known for dawdling. "If they're doing anything that shows a result—writing, creative work—it tends to take them a long, long time," Davison says. "It's a nice piece of work, but so much effort, time and stress goes into it that the creativity gets stultified." In math, these children may finish two problems in the time it takes everyone else to do 10.

They also tend to procrastinate. Faced with difficult tasks or long-term projects, perfectionists put them off until the very last minute. This allows them to avoid the fear of failure that the work arouses in them.

In a similar vein, some avoid work completely. If they don't attempt a task, they won't fail at it. Some children take such a long time on an English assignment that they never get to their math homework. In extreme cases, they may drop out of school.

Unwillingness to try new ventures is another trait. A child may resist playing a new game for fear of losing. Others avoid new subjects in school, afraid of failing.

Fear of failing is most evident in test anxiety. Children who clench up over tests may fear failure, even if they view a score of 99 as failure.

Jealousy is inevitable for the many perfectionists who view everyone else as perfect. As a result, they set themselves up for a lifetime of envy.

When these children don't get help, perfectionism takes a heavy toll. Obsessed with achievement, they drive themselves unmercifully, even when they're already getting top grades. But they're still never satisfied and can't enjoy their achievements. Competitive behavior and workaholism keep these children in constant tension. They find it impossible to relax, even away from school, because every activity becomes a testing ground.

Overemphasizing achievement makes children one-dimensional, says Dr. Michael Frey, coordinator of child psychiatry services at Lutheran General Hospital in Park Ridge, Ill. "If they're compulsive about academics, they don't develop other parts of their personality: social skills, humor, outside interests," he says.

One-dimensional children also suffer when they fail in their chosen field. "What about the kid who practices baseball and doesn't make it into the minors?" Frey says. "Now everything the kid's invested in is gone."

The overemphasis can have paralyzing results, Davison says. The child who never gets the chance to develop social skills may become extremely shy and withdrawn, fearful that any social blunders will repel potential friends.

One-dimensional children may become even more compulsive in adolescence. Anorexia and bulimia haunt teen-agers who never feel quite thin enough. Students who are obsessed with grades often cheat to ensure their success.

Once a perfectionist, always a perfectionist? Not necessarily. Some perfectionists have to hit bottom first, but they can and do change. Parents can help, or professional help may be required.

Tammy was one of the lucky ones. Her suicide attempt was a cry for help, and someone listened. Now, after extensive individual and family therapy, she's a successful—but not compulsive—student at a major university.

QUESTIONS ON CONTENT AND TECHNIQUE

1. What are the major causes of a child's perfectionism, according to Conroy?
2. The author lists one reason older children are vulnerable to perfectionism. What other reasons might there be?
3. What is the writer's attitude toward a perfectionist?
4. How does the article open and close? What is its effect?
5. How does Conroy create more interest for the reader through her sentence structure?

WRITING ASSIGNMENTS

Cause and Effect

1. Conroy took the adage "Practice makes perfect" and dispelled that folk wisdom. Take a widely held idea and show through cause and effect that it is not always true.
2. In the article, the writer points out that children of alcoholics and workaholics are at risk. Write an essay dealing with the effects of either on family members.

Education

1. Explain how an adult has taught you through attitude, manner, value system, body language, and example as well as words.
2. Relate an incident where practice and perfectionism helped or hindered you.

Chapter
10

Convincing Others

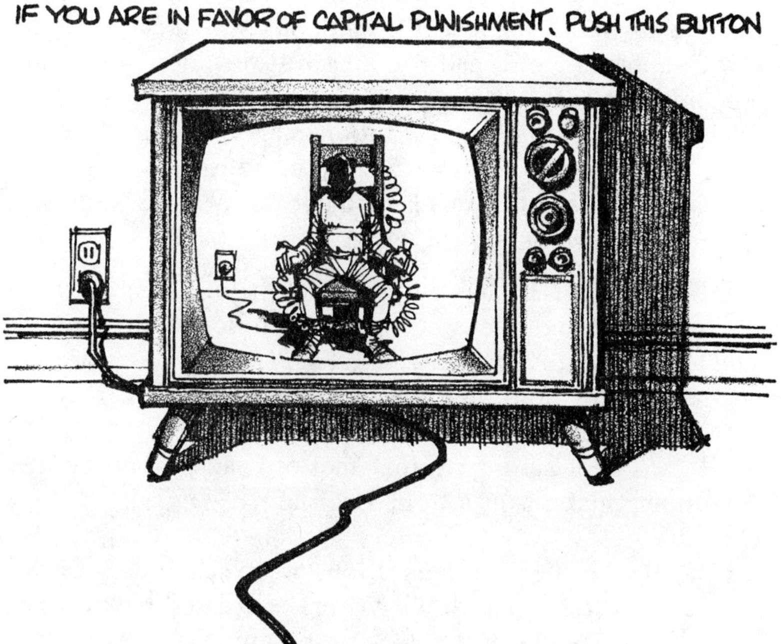

The Declaration of Independence, which helped launch our nation, is a prime example of reasonable argument aimed at gaining support for a cause. To see how our forefathers skillfully framed this document, we will highlight the principles of persuasion: gaining attention, stating the issue, recognizing an opposing point of view, developing your position, summarizing, and, finally, ending with an emotional appeal.

First, the colonists stated the issue: "It becomes necessary for one People to dissolve the Political Bands which have connected them with another" and institute a new government when the old one becomes destructive.

Then they developed their position, starting with the claim that the king of Britain was attempting to establish an "absolute tyranny," and buttressed this claim with a list of reasons that read like an indictment:

- "He [George III] has refused his assent to Laws the most wholesome and necessary for the public Good. . . .
- "He has dissolved Representative Houses [legislatures] repeatedly, for opposing with manly firmness his Invasions on the Rights of the People. . . .
- "He has kept among us, in Times of Peace, Standing Armies, without the consent of our Legislature."

All in all, 27 specific accusations were leveled against King George. Then the Declaration's writers expressed how reasonable they had been: "In every stage of these Oppressions we have Petitioned for Redress in the most humble terms. Our repeated Petitions have been answered only by repeated Injury."

They concluded their argument with an emotional appeal: "These United Colonies are, and of Right, ought to be, Free and Independent States," conveying the impression that the goal of independence was accomplished by the signing of the document. Of course, the end result was not that easy. The Declaration of Independence was a powerful shot, but only one shot, in the war of guns and propaganda that would not be resolved for another seven years.

Without its ringing words to convince and motivate others, however, the revolutionary cause would not have prevailed.

In this chapter, examples of argument will be presented. None of them has the sweeping aims of the Declaration of Independence but the writers use the same techniques to convince us of the righteousness of a cause or course of action. They accomplish this by emphasizing the facts that favor their viewpoints without resorting to falsehoods, which can destroy their credibility.

Donald J. and Louise K. Eberly, for example, seek to persuade us that a system of national service for young people would help solve some of the nation's problems. By using logical argument, they show what youths can do if organized for the public good. In another article, William Raspberry tries to convince us of the need to begin education reform early. And U.S. Representative Boxer uses logic to articulate why "whistle-blowers" who expose corruption should be honored and protected rather than vilified.

In everyday language, argument has come to mean a vocal dispute, a quarrel, or an orgy of name-calling. "I did not say that!" "You don't know what you're talking about!" Such sound and fury does little to advance one's cause or to change another's viewpoint. But when you use argument properly as a writing strategy, it can spark revolutions.

WHEN YOU WRITE TO CONVINCE OTHERS

- Focus on evidence that contributes to convincing readers of your point of view.
- Gain your audience's attention and respect by accepting that rather than one there may be ten points of view, and that truth, an elusive bird, rarely nests in any one place.
- State the issue fairly and indicate your position.
- Illustrate your major points with objective facts, statistics, quotations, testimony, comparison, and cause and effect relationships rather than your personal opinions and judgments.
- Recount the major elements within the issue and indicate the reasons that you have given as well as any real emotional feelings that you have.
- Assume that opposing views are not directed personally to you and that new facts might change your point of view.

It's Time for National Service

Donald J. Eberly and Louise K. Eberly

Donald J. Eberly, executive director of the Coalition for National Service in Washington, D.C., and his wife Louise K. Eberly, a free-lance writer, both taught in Nigeria during the 1950s.

WORDS TO KNOW

behooves be necessary for

innovative new

maligned spoken badly of

mandatory required

A five-year-old child misses his bus and stands crying on a busy road. A toddler in makeshift day-care is beaten for dirtying a diaper. An elderly couple die of cold in their home. Parks are vandalized and unsafe. Young people are blown away by drugs.

What's going on here, America? Why do we all have horror stories of unmet needs in our neighborhoods, towns, and cities? There is much that needs doing in our wealthy country and many of us volunteer our services, but they seem mere fingers in the dike.

There's a virtually untapped resource that could be filling many of these needs. Not just filling needs, but enhancing lives, exploring careers, building patriotism, and knitting up America's reputation as a caring, innovative society.

The resource is our young people. Yes, those same maligned young people often seen as bored with school, neglecting lessons to work for $90 jeans, or hanging around jobless and opting out of our society with crime and drugs. Have we forgotten that youth is naturally a time of energy, search, experimentation, and high idealism?

What can we do to tap this energy and idealism? One thing we can do is establish a National Youth Service Corps. Nine bills are before Congress right now to do just that. We can give them our support.

What would a national service program be like? Bill sponsors agree that it would start modestly with a few thousand recruits and would gradually increase as support staff was trained and work opportunities expanded. Volunteers from 18 to 24 years of age would apply through their local school or post office. Once accepted, they would be assisted in finding the right job for them in voluntary agencies like the Red Cross, the local hospital or library, or in a national park. Some would live at home and others would be off to the Grand Tetons or the South Bronx. The agency where the job was found would supply training, supervision, and a partial stipend. The government would pay the rest of the stipend, provide medical coverage, and award money for further education to those completing a year or two of service.

College graduates might be tutoring high school dropouts who in turn might be helping third-graders with their reading. Volunteers might be building a camp in a national forest where city kids could spend a week learning what nature is all about. Those monitoring air, water, and noise pollution could learn the scientific basis of their measuring devices as well as the causes of pollution. Others might be refurbishing abandoned housing. A highway rescue team might be manning a helicopter. Why not? Our young people successfully handled such demanding jobs in wartime. Why not ask them to help build our country in peacetime?

Have we any idea whether national service would work? Yes, there have been several programs in the last 50 years showing great promise for solving national problems with youthful energy. The Civilian Conservation Corps gave work and training to 3 million young men from 1933 to 1942. Roads, bridges, and lodges in our national parks attest to their useful work. Today, former CCC workers proudly bring their grandchildren to see that what they built still stands.

The Peace Corps, now 26 years old, has enhanced America's reputation abroad and is a source of pride at home. American know-how and can-do philosophy have given real assistance in developing countries, and the impact has been great considering the program's small size. The even smaller domestic Peace Corps, VISTA, has turned lives around for many disadvantaged young Americans. There is the Young Adult Conservation Corps of the Carter years, and current youth conservation corps in California, Michigan, Minnesota, Pennsylvania, and Washington. New York and San Francisco have local youth service programs, as do Israel, Indonesia, Nigeria, and West Germany, to name a few.

National surveys and polls for the past 20 years have shown that a majority of Americans think national service is a good idea. So what's holding it up? Some people worry about involuntary servitude. Only one of the nine bills calls for mandatory national service. Other people worry about undercutting the military. Several national service bills include voluntary military service as one option. Others worry about the cost. The National Service Secretariat, which has been studying national service for over 20 years, estimates a total cost of $11,000 per participant per year.

With the value of services rendered expected to outstrip program costs, and with the additional benefits of work experience, career exploration, and lower crime rates, national service is an investment worth making.

Research over the past 20 years has consistently shown a need for the services of some 4 million young people in such fields as conservation, education, health, child, and elder care. Innovative local programs, like one in Seattle, have demonstrated that the nation could easily absorb 100,000 youth service participants. Could it absorb 40 times that number? With a steady but gradual buildup over several years, the nation's ability to absorb youth service could be determined.

It behooves us to get behind a national service program. Our young people would benefit from the work experience and feeling of self-worth. Contributing a period of time and effort to serving the needs of our country ought to be the right of every young person. Being needed and serving builds loyalty to one's own country. We'd all benefit.

QUESTIONS ON CONTENT AND TECHNIQUE

1. Do the writers omit any problems that might arise with the establishment of the National Youth Service Corps? Discuss several that might surface.
2. What arguments of their opponents do they acknowledge?
3. What form of concrete evidence do they use to prove that National Service will succeed?
4. How do they catch the reader's attention in their early lines?
5. What does the phrase "mere fingers in the dike" mean?

WRITING ASSIGNMENTS

Convincing Others

1. "Being needed and serving builds loyalty to one's own country," state the authors. Argue pro or con.
2. Select a needed project in your own community and write a letter to an official giving reasons for its completion.

Social and Political Issues

1. The writers say that "youth is naturally a time of energy, search, experimentation, and high idealism." Using your teen-age years, can you recall some act in which those qualities emerged? Explain.
2. You are in the National Service and have a choice of your program. Explain your selection, your duties, and the possible effects on you and others.

When Do You Lie for a Friend?

Richard Cohen

Richard Cohen is a syndicated columnist with *The Washington Post.*

WORDS TO KNOW

analogous similar

flamboyant showy

ideologue an impractical idealist

paean song of praise

Suppose a colleague is nominated to the Supreme Court and the FBI pays you a visit for a background check on your pal. An agent asks the usual questions and then pops one that makes you pop sweat: Has your friend ever abused alcohol or used illicit drugs? Do you tell the truth about a certain party 15 years ago when you saw the candidate smoke pot—or do you lie?

It turns out that in the case of Douglas Ginsburg, President Reagan's fleeting Supreme Court nominee, a number of people lied. Not one of the people interviewed for Ginsburg's background check mentioned what Ginsburg himself later admitted: He had smoked pot. It was that revelation that sank his nomination.

For the FBI, Ginsburg was not its finest moment. The man had already worked at the White House and been confirmed as a federal judge. Twice before, the bureau had performed background checks on Ginsburg, and yet it seemingly could not find out what the press discovered almost instantly: Ginsburg was a man of his generation. Yes, indeed, the foul weed had passed his lips.

It's not likely any of the people the FBI interviewed will be prosecuted. Background checks are not conducted under oath, although the Justice Department, according to *The New York Times,* is considering whether it has a case. Legality aside, though, it's worth asking about the morality of the apparent lies—whether a person is justified in either withholding damaging information about a Supreme Court nominee or telling an outright lie.

E. M. Forster, the late English writer, said that if given a choice between having to betray his country and his friend, he would sooner betray his country. Forster's famous line was revived soon after Ginsburg withdrew his nomination because it seemed the nominee had, in fact, been betrayed by his friends. At least two were quoted in the press as saying they knew Ginsburg had smoked pot—although one later explained that he acknowledged only what Ginsburg had already admitted.

Of course, Forster was hardly speaking about marijuana. He was, instead, referring to those Cambridge University classmates and colleagues who later turned out to be Soviet spies. And in that context, the line is unforgivable—a homoerotic paean to male friendship as the ultimate bond. But the spies of the Cambridge set did real damage to their country and the Western alliance. Forster did not quite realize it, but as an Englishman, his chums had betrayed him, too.

But pot smoking is hardly treason. If anything, it's analogous to having held membership in a pro-communist organization at a time when naive and idealistic people joined by the thousands. As distinct from spies, these people did no real damage and, besides, were merely exercising their constitutional rights, Years later, in the McCarthy period, they were called to account for their associations, and some of them were severely penalized for them. Like Ginsburg's colleagues, they, too, were asked to rat on their friends. Some of them refused to do so—some, like Lillian Hellman, flamboyantly and famously. Before they could answer the question, they had to answer to themselves.. Silence was sometimes the result.

If possible, marijuana smoking is even less consequential than membership in a leftist organization during the McCarthy period. Yet the Ginsburg case proves the penalty can be just as dire. The one-time Supreme Court nominee was one of millions of persons who smoked pot in the 1970s. The stub was everywhere, considered an innocent enough indulgence and, indeed, touted as preferable even to wine or beer. In the near future, the United States is likely to have a president who at one time smoked pot.

Some commentators have blamed the press for Ginsburg's downfall. It invaded his privacy. Nonsense. It was the holier-than-thou ideologues of the Reagan administration with their unrealistic and unforgiving standards who brought the man down. Like McCarthyites in the 1950s, they cannot distinguish between naive and basically harmless activities and those that are truly dangerous. Just as there was a difference between being a leftist and a communist spy, so there's a difference between being an occasional pot smoker in the 1970s and a heroin or cocaine abuser today.

The colleagues and friends of Ginsburg who purportedly lied to the FBI had the wit to make that distinction. They were not, in Forster's formulation, putting friendship above country but rather were simultaneously serving both. They don't warrant an investigation. But if the Reagan administration wants one, it ought to direct it inward at the unrealistic and hypocritical standards it sets. Ginsburg's friends may have lied, but the larger lie is that Ginsburg's pot-smoking mattered at all.

QUESTIONS ON CONTENT AND TECHNIQUE

1. In what professional fields does Cohen suggest that lying can be highly detrimental? Give specific examples.
2. Look up "McCarthyism" in your dictionary or encyclopedia. What does the term "blacklisting" mean?
3. What is the effect of the use of the second person (you) in the introduction?
4. How does Cohen draw the reader into the dilemma?

WRITING ASSIGNMENTS

Convincing Others

1. The author raises the issue of privacy. Write an essay on one area where the government exerts too much or too little control over your life.
2. "Lying is never justified." Write an argument in favor or against this statement.

Philosophical Values

1. Suppose the press reveals that a presidential candidate has lied about his personal life. Do you think that person still should be considered as a candidate? Give concrete reasons for your position.
2. The writer quotes E. M. Forster as saying that if given a choice between having to betray his country and his friend, he would sooner betray his country. Have you ever lied, stretched the truth, or omitted certain facts when someone inquired about a friend? What was the result? Would you do it again? Why?

The Truth About Single-Parent Kids

Jill Jacobs Scott

Jill Jacobs Scott, mother of two children, is coordinator of the Newspaper in Education program for *The Denver Post*.

WORDS TO KNOW

apartheid separation of the races

callouses thickened and hardened skin

cynical relating all actions to selfish motives

demeanor behavior toward others

feisty full of nervous activity

menagerie collection of animals

I bristle when I hear the word "broken" to describe my home. I shake my head when I hear anyone explain a child's problems with the phrase: "You know, he's from a single-parent family."

I got furious when I heard the remark—from a married mother of three—that her child "doesn't hang around kids missing a parent. It's not healthy."

I heard that last statement from a former neighbor who thought I was still married. I reared up and shot back. My kids are healthy and self-reliant, I told her. They're doing fine in school. And before you point the finger at us, look at yourselves. Two parents, two incomes, children unsupervised as much as my own. Don't project your guilt onto me. I'm proud of how I'm doing with my family.

Single parents—we're a proud, feisty bunch. We hang tough and we hang together. And not only because our needs are the same. There's a subtle social apartheid that separates us from two-parent families. Just as many married couples are uncomfortable around singles, so are they uneasy about the single parent's children, fearful that divorce, and ensuing single parenthood, may be contagious. (Sometimes it is.) So when my kids were younger, we had little contact with two-parent children.

But that's changed. Parents of adolescents have little to say about whom their children befriend. So the barriers are gone, and now I see the differences between my kids and theirs.

It's made me more sad than proud.

True, my kids are self-reliant, quick to act and strong. When Jennifer, my 15-year-old, was getting the run-around on how to redeem a gift certificate at a local store, she demanded the manager and fairness. Her new friend, Jacob, who lives with his mother and father, was impressed. "I never would have done that," he told her. "My parents would have taken care of it."

But I see something else now with my kids, something I never saw before because there was no point of contrast.

My kids get cynical quickly. They hold onto anger longer. They quickly revert to a survival mode, while the other kids—the two-parent ones—still have a childlike wonder and a sense of feeling safe in the world.

Jennifer and Nathan know more about my finances than their friends do about their parents. More than once, Jennifer has asked me how much I spent for groceries this month, knowing my monthly budget, and could I afford a deluxe set of school pictures? A new friend, recently divorced with teenage children, was taken aback.

"My kids don't know how much money I make, and they shouldn't. You single parents figure you have to disclose everything, including money and family problems. Kids need to be protected against that. They'll learn it soon enough."

I disagree, but I have to admit that in my family, financial struggles have produced a certain hardness in Nathan, my 19-year-old. He announced this summer that if he had been in my place at 26 (the age I gave birth to him), he would have bought a new car instead of having him. "I'm going to have it easier," he concluded. "It's a drag sharing just one TV. I'm not going to have children."

Sensing a certain lack of softness in our house, I consented to getting a pet three years ago. I figured that a furry creature scurrying about would create a gentler aura around our struggles, a calmer demeanor to our daily trials. My kids wanted a dog, but a cat was easier to take care of. And I insisted that we get it from the animal shelter, not a pet store. Even that process, supposed to be a joyful family project, became a struggle. Jennifer's heart broke as she saw all the cats unchosen, and she agonized for weeks about all the ones left behind.

This feline became an element of softness sometimes, but other times was a reflection of the general atmosphere of the house: a menagerie of resourceful, independent beings who somehow get their needs met, but at the expense of a certain kind of warm dependence and predictability. My recently divorced friend brought his kids a puppy when they were youngsters. "It sat in our laps and panted lovingly at our feet," he told me.

And his children, now almost grown, retain a sense of childlike wonder that my kids have lost. I study these young adults who grew up with parents intact, and I am fascinated. They brush off hurtful remarks with a shrug and a "That's OK." They reminisce with their dad about fishing trips and family mishaps with the dog. In their conversations about the future, they relay a deep self-confidence that everything, after all, will be all right. They feel safe in the world; they still have a case of puppy love with life.

It makes me wistful. I look at my own kids, sturdy and lovely and strong, but with a strength that comes, as Jennifer puts it, "from fighting for everything I have."

I look upon my single-parent status with a different eye these days. Although I've never regretted leaving the man who is their father (my kids truly would have been damaged had I stayed), I do regret the vulnerability that's been stripped from my kids. And I hope when they're adults, they'll marry and buy dogs and all stay together. For as much as I'm proud of my single-parenting, I can see now that not having two people to lean on has left them with invisible callouses and sometimes those spots get tender.

QUESTIONS OF CONTENT AND TECHNIQUE

1. Explain some differences that Jill Jacobs Scott notes between "single- and double-parent" children.
2. In this opinion paper, where does the writer make inferences or assumptions that you might question?

3. Scott bases her argument on observation and personal examples. What other techniques of writing could she use to strengthen her position?
4. How does the informal conversational tone of the article affect you?

WRITING ASSIGNMENTS

Convincing Others

1. The writer "bristles" at the term "broken home." What word or phrase makes you bristle? Present your point of view on this controversial subject.
2. Jill Jacobs Scott wistfully envies the child from a two-parent family. Could you provide, from a child's point of view, several disadvantages that might occur in living in a two-parent home?

Social and Political Issues

1. "The grass always looks greener on the other side of the street" is an old proverb. Write how you envied or admired a person or situation and discovered later its flaws.
2. "Even that process, supposed to be a joyful family project, became a struggle." Relate an incident that you anticipated with joy and it became a struggle or tarnished in some way.

Let's Protect the Whistle-Blower

Barbara Boxer

Rep. Barbara Boxer (D) of California is a member of the House Budget and Armed Services Committees and the Congressional Military Reform Caucus.

WORDS TO KNOW

reprisal revenge

prestigious admirable

Major Peter Cole was one of our nation's most promising Army officers. A West Point graduate, he had served his country well for nearly six years. Then his shining career came to a premature, abrupt end because he refused to keep silent about wrongdoing in the military.

Shortly after Major Cole received a prestigious appointment to West Point, a seasoned military man took him aside and offered a few words of sage advice: "Peter, keep your mouth shut for 20 years and you will wear stars." But when Cole heard reports of widespread drug abuse at West Point and mysterious million-dollar "losses" of Army equipment in Germany, he made the biggest mistake of his life—he didn't take that advice. He didn't keep his mouth

Reprinted by permission of the author.

shut. Instead, he reported what he had heard to his superiors, and they thanked him by ruining his career.

While at West Point in 1969, Cole reported drug abuse among cadets to the Army Criminal Investigation Division and to the officer chain of command. Instead of probing the reports, Cole's superiors began investigating him for "honor code violations," and ordered Cole confined to the "psych ward" at Walter Reed Army Hospital in Washington. Cole was not given a hearing, access to a lawyer, or any other "due process" protection before confinement. In fact, Cole said that while at Walter Reed, he saw other officer-"patients," who claimed they were given electric shock treatments and drug injections against their will.

Sounds like a scene from the "Gulag Archipelago," doesn't it? But it happens to whistle-blowers in the United States, not just the Soviet Union, along with other forms of reprisal like negative performance reports, demotions or denial of promotions, even anonymous phone threats. It also happened to Navy officer Michael Tufariello, who found himself in a mental ward after protesting payments to Navy reservists for work never done. Cole, now a U.S. Army National Guard reservist, and Officer Tufariello, now retired from the Navy, should have been considered heroes. Instead, they were branded traitors.

Some whistle-blowers are federal employees, others work for private companies, but many are men and women who serve in our nation's armed forces. Federal and private sector employees have the benefit of established grievance procedures; military personnel are not so lucky. They live and work in an atmosphere where discipline, conformity, and unquestioning obedience to the orders of superiors are prized above all else. True, these values are the key to an effective defense in wartime. But they can also be misused by some to muzzle or punish whistle-blowers who reveal billion-dollar waste, fraud, and shoddy weapons that undermine our nation's security and jeopardize soldiers' lives.

I have introduced legislation to change that, giving military personnel the same due process rights already enjoyed by most Americans. H. R. 1394, the "Whistle-blower Protection Act," protects soldiers who report wrongdoing to the Inspector General (IG) or members of Congress from reprisal and requires the IG to promptly investigate reports of wrongdoing and retaliation. It also allows a whistle-blower who is dissatisfied with the IG's report to petition the Board of Correction of Military Records for a hearing. The bill also allows a whistle-blower to appeal the Board's decision to a U.S. Court of Appeals. A House Armed Services Subcommittee recently held hearings on the bill, and House action is expected early next year.

Why is it that extraordinary steps are needed to protect the whistle-blower? Shouldn't people who are already doing what's right be protected—even rewarded? Ideally they should. But the truth is that the whistle-blower in any industry—but particularly in the military—is the proverbial "boat rocker," the bearer of bad news. And sometimes that news can embarrass or even threaten the careers of their superiors.

Under current law, military whistle-blowers have virtually no due-process rights to independent legal counsel, hearings, or appeals to civilian courts. They cannot join unions or engage in collective bargaining to air their grievances. They are, in effect, second-class citizens in the eyes of the law. Their complaints, if formally heard, are reviewed by other military personnel, whose independence and judgment are often compromised by devotion to military discipline and the status quo. Hence, they are literally at the mercy of their superiors—some of whom may stand to gain the most if soldiers who know too much are stifled.

Without the invaluable disclosures of whistle-blowers, the American people and the Congress would never discover the needless, shameful waste of their hard-earned tax dollars. If we are truly serious about maintaining a lean, mean fighting force, we must protect the military men and women who blow the whistle on waste and corruption.

QUESTIONS ON CONTENT AND TECHNIQUE

1. Barbara Boxer has two purposes for her argument. What are they?
2. Where and why does she acknowledge her opponents' arguments?
3. What dramatic examples does she utilize to build her case?
4. How does her anecdote of Cole affect the reader?

WRITING ASSIGNMENTS

Convincing Others

1. Barbara Boxer lists whistle-blowers as heroes. Choose a controversial person in the public eye whom you consider a hero and attempt to persuade your reader to agree.
2. "They are, in effect, second-class citizens." . . . says the author. Choose

persons or groups you believe are also considered second-class citizens and persuade the reader how the group should be recognized.

Social and Political Issues

1. Choose a human rights issue and write to your U.S. Representative about it.
2. You are a whistle-blower in your job, church, union, or college. Write about an injustice that you feel deserves notice.

Raising High School Standards: The Cons

William Raspberry

William Raspberry is a columnist with the Washington Post Writers Group.

WORDS TO KNOW

punitive punishing

repertoire pieces a performer can present

Washington—Would Education Secretary William Bennett's proposed "leaner, meaner" high school curriculum help minority youngsters to close the achievement gap? Or would it merely raise an impossibly high standard, humiliating them and increasing their dropout rate?

In short, is it realistic to expect poor and disadvantaged inner-city high schoolers to "learn what the smart kids learn"? The temptation is to answer: Of course it is. Isn't the alternative to give up on these already hard-pressed children and to play into the hands of racists who insist on the genetic inferiority of blacks and Hispanics?

Here is a man, a lifetime educator, who resists the temptation.

Can poor kids learn what the smart kids learn?

"No," says my friend, "they can't. Not if the only difference between now and then is higher expectations, more rigorous standards and a tougher curriculum. No way."

I won't give you his name. His correspondence was personal, and I don't want to set him up as a target in a public controversy. I tell you only that he is white, liberal and a seasoned executive of an enterprise that has been involved in working for economic and educational justice. I ask you to listen to him.

"Why do so many of the kids of the very poor seem dumber than the kids of the middle- and upper-income families?" he asks. "Several things may be operating to 'dumb them down.'

"One is poor parenting by stressed and ignorant and often single young people, even adolescents—parenting that not only fails to stimulate the babies and toddlers and children, but which actually stifles their natural curiosity.

"This is bad when it derives from overly protective instincts, which may be natural for parents raising children in poor or hazardous environments; it's worse than bad when it is combined with punitive attitudes, which are more common among poor than among middle-income parents, because it is an attitude that recycles itself in conditions of poverty.

"In addition, some of those kids in poverty are in lead-laden environments where, after a few years, they are not just 'dumbed down,' they are brain-damaged as well. Plus, they are apt to have poor diets. The good eater will beat out the poor eater nearly every time.

"Moreover, when the kids get into the grades, they will be given homework to do—something that requires parental encouragement (which requires at least one parent on the premises with energy left to cope with that problem) and a quiet spot to work. How many really poor households can provide that?"

"Most teachers are poorly trained, with a very narrow repertoire of teaching skills. We have got to improve the skills of teachers so that they understand and know how to surmount the barriers to learning that those kids face. The knowledge to accomplish that is accumulating, but it is too rarely transmitted from research scholars to classroom teachers."

If we can be honest enough to admit the accuracy (in general) of that description, there's a good chance of getting these youngsters ready for Bennett's "lean, mean curriculum."

The logical approach, says my friend, is to "address the range of problems which are . . . not mysteries, but already well-known—problems with solutions, starting with prenatal care and running through parenting skills, good nutrition, clean environments, early childhood 'educare' or Head Start experiences, and then into schools staffed by teachers who care and are well-trained to provide that . . . nurture and teaching that all youngsters require."

He makes one last point: High school is far too late to begin. Simply setting high standards for children who come to high school years behind in academic achievement is to add insult to educational injury.

Are there realistic, non-budget-busting ways of intervening in the early grades?

There are. I'll look at one innovative proposal for doing so in a subsequent column.

Raising High School Standards: The Pros

Ben Wattenberg

Ben Wattenberg of the Newspaper Enterprise Association takes the opposite position.

WORDS TO KNOW

monger dealer

parity equality

It is no secret that the American education system has been under attack in recent years. The secretary of education has just come out with a report describing the sort of tough high schools we need. And education seems to be the favorite bogyman issue of just about every presidential candidate this year; if only we had better education, we are told, we would be more "competitive" in the world.

In this general context of the trashing of U.S. education, it has been noted that the high school dropout rate has been rising and is intolerably high. Conditions for blacks have been singled out for particular crisis-mongering. The president of the American Association of Community and Junior Colleges spoke of "the horrible high school dropout rate."

I do not propose to announce that education is without problems. There are real problems. However, looking at just one part of

Reprinted by permission of Newspaper Enterprise Association.

the issue—that high school dropout rates are supposedly high and going higher—it just is not so. In fact, there has been solid progress. Further, there is reason to believe that the progress has caused some of the problems.

A new Census Bureau report on educational attainment has the latest data. It shows that the dropout rate is not high, and it is not climbing; in fact, it has steadily declined for decades and is now at an all-time-low plateau. Moreover, the data for blacks are quite encouraging.

The best statistical way to measure a true, relatively current, dropout rate is to look at adults age 25–29 and see how many have finished high school. This picks up those teens who may have left school but then returned to get a degree either in a regular high school or via a high school graduate equivalency.

The census data show that in 1970 just 75 percent of young Americans of all races had taken their education at least as far as a completed high school education. By 1975 the rate had climbed to 83 percent. And in 1985—the new data—the rate is 86 percent.

The rate for blacks climbed much more sharply and is actually beginning to approach parity with whites. The black high school completion rate was 56 percent in 1970. It went up to 68 percent in 1975. In 1980 it was 77 percent. And in 1985 it was 81 percent, closing in on the white-only rate of 87 percent.

(Data for Hispanics only go back to 1974, when 53 percent graduated from high school. The 1985 data show a 61 percent completion rate—far behind whites and blacks, but a solid gain nonetheless.)

For confirmation, the census measurements of enrollment of 18- and 19-year-olds show the same general trends.

In an important way, these data are encouraging and remarkable. Uniquely among the nations, America is attempting to provide every youngster with a high school education. That is not the case in the more elite education systems in Europe and Japan.

Like most human advances, however, this one is not without second-order problems. When you try to educate everyone, you bring into schools many young people who in earlier years would have dropped out. Some of them are emotionally stunted. Some are behavior cases who are disorderly or violent. This can make it harder to keep discipline in a classroom; it can force a lowering of the general level of instruction, making school less interesting and less challenging to brighter students. Ironically, higher enrollment levels can harm quality.

So, it's right to stress that we have an education problem. We do.

But it is also in order to note that a good part of that problem stems from a remarkable success story.

QUESTIONS ON CONTENT AND TECHNIQUE

1. How do Raspberry and Wattenberg differ on standards?
2. Explain the term "leaner, meaner" high school curriculum.
2. In comparing Raspberry and Wattenberg's conclusions, look at their sources. How are they different?
3. Why does Wattenberg use the term "bogyman"?
4. Raspberry and Wattenberg use only two major sources. What other strategies or evidence could one use to argue both positions more effectively?

WRITING ASSIGNMENTS

Convincing Others

1. Many public schools socially promote students. Argue for or against any policy that promotes students on any criteria other than academic achievement.
2. Should proficiency exams be offered to all high school students after they are 16 to allow them to enter college or employment sooner? Give your position and defend it.

Education

1. If you were superintendent of your local high school, what program would you design to make dropouts stay in?
2. Raspberry says, "Most teachers are poorly trained." State what you consider are ideal characteristics of a teacher and using your own standard assess the quality of your high school faculty.

Johnny's Failures in Science and Math Have U.S. Worried

Jon Van

Jon Van contributed this report to the *Chicago Tribune*.

WORDS TO KNOW

deficit shortage of money

dogmatists those who believe in specific code or creed

flim flam trickery

illiterates those who cannot read

purveyors suppliers

You don't have to be a rocket scientist to realize that life gets more complex with each passing season, that technology is playing an increasing role in most areas of public and private life.

Technology is at the core of a wide range of policy issues, ranging from the "Star Wars" missile shield, to the foreign trade deficit, to new concern over a possible global warming caused by the greenhouse effect.

And at home, new video players and stereo systems, mostly from Asian countries, already come with so many instructions and gadgets that many U. S. consumers complain they cannot figure out how to use them.

Many of today's adults harbor a vague sense that things are getting too complicated too quickly. And now comes a drumbeat of warning that our children could grow up even further out of step with technology's grand march, ill-prepared for a world that will demand a work force ever more sophisticated in the use of mathematics and science.

A recent series of national reports by prestigious groups have documented the failure of American education to keep pace with technology's ever-stiffening challenge. To a great extent, the problem is being blamed on incompetent math and science teachers who too often fail to win the minds and hearts of even willing students.

Instead, they push the rote memorization of seemingly isolated facts, rules and formulas, and the only lesson most youngsters take home is that math and science can be as boring as watching paint dry.

Few educators—or parents, for that matter—are doing anything significant to convince children that learning math and science can indeed be pleasurable, and that in any case it is vital to their future success and well-being. One sad truth is that most American adults, even those with college degrees, are scientific illiterates.

Another is that the U. S. could wake up someday to find it is a has-been country with second-rate technology. Scientists say they are horrified because they cannot make their fellow citizens or the political leaders take this threat seriously.

So the scientists are issuing reports, holding seminars, giving lectures, and doing whatever they can to sound the alarm.

Last month, the American Association for the Advancement of Science issued a report entitled "Science for All Americans," which called for new science curriculums and better science teaching. In January, the National Research Council released its report, "Everybody Counts," which made a similar plea for mathematics.

Later this month, the American Medical Association and several other scientific and professional groups will hold a seminar on general science ignorance in this country and how to combat it.

The problem was documented anew in January by Jon Miller of Northern Illinois University's Public Opinion Laboratory, who revealed that a survey of 2,000 adults had found that only 6 percent meet minimum standards of scientific literacy.

The good news, for what it's worth, is that we're no worse off now than we were a decade ago. Studies in 1979 and 1985 produced virtually the same results. And a similar study of Britain's population found that people there are about as ignorant of science as Americans.

No one expects the average person to name all the quarks known to physics or to solve a differential equation in calculus, but Miller asked things that aren't quite that difficult. Using a true-false question format, he found that a majority of people don't know that electrons are smaller than atoms, that humans and dinosaurs never lived together on Earth, or that antibiotics can kill only bacteria, not viruses.

"The important point," said Miller, "is that in two of the world's oldest and most prominent democracies, at least nine out of 10 citizens lack the scientific literacy to understand and participate in the formulation of public policy on a very important segment of their national political agenda."

People who do not understand how science works or know the meaning of a few fundamental technical terms must take information on faith, often from politicians or industrial spokesmen who have vested interests in maintaining a monopoly on technical information.

The American Association for the Advancement of Science report put it this way: "Without the ability to think critically and independently, citizens are easy prey to dogmatists, flim flam artists and purveyors of simple solutions to complex problems."

Today's science professionals worry that not enough young people are being adequately trained to take their places. Declines in the quality and numbers of students applying to medical schools or entering biotechnology research make physicians wonder who will be on call to care for America's aging population in the next century.

Engineers worry about falling enrollments in engineering schools. They cite the failure of public schools to prepare enough young people adequately to study and succeed at engineering, as well as the increasing rejection by bright young people of the hard work required by college engineering courses.

In 1957, when the Soviets launched the Space Age by putting a tiny artificial satellite into orbit, Americans were shocked and embarrassed. For most of them, the atomic weapons that had ended World War II had confirmed the superiority of U. S. technology.

"The Soviets really did us a huge favor with Sputnik," said Samuel Hulbert, president of the Rose-Hulman Institute of Technology in Terre Haute, Ind. "That galvanized everyone overnight. What we're facing now is a gradual decline. Our losses in technology leadership to the Japanese and Europeans are taking place over years, not overnight, and we're not responding to it."

As scientists and educators remember it, the post-Sputnik era was a golden age of public concern backed up by federal funding for science research and teaching.

Average citizens demanded that their schools join in the national effort to regain America's rightful place on top of the heap in science. It became patriotic for the country's sons and daughters to study science and math. Graduate programs flourished, and college professors started to make good salaries—a new experience for many.

A key difference today is the general apathy about the tangled problems choking science and math education now. People who aren't scientifically literate themselves are unlikely to become upset at the failure to teach science to their children.

Money is needed to solve today's problems, of course, along with better teacher training and new curriculums. But what is most needed is for the average citizen to become convinced that this country is in big trouble—and to start demanding that America's leaders do something about it, fast.

QUESTIONS ON CONTENT AND TECHNIQUE

1. What are the effects that Jon Van predicts will occur if the declining apathy about math and science is not halted?
2. In what ways does he buttress and support his argument? Are there any suggestions that you might make to strengthen his appeal?
3. Why, according to the article, do only 6 percent of American adults meet minimum standards of scientific literacy?
4. What sources does the author use to build his persuasion? Can you think of any others that would be effective?

WRITING ASSIGNMENTS

Convincing Others

1. Write a persuasive essay, taking the position that knowledge of literature, history, or art is as important as science.
2. ". . . what is needed most is for the average citizen to become convinced that this country is in big trouble—and to start demanding that America's leaders do something about it, fast." These last words in the report

could trigger perhaps an issue or area that you wish to warn readers about. Try to persuade them to your point of view.

Education

1. "Many of today's adults harbor a vague sense that things are getting too complicated too quickly." Can you relate an incident that has happened to you recently in which you observed this? Perhaps your paper could suggest that not all technological progress is automatically beneficial.
2. Select the most valuable class that you ever had and explain what environment, methods of instruction, or experiences make it your choice.

Compassion from the Coroner's Office

Phillip D. Campbell

Phillip D. Campbell has been an investigator for the Los Angeles County Coroner's Office for more than six years. His point of view appeared in the *Los Angeles Times* on February 11, 1988, following a story on January 19 of a Colorado woman whose husband was killed in Los Angeles during a street robbery. Before she learned of the death, his body was cremated by the L. A. County Coroner's Office, which had waited 40 days for someone to claim it.

WORDS TO KNOW

bureaucrat one who works in a governmental agency

lament feel sorrow

myriad many

I cannot speak for the county, the Coroner's Office or their leaders. I cannot explain the wisdom of policy making or the deployment of personnel. I can only speak for myself and I would like to think that I speak for my co-workers and some of the people of this community whom we attempt to serve.

I may be violating department policy by writing, but I will take my lumps—on behalf of anyone who feels represented by my views—to be heard.

I have been an investigator for the Los Angeles County Coroner for more than six years and have served as a training officer for new investigators. I have been a police officer in a major California city. I am a California licensed embalmer. I have arranged and directed many funerals. I have counseled the bereaved, the deprived, the suicidal, the desperate and the criminal. I have a college education. I have suffered the loss of relatives and friends, some of whom have passed through the Los Angeles Coroner's Office.

The men and women who work at the Coroner's Office—I mean those who process the work—are human like the rest of the world. We suffer deaths among our families and friends as well. We understand the physical, spiritual, financial, and emotional strains put upon a family when the coroner must intercede.

Our office processes more death investigations in one day than most coroner offices see in a week. Most investigators in this state handle one to three cases per week. Our investigators handle two to five per day. There are between 100 and 300 bodies in our facility at any given time. In addition to myriad other tasks, our supervisors review every investigation at least three times. That's about 100 reviews per day per supervisor. Our physicians examine, or are consulted about, more than 17,000 deaths annually. Our aides and attendants answer hundreds of phone calls daily and move or handle bodies dozens and dozens of times per day. The people responsible for handling bodies and locating families work around the clock trying to keep up.

We collect bodies weighing from ounces to many hundreds of pounds. And from places ranging from mountain ravines to third-floor bathrooms too small for two people to get into at the same time—and one of the two is dead. We handle remains of people dead from only a few hours to many months and in conditions and states of decomposition that would stagger the imaginations of most people. I'm not writing an excuse for poor service, I'm offering a glance at our complex operation.

We receive calls daily from people demanding that their case get priority treatment. Each caller thinks he or she is more important than the last caller, or that he or she is the only one with a funeral to plan and with "friends and relatives coming from all over."

They don't seem to understand that every family we serve has had a death in the family and has plans to make. They all want to tend to their tasks and get back to the business of living. When those callers get their way, other families who patiently wait their turn get pushed back a few more hours or days.

We receive calls daily from people searching for a missing "loved one." Some are looking for a friend missing only a few hours while others are looking for a husband or wife missing for "a couple of years." That's not a misprint; "years," they say. And now they want us to drop everything else to help them look.

Trying to identify a person found dead without a single piece of paper on their person is a major task in itself considering that there are millions of people in this county, many of whom are transitory, undocumented, and alone.

But even if they are identified, trying to locate a family member is an entirely separate problem. Associating a dead body with a relative or friend across the street can be virtually impossible, let alone one in another state. Some out-of-state relatives have complained that we took too many hours to notify them of a death—in one case, four hours. I think that finding a relative in another state four hours after examining an unidentified male is just short of a miracle.

Seldom do people carry next-of-kin information on their persons, especially when they don't even carry personal identification. It can take weeks to learn where a local resident lives and whether or not they live alone, and then gain access to the home to search for relatives. Even California's Department of Motor Vehicle files often list former addresses at which the decedent is unknown.

I'm not suggesting that anyone—especially those who have suffered the loss of a friend or relative—should feel sorry for us, or that our problems should be theirs. I am saying that we have staff out on extended sick leave almost constantly due to back injuries, the result of moving bodies alone. We have employees who have tested positive for tuberculosis and hepatitis. We have suffered blood poisoning, infections, and infestations.

I am saying that our department loses employees as fast as it hires them because, among other things, they are overworked.

Because they have broken-down vehicles, useless equipment, and inadequate supplies. Because they are ashamed to enter private homes with torn, stained sheets. Because they are professionally humiliated when they have to drag a body-laden stretcher down the stairs alone. And because neither their employers nor the public they serve seems to appreciate them. They are physically tired, emotionally drained and under a great deal of stress.

Often we feel great compassion for the bereaved, but our hands are tied either by circumstances, by policy, or by law.

The Coroner's Office is not the enemy. It is a building. And we are not bricks in the building, we are sensitive, professional people with limited resources, and an important job to do.

The steady stream of new employees receives on-the-job training. For that we are sorry. We are sorry if we misinformed you, misdirected you or delayed you. We apologize if we were short tempered or if we gave you the "run-around."

And to those who have written or called to express your thanks, and those who do appreciate us but were unable to express themselves, we thank you. You keep us going.

It makes good copy to lament the plight of little people being beaten by the bureaucrats. Well, I'm not a bureaucrat. I, like my coworkers, am a thinking, feeling, compassionate person. If you have a loved one at the Los Angeles County Coroner's Office and you haven't heard from us, it isn't because we haven't tried.

QUESTIONS ON CONTENT AND TECHNIQUE

1. What major reasons does the writer develop as evidence of the efficiency and compassion within the coroner's office?
2. Does he use primarily emotional or logical appeal? Prove your answer by giving examples.
3. When Campbell says, "I'm not a bureaucrat," what stereotype is he rejecting?
4. What point of view (first, second, or third person) does the author use? Why has he chosen it?

WRITING ASSIGNMENTS

Convincing Others

1. You or your company has been misunderstood by a customer or patron. Explain your reasons and point of view, using Campbell's article as a model.
2. Convince your current employer in an imaginary letter that you deserve a 10 percent raise.

Social and Political Issues

1. Campbell thanks those considerate people who "keep us going." In your company, home, school, or community, tell how some person or group has kept you going in the face of criticism.
2. You have overheard a misinformed comment. Write a response giving your informed opinion and knowledge.

Chapter 11

Writing About Books

DENNIS THE MENACE

"HOW 'BOUT READING ME SOMETHIN' EXCITING, WHERE EVERBODY DON'T END UP LIVIN' HAPPILY EVER AFTER?"

Books are not for English classes alone.

Other disciplines—history, sociology, psychology, journalism, economics, the sciences—all require that students do reading beyond the class texts. Since instructors may assign reports in supplementary books, it may be necessary to use outside reading to write papers on specific subjects.

In this chapter we examine samples of reviews to see how the information from supplementary reading can help improve your term papers.

In the report on *Anything for Billy* by Larry McMurtry, Ed Hutshing concentrates more on the plot and characters of the story than the other reviewers. But even his review still gives readers background on the outlaws, dime novelists, and the Old West.

Robert Kirsch's critique on *The Underground Man* by Ross MacDonald focuses "on what has been his [MacDonald's] major purpose, to examine California as a microcosm of America."

For Lee Lescaze, his review of *The Complete Short Stories of Ernest Hemingway* serves not only as a criticism of the work, but provides an overview of this foremost writer's career.

And in John Gross's review of *A History of News from the Drum to the Satellite,* we are entertained with a capsule account of the development of news. Fleshed out with details from other sources, it could almost stand alone as a history of how people communicate to one another the events of their public and private lives.

Students who use these examples as models for their own book reports—or for more lengthy papers—will gain confidence in using their writing skills in classes other than English Composition and Literature.

WHEN YOU WRITE ABOUT BOOKS

- Check your purpose for writing: Is it to gain notes and information for a research or lengthy paper? Is it to convince the instructor that you have read the text and can critically select ideas from it, and using the tools from a particular discipline analyze it? Is it to present its value and/or significant flaws to a reading audience unfamiliar with it? Is it to highlight and illustrate a point you wish to make?
- Ask your instructors for samples of student book reports or forms that they want you to follow. Your report may be critical, interpretive, personal comparative, or a blend of all.
- Read the book carefully and make an informal outline and summary (whether called for or not) simply to get a feel for the author's overall structure and ideas.
- Analyze its subject matter according to what type of report you choose, jotting down details, paraphrasing, and quoting important passages.
- Keep in mind the audience. Are your readers informed or unfamiliar with the content of the book?
- Check that the report fairly reflects the author's position and research.
- Be certain that any reader can respond to your ideas and structure without needing the actual book.

Wild and Woolly

Anything for Billy
Larry McMurtry
Simon & Schuster, 382 pages,
$19.95

Reviewer: Ed Hutshing

Ed Hutshing is the book editor for the *San Diego Union*.

WORDS TO KNOW

alter ego other self

galore in abundance

pastiche a work that imitates other works

poignant deeply moving

"Billy gave me a chip-toothed grin. I would have guessed him to be no more than seventeen at the time, and short for his age at that. In fact, he was almost a runt, and ugly as Sunday. His dirty black coat was about three sizes too big for him."

This is Larry McMurtry's introduction for Billy Bone, otherwise known as Billy the Kid, in this flawless new book. At $19.95, it can hardly be called a dime novel, but that is McMurtry's model in this delightful pastiche and sendup of the Old West.

McMurtry's alter ego, the purported author who tells the story, is Ben Sippy, a Philadelphian addicted to dime novels and the lure of the Wild West, who has fled his wife and nine daughters to live his dreams of glory.

"'Howdy, Mr. Sippy, are you from Mississippi?' he said, and burst out laughing"—so the opening continues—and thus, Ben and Billy become friends as Sippy replies.

"'Oh, you've got a reputation,' I said. 'They say you're a cool killer.'

"'I am, but the cool killing don't start till around November,' he said giggling again. 'This time of the year we mostly do hot killing, Mr. Sippy.'"

Back home in Philadelphia, Ben Sippy's addiction to dime novels was such that he kept his butler busy going to the newsstand to get the latest works. He was first hooked on "Hurricane Nell, Queen of the Saddle" and "Mustang Merle's Mandate." Then Ben turned to writing the Wild West thrillers himself, with such titles as "Sandycrew, Man of Grit" and "Orson Oxx, Man of Iron." Ben came West when his wife threw out his precious collection of westerns.

Years later, Ben has begun writing his current work on Billy Bone to set the record straight and refute the myths that he feels other writers have saddled the young outlaw with. After all, Ben was there, rode with Billy to the very end, and the record is wild and woolly enough without exaggeration.

However, just as the reader is laughing at the escapades, the sudden realization comes through like a shot from a Colt that there is a poignancy to the narrative and to the characters. McMurtry is having fun, yet he takes his story out of the mere slapstick.

As Ben and Billy make their way around New Mexico and Mexico, they encounter a Mother Lode of characters.

There are gunslingers galore, both real and fictional, including Doc Holliday, Hill Coe, fearless cowpoke Joe Lovelady, Katie Garza, lady bandido and love child of Isinglass, as well as Isinglass' mistress, Lady Cecily Snow, an Englishwoman with a glacial heart and the deadliness of a diamondback rattler.

Still it is Billy—confused, at times lovable and, even in a sense, pathetic and sympathetic—around which the story turns. As Ben brings the tale to the racing finish and fatal roundup, the reader wishes it all didn't have to end that way, or any way.

McMurtry has brought another time, characters and locale to exciting life in the same way that he did in "Lonesome Dove." And the result is a novel that can stand equally tall in the saddle, or on the shelf with that Pultizer-prize winner.

QUESTIONS ON CONTENT AND TECHNIQUE

1. Is the book *Anything for Billy* fiction or nonfiction? Explain the difference.
2. What is "a dime novel"?
3. How is the outlaw portrayed?
4. Who were some other famous gunslingers not mentioned in the article?

WRITING ASSIGNMENT

Write a review of a biography or novel. Include your dominant impression of the character, an overview of the book, some passages, and your evaluation.

The Underground Man

Ross Macdonald

Reviewer: Robert Kirsch

Robert Kirsch, a novelist and book critic, wrote this review March 14, 1971, for the *Los Angeles Times*.

WORDS TO KNOW

didactic intending to teach a lesson

foible minor character fault

germane relevant

triteness being used too much

Certain crimes expose the terrors and nightmares of a culture, in the same way that dreams and fantasies reveal the dark terrain of the unconscious. Loeb and Leopold, Sacco and Vanzetti, the Manson case are examples. There are many more.

There is crime fiction and there is fiction about crime. The former is a genre which has produced some superb craftsmen; the latter is something more, a parable of human foible and violence, and some of the best novelists of the last hundred years have examined life and society through the acts and motives of criminals and their pursuers.

Ross Macdonald is one of those novelists who use the form but elevate it into serious literature. He is in a line of writers from Dostoyevsky to Raymond Chandler who have revealed the nether side of humanity and illuminated the worth of life in doing so.

He has been writing his Lew Archer series for two decades now. His latest novel, *The Underground Man,* is even more focused on what has been his major purpose, to examine California as a microcosm of America. In doing so, he has touched universality. The characters here evoke a glint of recognition to Californians. The young and innocent, haunted as O'Neill characters by the trauma of their domestic past, in flight sometimes through drugs and sometimes through a search for renewal in the hills and seas of this vast region; their elders caught in their own tangled histories, of divorce and adultery, of blackmail and greed.

Against the background of hillside inferno, so common here in the sere Southland, Archer with that compassionate cynicism seeks to untangle the web. As Chandler's Marlowe before him, he represents the tough decencies and obsolete chivalry of a man who has seen it all, twice.

The fire is a metaphor, a counterpoint to the purgatory of the soul, created by human beings, endured by them. Natural catastrophe may seem mindless but in this novel it is the catalyst which uncovers the sad and decaying truth. *The Underground Man* is not only a literal title but a figurative one as well. It is a work of art.

Southern California is evoked effectively; no writer since Raymond Chandler has done better in this regard. But I think Macdonald has more amplitude as an observer of life. Lew Archer is far more developed as a protagonist, particularly in the later books. He is closer to Macdonald himself, to his concerns, his thoughtful and penetrating understanding of the California experience.

All of this is free of didacticism. The taut and hard-boiled style remains, but it often carries more. "I followed them downtown," Archer says at the end of the book, "thinking that quite often nowadays the low-life subplots were taking over the tragedies. I gave a more prosaic explanation to a team of police detectives and a stenotypist."

A favorite theme of Macdonald is treated here, with more poignancy than ever. It is not so much the gap of generations, nor even the war between father and son, but that deeper problem in which the life of the young is determined by the patterns of the old; ultimately determined, so that no matter how long the cycles of generations, no matter how fashion or life style changes, the doom is seeded forever.

The adrenal response to the fire is basic and primitive. It seems against nature to be driving toward it, but Archer must, for the issue is there. "There was only one good thing about the fire. It made people talk about the things that really concerned them." Mood is caught in powerful and effective words. We sense the fire, smell it, see it, feel it. "The flames that from a distance looked like artillery flashes were crashing through the thick chaparral like cavalry."

Occasionally, but rarely, there are moments when Macdonald seems to acknowledge the almost ritual action of the private-eye story. He is hit over the head by a young man who is about to escape on a yacht. "The scene spun away," he writes. Yet, even here, Macdonald avoids triteness. The action is germane. Motives are surprising. What appears to be the kidnapping of a child turns out to be, however wrong-minded, a pathetic effort by a teen-age couple to save the youngster from the world they find abominable.

Is there blame here? Yes, but not in the uninformed and automatic sense. People are responsible for their acts, responsible to the law, which Archer, unlike most private detectives in fiction, respects. But there is another kind of responsibility which the rigidities of the law rarely take into account. This is, in the final analysis, a story of crime and punishment. But the crimes are shared and the punishment often built into life itself, in unhappy marriages, in the secret nightmare witness of children to violence and argument, in the endless pattern of private grudge, in love turned to hate; the victims are not only those who are the target of violence. Its fallout corrupts the innocent, exacts an exorbitant price in human suffering.

Lew Archer is not above all this. He has known life and it has slipped him some low blows. Interviewing a man, he says: "A kind of angry brotherhood had been growing between us. It was partly based in the fact, which he didn't know, that my wife had walked out on me and sent me divorce papers through a lawyer. And partly that we were two middle-aged men, and three young people had slipped away over the curve of the world."

It is not the apparatus that touches us so deeply. This is the surface entertainment. What penetrates is precisely what is underneath the town of Santa Teresa, much like Santa Barbara, what is locked in the dens of Northridge tract houses, in the files of juvenile courts, in the high school yearbooks, what takes place behind the fronts of houses in wealthy suburbs, or in ghetto slums. The secret world is Archer's domain and Macdonald's.

Yes, the characters are familiar: real estate men and forest rangers, middle-aged ex-schoolteachers who go away to paint, housekeepers who protect their fuzzy sons, women who marry for money, acquaintances who come out of the past and bring reminders of debts owed and incidents forgotten or buried. They are much like us.

Even the artifacts and machinery, the very nature of Southern California are molded into the story. It is a bulldozer, the ultimate symbol, which uncovers the ancient crime, while the fires blaze. It is a sports car which holds the secret. And the collision of the respectable and the longhairs, the solid people and the dropouts which center contention here. From children, there is no keeping of secrets. Of one young character, Archer observes: "He had to live out his time of trouble as she (his mother) had. And there was no assurance that he would. He belonged to a generation whose elders had been poisoned, like the pelicans, with a kind of moral DDT that damaged the lives of the young."

Where is Archer in all this? Goaded not only by conscience, by a respect for his craft, but something more, he revealed: "The hot breath of vengeance was growing cold in my nostrils and I grew older. I had more concern for a kind of economy in life that would help to preserve the things that were worth preserving."

Critics should not blow their own horns. But perhaps I may be permitted a small peep, for I recognized early the value of Macdonald as a novelist transcending the genre in which he appeared to work. His books are not uniformly good. But the occasional lapse points up his true strength as a novelist. He is a man of sensitivity, sensibility and wisdom, a gifted writer. It is restoring to know that the New York establishment has recognized that something good can come out of California. Many readers out here have known this about Ross Macdonald for years.

QUESTIONS ON CONTENT AND TECHNIQUE

1. According to Kirsch what was the purpose of the Lew Archer series and *The Underground Man* in particular?
2. How does the reviewer give the reader a sense of Macdonald's style?
3. What is the dominant impression of the book's characters as shown in the review?
4. What comparisons does he make? What is their effect?

WRITING ASSIGNMENT

Select a fiction book and model your review after Kirsch, creating a thesis statement and developing it through a brief synopsis of the plot, a sense of the characters and their interaction, a feeling of place, and passages illustrating thought and style. Include any biographical data that is relevant to the work.

Genius for Decisive Moments

[Bookshelf]
The Complete Short Stories of Ernest Hemingway

Reviewer: Lee Lescaze

Lee Lescaze is *The Wall Street Journal's* deputy foreign editor.

WORDS TO KNOW

derring-do daring action

jauntiness act of being lively in manner or appearance

presage predict

protagonist chief character in novel or drama

terrain ground

Ernest Hemingway, not yet 40, already was counting the days. When he published the collection of his first 49 stories in 1938, he was America's most famous writer. He seemed a man without limits, yet, with the mixture of dread and jauntiness that marks many of his best short stories, he closed that volume's preface more in the tone of a man with an incurable disease. "I would like to live long enough to write three more novels and twenty-five more stories," he wrote. "I know some pretty good ones."

The tone presaged what was to come. That moment was perhaps the top of Hemingway's arc. He hadn't yet written "For Whom the Bell Tolls" or "The Old Man and the Sea," but he was running out of stories, at least of good ones.

The best Hemingway stories catch people at times of great stress, balancing courage against cowardice or decency against loutishness. He wrote with genius of decisive moments.

In his fiction Hemingway faced the truth, as he wouldn't in his life. In a story he numbered among his favorites, "In Another Country," the protagonist, a patient in a Milan hospital after being wounded in World War I, modestly knows that his medals were awarded only "because I was an American" serving with Italian forces. In the story, boasting is impermissible, but the young American admits that sometimes "after the cocktail hour" he would imagine himself a war hero only to recognize that he was incapable of brave deeds because he was very afraid to die. It is an astonishing story to have been written by a young American who served in Italy in World War I and—both before and after the cocktail hour—boasted, exaggerated and told huge lies about his exploits and his wounds.

In another early short story, a young veteran feels the nausea "that is the result of untruth or exaggeration."

Hemingway's 1938 collection almost instantly became one of the key books of 20th-century American literature. For all the Hemingway parodies and endless imitators, and despite all the sad evidence (most fully elaborated in Kenneth Lynn's excellent biography published earlier this year) that not only the feet, but also the heart, of this once giant-sized cultural hero were made of clay, time hasn't diminished the stories' power.

Now, "The Complete Short Stories of Ernest Hemingway," (Scribners, 650 pages, $22.50) adds 21 stories to the canon, numerically not so far from Hemingway's modest goal. But his editors have upped the count by stretching the definition of short story to include several fragments from novels and two tales that Hemingway himself incorporated into his novel "To Have and Have Not."

More importantly, the later stories don't match the quality of his earlier work. As Hemingway grew older he lost his sense of balance. He began to boast in fiction as he boasted in life, no longer shadowing accomplishment with apprehension, or undercutting confidence with cowardice. It is most evident in the seven pieces included here that have never before been published.

"Black Ass at the Cross Roads" is full of unconvincing derring-do. "Landscape with Figures" gives us Hemingway as senior war correspondent, the expert who can explain it all to the less-experienced, not to mention less-brave.

There are also two stories in which Hemingway is the father betrayed by a weak son. They are cruel, unforgiving tales almost impossible to reconcile with the sensitivity in his great stories of Nick Adams coming of age. He knew what it is to be adolescent better than what it is to be a parent.

Youth had been Hemingway's best fictional terrain. The adults in "The Sun Also Rises" and most of the great short stories are young, their spirit even more youthful than their years. (The outstanding exceptions to this are the wonderful African stories "The Short, Happy Life of Francis Macomber" and "The Snows of Kilimanjaro.") The loss of youth obsessed him and he salted his later work with sentimental laments. Characters exclaim things like: "Everything was possible once." The young Hemingway knew better. He'd seen from the start that the world was a place of hard choices and closing options.

After Hemingway lost the narrative voice of a young man discovering the world, he never found another voice as good.

Some of the momentum of his fiction comes from Hemingway sharing his discoveries. He was a superb guide. The drinks and the meals in his pages are almost characters in themselves. It's hard to read Hemingway without getting hungry or wanting a glass of wine.

It is also hard from the perspective of our jet-plane homogenized world to remember just how many discoveries there were to make in Hemingway's time; how many places there were to visit without stumbling on the footprints of thousands of predecessors. Only in that sense is Hemingway becoming antique. The reporting in his stories about places and foreign people must have seemed exotic to most of his readers. No writer could describe such places with the same enthusiasm now. And when we read Hemingway on an Alpine idyll or a Spanish festival, we know that even if such places exist and we were to visit them, there would be no wide-eyed sense of discovery. Just the exhaust of tour buses.

QUESTIONS ON CONTENT AND TECHNIQUE

1. Does the reviewer feel Hemingway's stories are outdated or timeless? Explain.

2. What strategy does the reviewer use to avoid discussing all 21 short stories?
3. How does the reviewer contrast the real Hemingway with his characters?

WRITING ASSIGNMENT

If possible, select a collection of short stories. Choose one or two as examples of the writer's style and creativity. Include a biographical reference to the author that is relevant to the text. Share with the reader if the stories have lasting significance.

Account of Atlanta's Fall Praises Sherman

War So Terrible: Sherman and Atlanta
James Lee McDonough and James Pickett Jones
W. W. Norton, $19.95

Reviewer: Stephen Davis

Stephen Davis, associate editor of *The Blue and the Gray* magazine, wrote this review especially for *The Atlanta Journal-The Atlanta Constitution.*

WORDS TO KNOW

culpable deserving blame

hoodwinked deceived

petty minor

poignant deeply moving

scrappiness quick to quarrel or fight

We Atlantans have always thought Gen. William T. Sherman was a little off his rocker. Early in the Civil War, in truth, the general suffered what we would today call a nervous breakdown. Some Northern newspapers actually headlined that he was insane. Even Sherman's own soldiers spoke of the wild look that their "Uncle Billy" would sometimes get in his eyes.

And so it's always been convenient to discredit Sherman's generalship and find some other reason for the Yankees' capture of our city in 1864. Southern troops were badly outnumbered. They were starving, or poorly equipped. Confederate President Jefferson Davis messed up somewhere. Or we just had bad luck.

The most important point, however, in the new book on the Atlanta Campaign of 1864 is that Sherman whipped the Rebel army and took Atlanta because he was simply a better general—tougher, more aggressive, or downright smarter—than the Confederate leaders he faced. That's saying a lot. But James L. McDonough and James P. Jones make the point convincingly in "War So Terrible."

To be sure, in May 1864, Sherman's Union armies began the Atlanta Campaign north of Dalton with a decided numerical edge of some 100,000 men to maybe 65,000 or 70,000 Confederates. But in the first few days of operations, Sherman fooled his Rebel counterpart—General Joseph E. Johnston—by slipping a strong column around his flank and forcing a Southern retreat. Compounding the Reb's troubles was that Johnston, by personality, was just not an attacker. Time and again—north of Calhoun, at Cassville and Pine Mountain—he ordered a retreat from strong positions. It was Sherman who ordered the attacks, and so by his smarts and scrappiness managed to push the Confederates back across the Chattahoochee River by early July.

Missing chances to strike a blow, failing to inform his superiors of his plans, and soon dropping back into the very fortifications of Atlanta, poor Johnston clearly had to go. President Davis replaced him with a general of decidedly opposite temperament, the bulldog attacker John B. Hood. In three bold but rather badly managed attacks during mid-July, Hood lashed his army at the Federal lines outside the city. The result was thousands of Confederate casualties, but no gain. Sherman kept up the pressure, opening fire on Atlanta with big siege guns while extending his powerful lines around Atlanta. Finally, having cut three of the four railroads that fed Hood's army, in late August Sherman made a lunge for Jonesboro and the last rail line. Here, too, the Confederate leadership was . . . well, hoodwinked. Sherman stole a march and the confused Southerners responded with too little, too late. Even a tough battle at Jonesboro couldn't save the railroad, and on the day the Yankees tore up the tracks, General Hood ordered Atlanta abandoned. Sherman's men marched in on Sept. 2.

Aided by an array of photographs and maps, "War So Terrible" chronicles these day-to-day events in a manner both informed and entertaining. Brisk, effective descriptions of pitched battles—

especially Resaca, New Hope Church and Pickett's Mill—help counter the oft-held idea that the campaign's early stages were marked more by maneuver than fighting. Stories of the petty bickering among officers of both armies are as well-told as the terrifying effects of Union bombardment on Atlanta's civilians. Narration blends with analysis, too, as McDonough and Jones assess commanders' faults (chiefly Joe Johnston's) and evaluate strategy, particularly whether Confederate cavalry might have forced Sherman's retreat by pouncing on the Federals' railway supply lines. Not forgotten are the common soldiers, from whose letters and diaries the authors quote poignant hopes and fears.

Both in research and interpretation, this study is far superior to the last book we've had on the Atlanta Campaign, Samuel Carter's "The Siege of Atlanta, 1864" (1973). Yet there are oversights. A significant question left unanswered is how much of Atlanta the Yankees actually burned before they left, or to what degree General Sherman is technically culpable for his men's undisciplined torching. Nashville artist Jim Moon's maps are generally good, but the authors failed to commission diagrams showing Sherman's "grand wheel" toward Jonesboro, or the key movements of that critical battle.

Some may argue that McDonough and Jones, both accomplished scholars of the Civil War, should have footnoted their text. More disconcerting to me, however, is my discovery of the authors' unlicensed literary borrowings. In reading their account of the big snowball battle, March 22, 1864, which entertained thousands of Confederate soldiers in their camps near Dalton (pp. 63–64), I realized that McDonough and Jones had lifted, without quotes or attribution, exact phrasing from an article I wrote and had published more than a decade ago in "Civil War Times Illustrated."

But enough of technicalities. In the end, how is the Atlanta Campaign to be measured? By four months' hard campaigning, throughout which scarcely a day passed without some bloodshed, William T. Sherman led his forces a hundred miles into enemy territory, cowed and repeatedly beat a strong Rebel army, and captured one of the South's most heavily fortified supply and communication centers.

The authors persuasively argue that this dramatic feat did more toward hammering the Confederacy's coffin than Grant's bloody operations against Robert E. Lee in Virginia. At the very least, Atlanta's fall ensured President Lincoln's re-election in November 1864, and set the stage for the Federals' notorious March to the Sea. All of this leads McDonough and Jones to conclude that while Sherman may have botched a battle or two, "from the standpoint of strategy, logistics, and communications, the general had no superior on either side of the war; possibly no equal."

This kind of praise may be a little steep. But maybe it's time, after all, for us to give "Crazy Billy" the respect he is due.

QUESTIONS OF CONTENT AND TECHNIQUE

1. McDonough and Jones's book has a thesis. Where does Davis point it out?
2. What sources have the authors used to develop their review?
3. A comparison is used in the review. Locate and discuss it.

WRITING ASSIGNMENT

In your nonfiction review, highlight some unusual event, technique, or knowledge that the writer specifically offers. Compare the author with other authors, indicate your sources used, and pinpoint the purpose of the book.

Roots of Journalism

A History of News
from the Drum to the Satellite
Mitchell Stephens
Viking, Illustrated,
401 pages, $24.95

Reviewer: John Gross

John Gross writes for the New York Times News Service.

WORDS TO KNOW

disseminate spread around

precursors forerunners

prodigy extraordinary person

"What's new?" It is one of the basic human questions.

Whether through curiosity, or boredom, or because they think it will help them, people have always been eager to learn the latest developments.

In the words of a 16th-century English pamphlet—one of the many excellent quotations in "A History of News" by Mitchell Stephens—we are marked by "the thursty desyer that all our kynde hath to know."

Stephens' subject is news itself, rather than newspapers or newscasts. He has set out to write a history of its changing (or unchanging) character, of how it has been gathered and disseminated, of the forces controlling its distribution.

In the beginning was the spoken word. Wherever people met—on a footpath, in a market place, around a well—they kept one another up-to-date.

In time, elaborate oral systems developed for spreading the news further afield. Stephens describes the role of runners and news criers, and the information networks of preliterate societies, the "bush telegraphs" that could so often astonish Europeans and Americans with their speed and effectiveness.

There are limits to what we can hope to learn about the history of oral news. But one thing seems clear: Even when written news became available, it took a long time for it to compete effectively with gossip and the word-of-mouth report.

There were newspapers in 18th-century London, but if you wanted to find out what was going on in the wider world, you generally did better to visit a coffee-house.

For practical purposes, the history of written journalism can be said to have begun in Rome, with two remarkable productions—the "Acta Senatus," transactions of the senate, and the "Acta Diurna," a daily summary of current events, including law reports and human interest stories.

These were handwritten news sheets, published daily (over a period of nearly 300 years) by being posted up in public places. Copies of them, which could be bought from scribes, were widely read both in Rome itself and throughout the Roman empire.

There is a faint parallel in the bulletins that began circulating in China around the same time, but these were intended for government officials rather than the public.

In Europe itself, there were no further examples of written news until a few handwritten newsletters made their appearance in the 15th century.

In a world where rulers were determined to keep tight control over what could be published, the introduction of printing didn't initially transform the situation.

For a century and more, its chief journalistic consequence was the news book—a pamphlet, often in verse, sometimes recounting a battle or a royal marriage, but rather more likely to be devoted to a crime, a supernatural prodigy, a man-bites-dog sensation.

Stephens quotes entertainingly from this subliterature, with its gory details and tall stories; he leaves you in no doubt that the most traditional papers in present-day America are the *National Enquirer* and its rivals.

The first printed newspapers, "corantos" made their appearance at the beginning of the 17th century. Like their immediate precursors, the handwritten newsletters of 16th-century Vebucem which gave the world the word "gazette," they were primarily concerned with matters affecting foreign trade.

Many of them were printed in the great commercial center of Amsterdam—among others, the earliest surviving newspaper in English.

This began its life, in 1620, with a misprint (it was dated "The 2. of Decemember") and a cry of editorial despair ("The new tyding out of Italie are not yet com").

Stephens goes on to describe the subsequent growth of newspapers in England itself, especially during the English civil war—a period that saw such varied innovations as headlines (of a sort), newsboys and newsgirls, and above all, what he calls "spirited coverage of national news."

At the heart of "A History of News," for all its broader concerns, is a miniature history of the rise of the newspaper in Britain, the United States and, to a lesser extent, France.

This is very well done. There is a particularly useful account of the development of reporting—an art that took newspapers a long time to master; and at every stage, Stephens' wide knowledge of his subject furnishes him with striking facts and analogies.

He is excellent on the unifying influence of the colonial press during the period of the American Revolution—for example, the part it played in creating an American national consciousness.

Only toward the end does he falter. His coverage of radio, television and recent developments in the press is too skimpy for him to be able to add much that is news, and he skirts around some of the most important contemporary issues.

Throughout the book, for instance, he stresses the role of news in binding a society together, reinforcing a sense of common aims and interests; but this makes him seriously neglect the adversarial and critical role that journalists are free to play in a democracy.

He might have been less inclined to slight this aspect of the story if he had found room for an account of the press under less open regimes.

All in all, then, a lively and original historical introduction; but less satisfactory as a guide to the present or a pointer to the future.

QUESTIONS ON CONTENT AND TECHNIQUE

1. Where does the book falter according to the reviewer?
2. Would you call the review favorable, mixed, or unfavorable? Explain your choice.
3. How does the writer prove the newspaper has been influential in many nations or empires?
4. What does Gross choose to quote and why?

WRITING ASSIGNMENT

When you write the nonfiction book review, be sure to note cause and effect. Use concrete examples, anecdotes, or passages to indicate the significance of the theme. Do include your opinion of the book and the audience to whom it is directed.

Glossary

acronym A word formed from the initial letter or letters of a term. *Example:* acquired immune deficiency syndrome (AIDS).

allegory A narrative (story) in which the characters and the events stand for a set of ideas. The best known allegory is *Pilgrim's Progress* where Pilgrim represents every man in his journey through life.

anecdote A short account of some interesting or humorous incident. (See Bob Greene's "Today's History Lesson," Chapter 4.)

appositive A noun that follows another and explains it. *Example:* Harriet, my sister, is older than I am.

argument A writing strategy in which reasoning is aimed at determining the truth or falsehood of something. The writer seeks to convince the reader to adopt his or her position or point of view. (See introduction to Chapter 10, "Convincing Others.")

biographical Relating to material that deals with the life of the author. *Example:* If one were writing on *The Grapes of Wrath,* one might want to include that Steinbeck himself had worked as a supervisor in the lettuce fields of Salinas.

cause and effect A writing strategy in which the writer seeks to show the influence of one person, group, or event on another. (See introduction to Chapter 9, "Cause and Effect.")

characterization The act of revealing one's personality through description, dialogue, and action.

classification A writing strategy in which the writer takes a group and subdivides or categorizes it in order to understand it better. *Example:*

types of murder: first degree, second degree, third degree. (See introduction to Chapter 8, "Classification and Division.")

cliché A phrase once original but now too commonly used. *Example:* It's raining cats and dogs.

closing The conclusion of an essay in which the writer usually summarizes the main ideas and satisfies the reader's interest.

comparison and contrast A writing strategy in which the writer finds likenesses or differences between two objects, persons, events, or concepts. (See introduction to Chapter 6, "Comparison and Contrast.")

critique An evaluation of any writing to determine its nature, its limitation, or its agreement based on standards. Book reviews or reports serve this function.

definition A writing strategy or mode to explain the meaning of a word or phrase. The writer answers the question What is *x*? (See introduction to Chapter 7, "Definition.")

description A writing strategy that gives the characteristics of an object, landscape, animal, or person, particularly focusing on the senses of sight, sound, touch, taste, and smell. *Example:* The cold, wet nose of the furry puppy brushed against Jacob's bare arm.

dialogue Conversation between two persons. Normally dialogue enlivens writing. Note the difference between (a) and (b): (a) Mrs. Murray scolded her son Henry for not eating his meal. (b) "Henry, you haven't eaten your vegetables."

"But, Mom!"
"No 'buts,' just eat!"
"Aw, do I have to."

dominant impression The main idea or feeling that the writer wants to share with the reader.

essay A writing that explains, shares, or interprets the writer's personal feelings or findings on a limited subject.

example A fact, incident, or item that may be taken fairly as typical of a group. Also a writing strategy that expands a topic by a series of definite illustrations. *Example:* The average American knows several revolutionary patriots: Patrick Henry, Paul Revere, Thomas Paine.

fragment A nonsentence that is normally not acceptable in standard English. However, immediately following a question or with dialogue, it is correct. *Example:* (a) Why did he leave? Because he was late to class. (b) "Can't run anymore—just can't."

generalization A general concept, idea, or notion that is indefinite. A statement with no example, supporting details, or imagery to indicate its particular application. *Example:* Crime doesn't pay.

glossary Brief definitions of terms used in a text in the context of their particular usage.

hyperbole See *overstatement.*

image The representation of something sensed or seen. Images may be seen, heard, smelled, tasted, or touched (see *metaphor, simile,* and *symbol). Example:* The rib-marked old horse, its head inches from the ground, shook its grey mane as it wheezed up the dusty winding road.

introduction A short passage preparing the reader for the main idea and essay to follow. Its purpose is to arouse interest and lead into the subject.

metaphor A figure of speech in which two different objects are identified with each other. *Example:* My love is a rose that never fades (see *simile*).

mode A type, strategy, or method of writing. Rhetorical (writing) modes are identifiable forms: description, narration, process, argument, classification.

narration A writing strategy that develops its form in chronological order with a beginning, middle, and end. A story, fiction or nonfiction, of any length from anecdote to novel.

overstatement An exaggerated comment for literary effect (a hyperbole). *Example:* The ice-cream cone was a yard high.

parable A short, allegorical narrative. Many famous parables appear in the Bible, for example, the Parable of the Lost Sheep.

parenthetical elements Any words, phrases, or sentences that interrupt the main idea or clause but are not essential to the meaning. *Example:* Mary—and I've known her for years—is very reliable.

person A writer selects a point of view (first, second, or third person) for an essay.

	Singular	*Plural*
First person:	I, me, my, mine	we, us, our, ours
Second person:	you, your, yours	you, your, yours
Third person:	he, it, she	they, them, theirs
	his, its, her, hers	theirs

personification A thing or idea that is represented as having human traits. *Example*: The sky was weeping.

phrases A group of words not containing a subject and a predicate. Some common phrases are prepositional (on the way), infinitive (to run a mile), participial (racing against time), verbal (have been teaching), absolute (their eyes swollen shut).

plot The structure of the action in fiction or drama. What happens to the characters, the conflicts met, and how they are resolved.

point of view The position of the writer in the essay. Is he writing in the first person (I), the second person (you), or the third person (he or they) as an observer? Is he, in other words, writing about himself, to teach you, or writing about others?

process A writing strategy that tells the reader step-by-step how to do or make something or how something works. (See introduction to Chapter 5, "Process.") *Example:* How to Discourage a Car Thief.

purpose The purpose or intent of the writer is usually to entertain (stir emotion), to inform (explain), or to persuade (take a position and seek to convince another of it).

rhetorical modes See *strategies.*

sensory detail Concrete or specific images that evoke the reader's senses of touch, taste, smell, sight, and sound (see *description* and *image*).

sentence patterns The order in which grammatical elements appear. The most common pattern is subject–verb. Often writers will vary this basic pattern by putting an adjective, adverb, phrase, or clause at the beginning of the sentence or inverting the sentence completely. *Examples:* The bride and groom walked slowly down the aisle. Slowly, the bride and groom walked down the aisle. Down the aisle, the bride and groom walked slowly. Slowly down the aisle walked the bride and groom.

simile A figure of speech in which one object is likened to another, using the prepositions "as" or "like." *Example:* The porcelain doll had cheeks like roses.

slant (bias) The writer seeks to influence the reader by the choice of words to adopt a certain point of view. *Examples:* Eighteen-year-old Stabs Teacher (factual). Hoodlum Stabs Teacher (slanted). Former Boy Scout Stabs Teacher (slanted).

sources Books, magazines, periodicals, interviews, documents, newspapers that a writer uses for background to prepare an essay.

strategies Modes or forms of writing that help the writer develop her material (see *description, narration, example, process, comparison and contrast, definition, classification, cause and effect, and argument*).

style The distinctive or particular technique of a certain writer. Compare the difference in style between Andy Rooney and Russell Baker.

summary The reduction of a work to one-fourth or one-tenth of its original length, giving its major ideas in the order set by the author.

support Facts, details, quotations, examples, statistics, and anecdotes that provide evidence for the general statements of a writer. *Examples:* Many Americans have mental health problems (general). One out of six Americans will seek some type of mental health treatment during his or her lifetime (support).

symbol Something that represents something else. *Examples:* The flag is really only a piece of cloth but it represents a nation. The color red often represents blood or life.

synonym A word that is similar or means the same as another. Writers avoid using the same word too often. *Examples:* There are many factors to consider in selecting a garment. Instead of the word "factors" used over and over, a writer might choose words such as "qualities," "points," or "decisions."

synopsis A brief outline giving the general view of an essay or narrative. A quick summary or condensed statement. *Example: Huckleberry Finn* is the story of a wayward boy who encounters many adventures on a raft floating down the Mississippi.

theme The basic idea, special view of life, or values of a piece of writing. The theme of the Parable of the Lost Sheep is that God cares about all children whether saint or sinner, whether within or outside the fold.

thesis Major idea or concept that the writer wishes to communicate to the reader. It is the bedrock on which the structure of the essay is built.

tone The attitude of the author as reflected in the structure of the writing. He or she may be humorous, whimsical, informal, or appear serious but have an underlying tone of merriment, as Mark Twain exhibits in his mining yarns.

transition Any word, phrase, clause, or paragraph that leads the reader from one important idea to another. Some transitional words are however, on the other hand, yet, moreover, furthermore, nevertheless. Key words also alert the reader to changes: first, second, third, finally, another, in conclusion.

understatement Deliberately saying less about an event or person in order to gain effect. Known for understatement, the British might say of the war hero Montgomery: "Yes, General Montgomery did rather well in North Africa."

Index